Lecture Notes in Computer Science 6874

Commenced Publication in 1973
Founding and Former Series Editors:
Gerhard Goos, Juris Hartmanis, and Jan van Leeuwen

T0213448

Yuhua Luo (Ed.)

Cooperative Design, Visualization, and Engineering

8th International Conference, CDVE 2011
Hong Kong, China, September 11-14, 2011
Proceedings

 Springer

Volume Editor

Yuhua Luo
University of Balearic Islands
Department of Mathematics and Computer Science
07122 Palma de Mallorca, Spain
E-mail: dmilyu0@uib.es

ISSN 0302-9743   e-ISSN 1611-3349
ISBN 978-3-642-23733-1   e-ISBN 978-3-642-23734-8
DOI 10.1007/978-3-642-23734-8
Springer Heidelberg Dordrecht London New York

Library of Congress Control Number: 2011935215

CR Subject Classification (1998): H.4, C.2, C.2.4, D.2, H.5, H.3

LNCS Sublibrary: SL 3 – Information Systems and Application, incl. Internet/Web
and HCI

Typesetting: Camera-ready by author, data conversion by Scientific Publishing Services, Chennai, India

Printed on acid-free paper

Springer is part of Springer Science+Business Media (www.springer.com)

Preface

This volume comprises the proceedings of the 8th International Conference on Cooperative Design (CDVE 2011), which was held during September 11–14, 2011, in Hong Kong.

The papers in this volume present the most recent research and development results in the field of cooperative design, visualization, engineering and other cooperative applications.

The papers convincingly show us that cooperative working provides higher capability for solving complicated problems and raises the quality of production, client satisfaction and security.

Cooperative working has been applied to various application fields. These proceedings include a group of papers reporting on cooperative design in architecture, furniture production, concert hall interior set-up etc. How to include the clients into the cooperative design phase is one of the key issues to be solved. Parameterizing the design to facilitate the participation of the clients in customizing the final product design is one of the innovations presented here. Papers that deal with the problems in cooperative decision making are also included.

Cooperative technology has been applied to finer phases of the product life cycle more than ever. Examples include cooperative disassembly process planning and complex equipment maintenance such as aircraft maintenance where security is vital.

Cooperation is extended from human cooperation to machine cooperation. Cooperation among sensors in sensor networks has proved to be much more efficient than without the application of cooperative technology. Cooperative working between the different life cycle phases has also received more attention. Even when the phases in the product life cycle do not occur at the same time, cooperation makes a big difference in the life cycle management. We can consider life cycle management as an asynchronous cooperative working process along time which benefits all the phases of the product life cycle.

New user interfaces have appeared for cooperative design and cooperative learning. Typical examples are the multi-touch devices that have been used in various applications. This volume deals with the application of these new user interfaces.

We are happy to see that the research community has begun to study cooperative entities as a whole. Researchers have started to model and simulate the behavior of large-scale entities of cooperative organizations at a higher abstract level.

I would like to take the opportunity to thank all of our Program Committee members and Organizing Committee members for their continuous support of this series of conferences. To begin is difficult. To continue and persist is even more difficult. I would also like to thank all of our authors for their wonderful work in the research of this field and their willingness to share their experience and results with the community. I would like to thank all the reviewers for their generous help in reviewing the papers and thereby helping to ensure the quality of this conference.

September 2011

Yuhua Luo
CDVE2011

Organization

Conference Chair

Yuhua Luo   University of Balearic Islands, Spain

International Program Committee

Program Chair

Dieter Roller   University of Stuttgart, Germany

Members

Jose Alfredo Costa
Peter Demian
Susan Finger
Matti Hannus
Shuangxi Huang
Claudia-Lavinia Ignat
Ivan Jelinek
Mikael Jern
Harald Klein

Jean-Christophe Lapayre
Francis Lau
Pierre Leclercq
Jos P. Leeuwen
Kwan-Liu Ma
Mary Lou Maher
Toan Nguyen
Moira C. Norrie
Manuel Ortega

Niko Salonen
Weiming Shen
Ram Sriram
Chengzheng Sun
Thomas Tamisier
Carlos Vila
Nobuyoshi Yabuki

Organizing Committee

Chair

Francis Lau   University of Hong Kong, China

Members

Alex Garcia
Tomeu Estrany

Jaime Lloret
Guofeng Qin

Reviewers

Jose Alfredo Costa
Marc Aurel
Peter Demian
Rafael Duque
Sylvia Encheva Susan Finger
Takayuki Fujimoto

Shuangxi Huang
Claudia-Lavinia Ignat
Jessie Kennedy
Mi Jeong Kim
Harald Klein
Jean-Christophe Lapayre

Jos P. Leeuwen
Guoxiang Liu
Jaime Llore
Mary Lou Maher
Suhas J. Manangi
Toan Nguyen
Witold Nocon
Moira C. Norrie
Manuel Ortega
Sebasti Galms Grzegorz Polakw
Guofeng Qin

Dieter Roler
Niko Salonen
Weiming Shen
Ram Sriram
Chengzheng Sun
Kubicki Sylvain
Thomas Tamisier
Carlos Vila Pastor
Xiangyu Wang
Nobuyoshi Yabuki

Table of Contents

Part 1: Cooperative Design

Part 2: Cooperative Applications

Part 3: Cooperative Engineering

Part 4: Cooperative Visualization

Part 5: Basic Theory and Technology

Concert Halls in Cooperative Virtual Environments

A. Benjamin Spaeth

casino IT, CAAD Laboratory of the Faculty of Architecture and Urban Planning,
Stuttgart University, Geschwister-Scholl-Str.24D, 70174 Stuttgart
spaeth@casino.uni-stuttgart.de

Abstract. The integration of simulation tools into an architectural design and decision process comprise a large potential. The design of acoustic spaces like concert halls or theatres is very complex in regard to the design and evaluation of its acoustic quality. To enable evaluation and discussion between different participants of an acoustic design and decision process an adequate cooperative and interactive design environment was searched. As the acceptance and the reliability of cooperative virtual environment rises with the number of addressed senses and the quality of representation the combination of a high quality visual simulation (COVISE/COVER) with a high quality acoustic simulation (RAVEN/VA) is achieved. The paper describes the system architecture in regard to its cooperative aspects and points out possible cooperation modes. Different application scenarios of the virtual acoustic environment, like education scenario or planning scenario are described through case studies. The experiences from these scenarios are summarised in the conclusions.

Keywords: virtual acoustics, virtual reality, architectural design, design tools.

1 Introduction

Concert halls make high demands on the aesthetic and acoustic quality of the architectural design. Moreover they are often in the focus of public perception. Many different decision makers and observers with different qualifications and intentions are involved in the design process. As the design itself is very complex in regard to acoustic, functional and aesthetic requirements, it would be helpful to have a most realistic representation of both visual and acoustic properties. There are already simulation tools existing like Catt Acoustics [1], Soundplan [2] or Ease [3] which are able to simulate and auralise the acoustics of an enclosure. Although these applications provide very precise acoustical simulations they are limited in their visual representation and their interaction and collaborative possibilities. As Kieferle and Wössner [4] already declared the combination of different senses in an interactive collaborative virtual environment hold a big potential and should be achieved. As there are existing systems for real time visual interactive environments like COVISE/COVER [5] as well as systems for real time acoustics simulation and auralisation like RAVEN/VISTA [6] the obvious challenge was to combine these two

Y. Luo (Ed.): CDVE 2011, LNCS 6874, pp. 1–6, 2011.

systems to a performing audio-visual cooperative environment. Inside an immersive strongly realistic simulation of the future concert hall, laymen and planners can discuss acoustical and architectural phenomena directly and can percept the spatial audio-visual result of their design decisions in a very natural way.

2   Collaborative System Architecture

The presented system is a combination of a collaborative interactive real time virtual environment called COVISE/COVER [5] and a real time room acoustics simulation called RAVEN/VA [6]. The core intention is to integrate the advantages of both systems into a single system which is feasible in an architectural design context. The simulation of room acoustics is an expensive process in terms of computational power. Although the acoustical system uses pre-calculation methods the acoustical simulation (RAVEN/VA) is able to calculate about 40 polygons in real time. The visual system (COVER) which is using a pre-calculation method of light information by embedding it into a texture map handles several ten thousands polygons. Due to different data formats and different geometrical resolutions of the systems the use of two different models is necessary.

The COVIES/COVER architecture is a cooperative environment based on a hybrid communication model which is a combination of server/client and peer-to-peer communication. Due to security reasons and band width economy COVER uses a replicated application model where every client hosts the complete application and is just sharing navigation, synchronisation and interaction data. The object data like CAD models are distributed in advance and are available locally on every client. The server handles session information and application status [5].

The integration of the room acoustical simulation into the cooperative environment follows the above described replicated application model. It is realised by a local calculation of the acoustics simulation on every client. The acoustic simulation is based on distributed model and material properties information. Thus the clients remain independent from hardware performance and network band width of the involved clients [6].

Figure 1 shows the scheme of the client side integration of the simulation into the COVER architecture. The visualisation and the acoustical simulation module are communicating through TCP protocol on a local network. The user position and interaction data are distributed to both applications by the tracker daemon. Thus both applications calculate the corresponding output although they are using different models. This requires certainly that the models are persistent in terms of origin, scale and orientation.

The indispensible sound source is implemented as a nonstandard VRML node into the COVER model. It is realised through a COVER plugin. Due to the VRML node characteristic of the sound source its position data is distributed through the cooperative architecture of COVER automatically. Thus the sound source can be moved during run time.

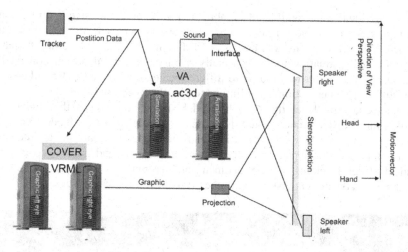

Fig. 1. Diagram of system architecture [7]

3 Cooperation Modes for Architectural Design Purpose

In an architectural design context the user groups are limited in terms of number and size of the groups. COVER supports explicitly this kind of user scenario.

The replicated application model of the COVER architecture provides different cooperation modes. Through the takeover of this replicated application model by the acoustical simulation integration these cooperation modes remain available. In the independent cooperation mode every client can act independently from other clients, whereas in the master-client cooperation mode, one client is promoted to a master roll which guides the other clients through the model. The first scenario corresponds to a group of different users with different interests on the design task which are invited to explore the model. Every client is acting and calculating independently, while the position data of every user is distributed and represented in all other models. The second scenario represents a group of different planning disciplines which intend to solve a specified design problem. Every user is following the master's action, interaction and position. While the interaction data is distributed from the master to the clients the visual and acoustical output is calculated locally on the client whereby every client produces the same output.

4 Different Application Scenario

As the combined audio-visual system allows very realistic and individual perception of abstract but relevant acoustical values like reverberation time or early decade time it is a valuable tool being used in the education of architecture students to better understand room acoustics. Through the immersive simulation the abstract values of room acoustics commonly represented by figures in tables and graphs in schemes become individually perceptible in combination with an immersive 3-dimensional visual representation of the considered space. As human senses work dependently the combined and synchronous addressing to different is a valuable aim of spatial simulations and evaluation tools. Especially in an architectural design context the evaluation of space improves the more different categories of senses are addressed. Architectural space perception is not limited to visual perception [8].

On the pedagogic level the twofold model architecture forces the students to simplify a much differentiated visual model into a simple acoustical model. Thus the geometrical impacts to room acoustics and the representation of architectural structures into acoustical properties have to be understood and transferred into the acoustical model. Deciding relevant geometry and assigning adapted properties leads the students to a deeper understanding of the principles of room acoustics.

Fig. 2. Virtual acoustics model of the Golden Hall, Musikvereinsaal, Vienna

On a higher education level, the system is used for students' presentations, in order to make the design evaluable. The design and the evaluation of acoustical spaces are often funded on well-known and proofed acoustical concepts [9], [10]. So the conceptual evaluation is based on a rough comparison between existing and new design. Thus it becomes very difficult to evaluate spatial-acoustical concepts which exceed common design principles. Exploring genuine new designs in the combined virtual environment a realistic impression of acoustical performance in conjunction with the spatial experience enables a chargeable architectural evaluation without corresponding precedents.

Fig. 3. Student's design for a concert hall for spatial music (three stages)

Fig. 4. Virtual acoustics model of the Neue Stadthalle Reutlingen

Testing the acceptance of the system it is used in a realistic planning process where different groups of planners and decision makers are involved. For the design of the "Neue Stadthalle Reutlingen" the involved parties are located in Reutlingen, Berlin and Stuttgart. Using the collaborative virtual acoustical environment the different planning groups are able to share design advances. Through the individual perception of the design acoustical engineers, the architect, members of the orchestra and representatives of the client can get into communication about the design of the concert hall. Considering personal comments the majority of the users appreciate the combined perception of visual and audible presence. Only some users' audible perception is irritated by the visuals. Due to the realistic 3-dimensional impression, interaction possibilities and the free movement abilities in the scene even orchestra musicians feel a high acceptance of the virtual representation.

5 Conclusion

The presented system allows different people at the same time at different places to percept an audio-visual representation of an acoustical design. The system combines highly visual quality with highly realistic acoustical auralisation by providing interaction and collaborative possibilities. Considering the different scenarios one can state that the system is feasible for education purpose as well as for research issues like evaluating and designing innovative acoustical concepts. The integration of the acoustical simulation into the replicated application architecture of COVER provides cooperation methods like independent client cooperation modes as well as master-client modes.

References

1. Dahlenbäck, B.: CATT-Acoustic, Gothenburg (1998), http://www.catt.se
2. Braunstein + Berndt: SoundPLAN Acoustics,
   http://www.soundplan.eu/start.php?Spr=eng
3. Ahnert, W.: EASE,
   http://www.ada-acousticdesign.de/set/setsoft.html
4. Kieferle, J., Wössner, U.: Showing the invisible. Seven rules for a new approach of using immersive virtual reality in architecture. In: 19th eCAADe Conference on Education and Research in Computer Aided Architectural Design in Europe, Helsinki, pp. 376–381 (2001)
5. Wössner, U.: Virtuelle und Hybride Prototypen in Kooperativen Arbeitsumgebungen. Dissertation. Universität Stuttgart, Stuttgart. Fakultät Energie-, Verfahrens- und Biotechnik (2009)
6. Lentz, T., Schröder, D., Vorländer, M., Assenmacher, I.: Virtual Reality System with Integrated Sound Field Simulation and Reproduction. EURASIP Journal on Advances in Signal Processing, Article ID 70540, 19 pages (2007), doi:10.1155/2007/70540
7. Spaeth, A.B.: Room acoustics in the architectural design process. In: 26th eCAADe Conference on Education and Research in Computer Aided Architectural Design in Europe, Antwerp, pp. 367–374 (2008)
8. Schricker, R.: Kreative Raum-Akustik für Architekten und Designer. Deutsche Verlags-Anstalt, Stuttgart (2001)
9. Fasold, W., Veres, E.: Schallschutz und Raumakustik in der Praxis: Planungsbeispiele und konstruktive Lösungen. 2. Auflage. Verlag für Bauwesen, Berlin (2003)
10. Mehta, M., Johnson, J., Rocafort, J.: Architectural Acoustics: Principles and Design. Prentice-Hall, New Jersey (1999)

Design Offered Up: Control and Open Outcomes in a Digitally Enabled Design Process

Anne Filson and Gary Rohrbacher

College of Design, University of Kentucky, Pence Hall, Lexington, KY 40506
{anne.filson,gary.rohrbacher}@uky.edu

Abstract. This paper presents the design of a digitally fabricated, customizable line of furniture and casework objects that leverage parametric technology and social networking to produce a highly collaborative distributed digital fabrication workflow. It describes how a furniture system, serving as an apprehensible model for architecture, was designed concurrently with the networked, multi-agent workflow that manufactures it and the layered user input that defines it. The furniture object designs are inextricably linked to their fabrication by a distributed network of small fabricators that supplant the single large manufacturer, and to their open outcomes that balance professional design expertise with user input. The paper concludes with describing how this model challenges the architectural profession's prevailing focus on the transactional and object oriented capabilities of recent digital innovations. By using such tools to design the objects within their systemic and networked relationships, architects might successfully create outcomes that better respond to society's increasingly complex demands.

Keywords: Collaborative Design, Emergence, Network Theory, Parametric Modeling, Open Design, Networked Fabrication, Multi-Agent Systems.

1   Introduction

The AtFab project began as a research investigation into how architects can assert professional expertise and leverage the knowledge of others in order to produce better, more relevant design outcomes. This paper documents how our team of architects pursued a design project that entailed developing a line of CNC fabricated furniture objects. We sought to test whether balancing design control and open outcomes might produce an effective working model for addressing larger, more complex architectural challenges. In this process, we designed the furniture objects themselves, the workflow that would produce them, as well as the interface and inputs that would engage others in the process. In contemporary architectural scenarios, our profession maintains a residual pre-digital mindset, where project realization and the input of others remain ancillary to an object-oriented design process. Digital innovations that range from building information modeling and parametric definitions to digital fabrication and "social" networking among the delivery team have great potential to change this prevailing mode of working. However, much of our profession deploys these innovations to exclusively define object physicality [1]

Y. Luo (Ed.): CDVE 2011, LNCS 6874, pp. 7–13, 2011.

and/or to serve the transactional structure of architect-client-constructor relationships [2]. In contrast, our team sought to engage these tools in an iterative design process that inextricably links the design of the object with the workflow in its production and the productive engagement by users. The investigation focused on combining this redefined scope and digital tools to yield a working model for achieving highly responsive design outcomes that will serve the increasingly complicated demands on our profession.

2 Design Research Process

The team's research focused on developing a line of furniture which proved to be apprehensible enough to test the design, communication and construction process, while possessing the analogous structural, material, functional and contextual requirements of architecture. Calling the line AtFab, the team sought to derive the widest array of objects from the simplest system possible. The design was inspired by John Holland's notion of emergence, "this sense of much coming from little [3]." The project used the construction joint as the "little," assuming that "much" was a wide proliferation of furniture types. The construction joint, which we called the S/Z Joint, was developed for its sound 3-sided relationship between two flat shapes cut from any thickness of sheet material by any CNC cutting machine. The study further defined sets of functional and structural criteria that drove combinations and re-combinations of the S/Z Joint to maximize the quantity and variety of outcomes, toward achieving "much" {Fig 1}.

Each furniture object is comprised exclusively of flat pieces that are cut from sheet materials by a basic 3-axis CNC router. The team refined the 2D furniture pieces to be

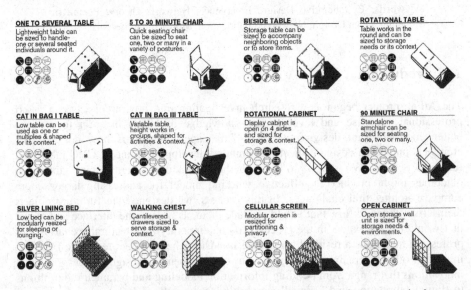

Fig. 1. Resulting Furniture Objects alongside roster of structural & program criteria

rudimentary in shape, in order to allow intuitive assembly by anyone with a basic fastening method. Each furniture object was also designed to undergo parametrically controlled transformations in dimension, shape, and/or material thickness, which would enable users to tailor the object to specific needs and contexts. The parameters would yield an infinite range of variations as well as extreme transformations of each furniture object, which could introduce of unanticipated programmatic affiliations. With furniture objects that are adaptable to a multitude of specific needs, the team brought the system closer to functioning as emergence does in nature [4].

The investigation developed a designer/user/fabricator workflow that would support digitally enabled, distributed, and collaborative manufacture. By looking through the lens of network theory, and identifying links and nodes [5] in the manufacturing process, we found a framework for fine-tuning the design to leverage digital tools, and to facilitate the agents in the process and the relationship between them.

AtFab engages the increasing number of CNC fabricator networks that are uniting everyday consumers with CNC fabricators.[1] Through several iterative phases, the team collaborated with a dozen independent fabricators, found through the networks, operating CNC laser cutter, router, and water jet machines both close to home and a continent away. We collaborated with this group, by emailing them a package of .dxf files and simple instructions, in order to fabricate partial and full-scale prototypes of the furniture objects. The research team found that fabricator feedback aided us in streamlining the workflow process, and in the development of the furniture design for the process. We discovered .dxf formats, defined origins, and simplified layering nomenclature ensured the cleanest translation into the seemingly infinite variety of proprietary CAD/CAM softwares that run the machinery. Early verbal communication confusion drove us to simplify the designs to reduce our cut types to holes, and inside and outside cuts, and eliminate any option for tool path offsets. Results that produced joints with fits that were too loose or tight inspired the inclusion of a small test pieces located within every cut file, to help fabricators calibrate material thickness to joints before cutting the overall file. Idiosyncrasies and differences between machines and materials substantiated our early assumption to include a parametric definition for adjusting kerfs in the S/Z joint. Kerfs were incorporated into the furniture design and could be minimized for the sharpness of a laser through plastic, maximized for a router bit through solid hardwood, or between for a water jet through aluminum. Also, as the team realized that the language and units of cost estimating varied by machine and material we began to generate linear inches of cutting, sheet material requirements and square footage into an accompanying instruction file.

In the assembly step, the team tested how effectively the designs avoided pitfalls of the "IKEA effect," where consumers find themselves too challenged by the construction task [7], and sought extremely intuitive assembly of each furniture object without instructions. We asked some of our fabricators, students and others to put

---

[1] Networks like 100kgarages.com and Ponoko.com are enabling consumers to connect with local CNC fabricators, while digital fabrication storefronts like Tech Shop, Shapeways and MGX provide either full fabrication services or self-serve/DIY CNC equipment for urban consumers.

together full and partial scale furniture prototypes with only an axonometric drawing of the finished object as reference. Our test subjects successfully assembled 9 of the 12 furniture objects quickly without prompting. We found that assembly of the remaining 3 larger, more complex pieces (Silver Lining Bed, Cellular Screen & and 90 Minute Chair) presented more challenges. While the team felt these designs could not be further reduced to achieve the same construction ease without compromising function, we did find that users could be prompted with the help of pictogram keys etched discretely into the surface of each piece.

The task of eliciting productive user input into the worfkflow, which followed our system design and manufacturing research, required more iteration and nuance than testing collaborative fabrication and construction. The team studied interactive conditions first by simulating them with animated transformations of the 3D furniture models. Animations in this case were analogous to sketching and enabled the team to visualize transformations that could best maximize the range of outcomes, through the most minimal sets of adjustments. Once the most generative transformations were understood, the team translated the animated 3D choreography into parametric definitions using both Rhino's Grasshopper plug-in as well Revit's parametric capabilities. In designing the parametric definitions, the team found it necessary to define limits that would ensure successful outcomes while maintaining openness for unanticipated scenarios. The dimensions of a standard CNC bed and material dimensions, as well as the structural integrity of each furniture object and the scale of a human, served as the underlying criteria for limits. Parametric definitions enabled adjustment to material thickness and kerf on the furniture objects to maximize user choice in material. The furniture designs were refined to locate transformations in dimension, shape and module between the S/Z assemblies, keeping changes in size and shape independent of each object's fundamental construction. Both Rhino and Revit enabled the team to extract 2D profiles of each transformed furniture part, and efficiently nest them onto a 2D "sheet" that could be exported as a .dxf file and sent to our fabricators for cutting.

The team defined design criteria for an automated version of this step in the workflow that could supplant the overlapping software and manual steps in our simulation. An automated, potentially asynchronous, system would rely upon an online interactive graphic user interface, which would re-contextualize our parametric interactions turning them outward to the user and refining them for clarity and usability. The UI would input dimensional data selected by the user into an XML design table, which is linked to a SolidWorks parametrically defined 3D model of the furniture object. SolidWorks would make automated extractions from the model and produce 2D .dxf cut files, which would be bundled with specifications and instructions for download. The team is presently taking steps to realize a version that will ultimately be placed online for use by a wide range of consumers, who can download their customized Open Source furniture files that would be licensed through Creative Commons [8]. As open furniture objects, they are attributed to the designer, but re-mixed and shared non-commercially from one user to the next. This online stage would ideally provide crowd-sourced feedback to further develop the object, interface and system design. {Fig 2}

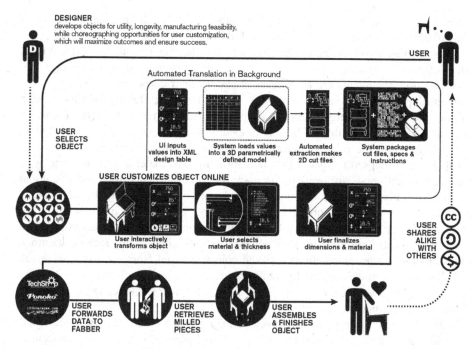

Fig. 2. Collaborative Workflow Diagram

As the research team relinquished some design scope, going deep to script the details of exact furniture design outcomes, we had successfully expanded other scope, going broad to define nested sets of design parameters. We couldn't know every shape, size, material or pattern, but we made an intensive strategic design effort to define digital and logistical conditions in the interface and workflow that ensured the furniture objects would maintain structural and functional integrity, and could be easily manufactured and assembled in a wide array of contexts. The team found much design involved in choreographing the means and terms of customization, so that variety in function and context was as feasible as adjustments for taste and preference. Furniture objects and their parameters were evaluated for a capacity to maximize difference at opposite ends of the growth spectrum. Some examples included watching the rotational cabinet become a wardrobe or a low TV stand, a coffee table become a workbench or an altogether unknown storage unit, the 5 to 30 Minute Chair become a bench for three or a chaise for one. Our expertise was equally tasked in designing to enable users to determine cost and materiality of the furniture object, to facilitate infinite options for time, place and terms of its fabrication, and even to expand conditions of ownership in the design. Parameters, or relationships enabled by digital tools, became our design focus in all of these instances.

3 Conclusions and Discussion

The team arrived at two significant insights in the pursuit of this expanded design scope in the development of AtFab. The first revolved around the vast opportunities of a distributed manufacturing scenario and the other around articulating the recast role of designers to create open-ended scenarios.

Designed as a connecting agent, AtFab erodes the conventionally assigned roles of designer, fabricator and consumer in the process of manufacture and consumption; the agents are no longer defined by their corporeal limits, but by the relationships that sustain the process [9]. The resulting fluidity of this erosion allows the manufacturing process to adapt to a wider array of delivery conditions that increase the possibility of finding relevance, or as in nature, ensuring survival. By relying upon the relay of information rather than the conveyance of material [10], AtFab collapsed the geography of transaction and material procurement. As a result, finished goods are available in more places, at the same time redundant and excessive materials and goods transport can be minimized or altogether eliminated. AtFab's manufacturing process also enables distributed manufacturing to reconstitute the fabricator from a whole multinational single manufacturer, with a supply and distribution chain, to a network of individual small, local fabricators. This model supports interactions between consumers and fabricators that are much smaller, but are abundant and found anywhere at anytime. Such exchanges can be more efficient, adaptable, and responsive than a centralized source, and can be more locally and personally engaged.

AtFab's multi-agent maker network demands categorization outside designer-centric, user-centric or author-less models being pursued across our architectural profession. We found its analog in conceptual artist Sol Lewitt's challenge to the prevailing concept of the artist in the 1960's. To produce his earliest wall murals, "Drawing Series Composite, Part I-IV," Lewitt outlined a simple set of drawing parameters and left particular elements in the material execution open to participants' interpretation. Lewitt's parameters proved elemental enough to yield almost infinite outcomes depending on the site, user and materials but clear enough to consistently generate an artwork to his standards [11]. Similarly, AtFab's model leverages the architect's expertise in envisioning, innovating, thinking systemically, and implementing to define the most productive parameters that support the input of users, who are expert in knowing their own needs and desires [12].

The project ultimately illustrates an apprehensible model for architects to engage BIM, parametric tools, social networking and digital fabrication and implicate them in the relationships that define the multi-agent system of design and construction. Without these tools, this inclusive process wouldn't be possible, but without Design Thinking [13], the full advantages of these tools will never be fully utilized. Designing relationships alongside objects, architects can simultaneously open up more opportunities for design, and create strategies that respond to the indeterminate unknowns that inevitably compromise the perceived perfection of a closed design. Prior to the innovations of these tools, we could not have conceived of such a role beyond the singular designer-singular outcome. Today, we're empowered by them to offer design up, rather than hand it down, and in so doing address the increasingly complex architectural challenges faced by our profession, clients and societies.

References

1. Schumacher, P.: Parametricism as Style: Parametricist Manifesto. Presented at 11th Architecture Biennale, Venice (2008)
2. Introduction. In: Bernstein, P., Deamer, P. (eds.) Building (in) the Future: Recasting Labor in Architecture, pp. 17–20. Princeton Architectural Press, Princeton (2010)
3. Holland, J.: Emergence from Chaos to Order. Basic Books, New York (1997)
4. Ibid, p. 24
5. Barabasi, A.-L.: Linked: How Everything is Connected to Everything Else and What It Means. Plume, New York (2003)
6. Norton, M.I.: The IKEA Effect: When Labor Leads to Love. Harvard Business Review 87(2), 20–21 (2009)
7. Creative Commons with Attribution and Non-Commercial Use, http://creativecommons.org/licenses/by-nc/3.0/legalcode
8. Deleuze, G., Guattari, F.: Capitalism and Schizophrenia. University of Minnesota Press, Minneapolis (1987)
9. Delanda, M.: A Thousand Years of Nonlinear History. Zone Books, New York (1997)
10. Lewitt, S.: Paragraphs on Conceptual Art. Artforum 5(10), 79–83 (1967)
11. Suri, J.F.: Thoughtless Acts. Chronicle Books, San Francisco (2005)
12. Brown, T.: Design Thinking. Harvard Business Review (June 2008)

Design Interaction via Multi-touch

Marc Aurel Schnabel[1] and Rui (Irene) Chen[2]

[1] The Chinese University of Hong Kong, SAR, P.R. China
marcaurel@cuhk.edu.hk
[2] The University of Sydney, NSW, Australia
rui.chen@sydney.edu.au

Abstract. We present a multi-touch-tabletop tool for design-collaborations and -communication tasks employing three-dimensional digitalized models. Our system allows users from various disciplines to communicate and share their ideas by manipulating the reference and their own input simultaneously by simply using intuitive gestures. Haptic and proprioceptive perception of tangible representations are perceived and understood more readily whereby our system provides an increased potential to compensate for the low spatial cognition of its users. Our integration of combining both model-based and participatory approaches with multi-touch tabletop system setups differs considerably from conventional visual representations for collaborative design. Since the multi-touch design interaction allows users to engage intuitively within virtual design environments, it is presenting a next generation of common graphical user interfaces.

Keywords: Multi-touch, collaboration, interaction, haptic, design.

1 Introduction

We employed a multi-touch tabletop combined with 3D digitalized models for design collaboration and communication tasks. Designers communicated and shared their ideas using intuitive and natural gestures to manipulate the same references, simultaneously. Other studies have presented that 3D shapes can be perceived and understood more readily through haptic and proprioceptive perception of tangible representations - versus through visual representation alone [1]. As a result of this, Chen and Wang [2] established a framework to integrate 3D visualization and tactile sensory in design learning.

As a next step in this development we developed natural user interactions into design activities [3]. Hereby Graphical User Interfaces (GUI) brought a new approach that was more effective than their conventional predecessors. *Natural User Interfaces* (NUI) have advanced user experiences, and multi-touch and gesture technologies provide new opportunities for a variety of potential uses in design activities. Current research studies how to control the design of interactive interfaces. Tabletop interfaces have already emerged in the past decade, and attempts have been made to move away from the conventional mouse input and desktop screen metaphors, which limit the information sharing for multiple users and impediment the direct interaction for communication between each other due its built-in restrictions.

Y. Luo (Ed.): CDVE 2011, LNCS 6874, pp. 14–21, 2011.

With the use of a multi-touch tabletop for instance, more than one designer can manipulate entities on the tabletop, and can communicate his or her ideas directly. This makes designing more effective, which increases the overall efficiency. Designers can also collect real-time data by any change they make instantly. Our multi-touch tabletop system has integrated the *Unit3D*-tool [4] into the platform. The possibilities of Uniy3D make designing flexible, direct, instantaneous and enjoyable; it is deeply engaging and expressive. Unity3D is not only influences the game industry, but also it is a development for creating highly interactive 3D content as the interface of multimedia devices such as mobile phones, pocket-computers, etc. It allows designers to work remotely in a collaborative way to integrate the design process by using the individual (mobile) devices while interacting in a common platform.

2   The Multi-touch Tabletop

2.1 Model -Based Approach Integrated into the System

Digital architectural models can be built within Unity3D or imported into it. Designers can choose from the various components from the built-in menus. However, in the past these objects are usually only used to build game environments for Unit3D applications. The innovative idea is to build 3D architectural models instead for the purpose to explore and communicate the design. Since architectural models have been largely applied to present the design proposal and range in detail from very simple formal massing models of just a few cubic blocks, through to basic interior/exterior walkthrough models, on to detailed models complete with furnishings and landscaping. This improved visual communication offers stakeholders an immediate and three-dimensional access to the design.

Architectural modelling is an essential part of the process towards creating an accurate building [5]. The architectural concept is reflected in, communicated through and expressed with digital models – hence it forms the crucial stage for all types of architectural building design, no matter what type of building. Since (digital) architectural models are those elements that enable users to view an interior as well as the external appearance, the making digital models for an architectural concept is known as architectural concept modelling [5]. It is a technology allowing the user to apply their imagination and thoughts in a variety of ways, and to examine or reflect on the outcomes.

These models assist users to pursue a particular line of thoughts to intersect idea with tactile reality, satisfying for example combinations of furniture arrangement, floor plan layouts, spacing and massing. By changing the variables, a user of a digital model gets instantaneous representation, iterating towards a final design.

Naturally, our multi-touch tabletop system benefits a variety of users such as developers, builders, or contractors; all stakeholders of a building process form idea to realisation.

2.2 Participatory Approach Integrated into the System

Naturally, our multi-touch tabletop system benefits a variety of users such as developers, builders, or contractors; all stakeholders of a building process form idea to realisation.

Some of the reasons for all stakeholders to be involved in participatory design are:

- *Inclusive* opening up the design of the process to include multidisciplinary requirements; from direct and indirect intentions, and giving the beneficiaries the chance to voice their needs at the earliest stage.
- *Negotiation* between the different stakeholders to reach agreement about what is to be monitored and evaluated, how and when data will be collected and analysed, what the data actually means, and how findings will be shared and action taken [6].
- *Learning* - a focus on cumulative learning by all the participants as the basis for subsequent improvement and sustained action. This action includes local institution building or strengthening, thus increasing the capacity of people to initiate action on their own.
- *Flexibility* in adapting the evaluation to the wider external environment and to the set of different conditions and needs from multidisciplinary, as these factors change over time.

In architectural design, the participatory approach offers to bridge between architects, builders, developers and everyone else who needs to participant in the building and design process. This collaboration throughout the building process can benefit both each stakeholder as well as improve the overall outcome. Architectural and building design solutions are richer when end-users are involved early on in the design process [6]. Hence, there is an increasing need for the building and design/production process to engage collaboratively between teams of architects, between architects and engineers, and architects and builders as well as clients, users, and general public. Our system integrates participatory possibilities in order to make use of these benefits.

2.3 Prototype

The setup of our prototype is illustrated in Figure 1. It shows the interaction between the participants (actor), system hardware, and Unity3D. The designer uses multi-touch gestures to interact with a device (e.g. multi-touch tabletop, smart phone, etc.); the multi-touch gesture events are passed to Unity3D via TUIO (event handler and proxy) [7]. Unity3D then takes the user input, and acts upon it according to the game logic and creates a representation of the 3D world database on the user's device (visualization). The designer, seeing the visualization, makes decisions, and uses gestures to signal them. Stakeholders can then jointly interact, view and access the design and discuss elements they see in front of them. The multi-touch is then extended not only to the gestures of one person, but also to the whole participating group. Hence, the design becomes the connecting element between the designer and its stakeholders as well as between the physical and virtual realm.

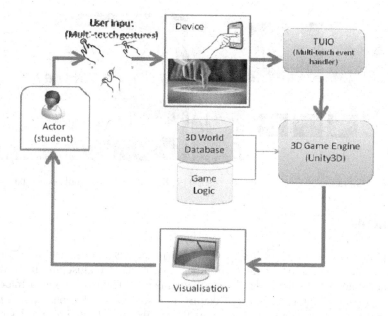

Fig. 1. Interaction diagram between participants (actor), system hardware, and Unity3D

The system setup shall be configured as follows. Every user installs a copy of the free available Unit3D application on their devices. With that in place designers or collaborators can model their desired design according to their needs. Since Unit3D allows for different modes of representation, designers can develop their models from rough ideas or sketches to detailed representations.

In order to set up the TUI systems, users also install a Community Core Vision (CCV), which is an open source/cross-platform solution for computer vision and machine sensing [8]. It takes a video input stream capturing the gesture movements by users, such as finger down, finger moved and finger released, on the screen as events sending them to the system as source images and outputs tracking data, which coordinates. Users adjust their settings to change background, smooth levels, brightness, etc. allowing a calibration of the system as the example shown in Figure 2 left.

The benefits of CCV is its use as an interface, with various web cameras and video devices, as well as its ability to connect to various 'TUIO/OSC/XML' enabled applications and to support multi-touch lighting techniques including: FTIR, DI, DSI, and LLP [8]. Users just need to calibrate following the instructions to ensure the movements from users can be recognized by the systems precisely. Users also need to install the appropriate video drivers according to the video camera they use. The Sony PlayStation camera is used in our system for reasons of quality and ease of use.

Finally the TUIO has to be installed; it is the bridge between the hardware and the other underlying applications so it allows all applications running to be interoperable. Then users connect their mobile device, video cameras and the multi-touch tabletop (e.g. Figure 2 right) and run the applications. Once models are loaded or imported, users can not only visualize but also collaborate in with their set-up.

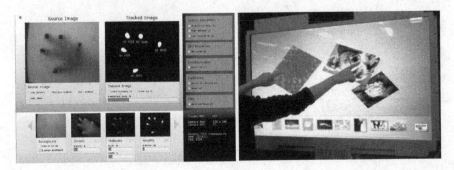

Fig. 2. L: Calibration by *Community Core Vision* [9] **R:** *Astri's* Optical multi-touch panel [10]

3   Benefits

The exploration of the relationship between human beings and the natural world and the subsequent implication on interaction has deep roots in philosophy, in particular Phenomenology, which also radiated into the domains of Human Computer Interfaces (HCI). Phenomenology is the tenet of empirical observation on events that are based on other theories but cannot be directly explained through them. From a designer's perspective, the connection between the real and the virtual is a natural one, as the development of a design includes thinking in virtual realms about real objects [6].

In design activities, people create an external representation of information, often of their own ideas and understanding. Our system provides a common ground for multiple users to express their ideas with immediate correspondence from the representation showing on the multi-touch tabletop. It aids users to make their ideas more concrete and explicit, and once externalized, they can reflect how well their work sits within real context or situation or communicate and collaborate with stakeholders. During a design process, iterations and reflections refine the design itself. In collaborative setting users have varieties of reflections and ways to communicate them; often these variations lead to issues that need a clear visual representation. A conventional screen based or physical model environment restrains active communication and engagement of all users in the favour of the computer operant or model builder. The prototype demonstrates how this tabletop innovatively replaces the typical desktop metaphor.

We integrated for our system Unity3D with multi-touch tangible interfaces. Unity3D provides a game development tool as part of its application package that has been designed to let users focus on creating new games. However, it does not limit the usage to design additional game scenarios, and allows users to build their own 3D environments, per its customizable and easy-to-use editor, graphical pipelines to openGL [4]. It creates Virtual Reality (VR) environments, which can simulate places of the real world, as well as new designed VEs, thus helping architects and designers to vividly represent their design concepts through 3D visualizations, and interactive media installations in a detailed multi-sensory experience. Stereoscopic displays advance their spatial ability to consider design aspects, from details to urban scales.

3.1 Visualization and Tangibility

Visualization is the key in design development. It is an important part of geometrical thinking and modelling, which allows communication of idea to one self or to others. Visualization is crucial in solving problems that lie within three dimensions [11]. Already simple translations or modifications of elements in space can be a challenge for designers. Generally, people have difficulties for example rotating an object in their minds to see how it would look from a different angle. 3D modelling processes usually provide 3D panorama views that allow users to visualize each building element more accurately. Subsequently, it reduces time and errors of inaccurate imaginary views. Besides reducing error during actual construction, our system assists in clash-detection and the use of certain constrains, material requirement or structural issues.

Our prototype makes use of hardware-accelerated 3D graphics and built-in shaders, visual effects, etc. [3]. Particularly, during the initial 3D modelling process, the system offers an easy visualization process for laypersons and experts.

The main benefit however, comes from the integration of a multi-touch device via the Protocol for Tangible User Interfaces (TUIO). This protocol is simple and adaptable designed specifically to meet the requirements of tabletop Tangible User Interfaces (TUI) [12]. TUIO provides the communication interface between the tangible interface controller and the underlying application layers bridging between Unity3D and the TUI devices [13]. With this in place, users are able to manipulate sets of objects or draw gestures onto the multi touch surface with their fingertips [7]. It was designed in respect to the findings presented in the case studies above [13, 14], where users design using common gestures to generate their design proposals. The interface subsequently connects the VE of the digital model to the physical environment of the users' interaction and hence interacts directly with both realms. Physical objects are tracked by a sensor system and are identified and located in position and orientation on the table surface similar to an AR environment [13, 15]. Physical models can easily be transferred to virtual realm and users can manipulate and explore them in both environments.

3.2 Flexibility and Speed

The core-system of our prototype offers console-like 3D graphics for any web browsers [4] providing a flexible communication-and use-environment for stakeholders: all models can be viewed locally or remote through web browsers. Collocated or remote partners are able to engage within the 3D environment either synchronously or asynchronously.

Our system allows users to switch the target platform while they work and can use a larger variety of device for visualization, modelling and communication: smart-phones, net-books, computers and game consoles.

Based on game technologies or prototype allows for real-time visualisation, animation and special effects. This makes 3D modelling, visualization, changes, and collaboration not only faster but also easier compared to current standard modellers such as *Maya, Rhinoceros,* or *3dStudio Max* [4]. These programs require a higher set of operation skills and considerable time to implement changes, or amendments that are not pre-rendered or modelled. The advantage of our system is that encourages users to try out different scenarios in order to reach a solution, since these tries can be carried out in real-time and with great ease of operation.

3.3 Spatiality

To be able to encode spatial information architects requires skills of spatial understanding. Marshall's study [16] has showed that TUIs offer significant cognitive benefits to individuals with low spatial cognition. In a participatory approach, not all the people are expert on how to imagine and retrieve spatial information. Our prototype with its TUI provides a great potential to enable users from any background to be less challenged since the design in accessible spatially in a physical and/or virtual environment, hence offering a clearer understanding and communication of spatial issues.

4 Conclusion and Summary

We presented a prototype of a multi-touch tabletop system that offers real-time visualization to process information and ease to use by any user laypersons or experts. The flexibility and tangibility means that our prototype can be used on a variety of computational devices and allows multiple users to access and interact on a design proposal remotely or collocated. The multi-touch tabletop system offers spontaneous involvement providing for an exploration of a broader scope of stakeholders. It offers a structured support by collecting data of the design development and outcomes. It integrates effectively and efficiently design-developments from the early stage onwards. Additionally our system proposes to overcome challenges of spatial cognition through its different TUI, hence aiding the communication within the design process and contributing to an integrated approach to design.

It is of advantage in collaborative design allowing users to interact with both physical and virtual objects, whereby a tangible interface enables them to construct expressive representations passively [9], and at the same time communicating with other participants during the design process. We presented a prototype that enables multiple users to actively generate, interact and communicate spatial designs that goes beyond possibilities of conventional media and interfaces. Users can manipulate the same reference synchronously and asynchronously within the same scene with physical and virtual objects.

There have been earlier attempts to create a 'design-table' with similar interaction as presented here. Yet these prototypes have not developed to common use and acceptance. Our system captivates through its simplicity and mostly readily available applications and instruments.

Akin to the findings of Dorta et al [17] in their 'Augmented Design Studio' the implementation of hybrid technologies and design environments proves to be and efficient and effective collective ideation space. Spatial user interfaces allow the design of architecture to be 'touched' by a multiple persons using 'multi-touch' gestures. 'Multi-touch' extends its meaning from a technical HCI concern to a social – collective intelligence and collaborative designing.

References

1. Gillet, A., Sanner, M., Stoffler, D., Olson, A.: A Tangible interfaces for structural molecular biology. Structure 13, 483–491 (2005)
2. Chen, R., Wang, X.: Tangible Augmented Reality: A New Design Instructional Technology. In: Tidafi, T., Dorta, T. (eds.) Joining Languages, Cultures and Visions / Joindre Langages, Cultures et Visions – CAADFutures 2009, Montreal, Canada, pp. 572–584 (2009)
3. Kaltenbrunner, M., Bovermann, T., Bencina, R., Costanza, E.: TUIO - A Protocol for Table Based Tangible User Interfaces. In: Proceedings of the 6th International Workshop on Gesture in Human-Computer Interaction and Simulation, Vannes, France (2005)
4. Unity3D (2010), http://unity3d.com/unity (viewed November 30, 2010)
5. Netstarter, 3D architectural modelling now (2010), http://www.netstarter.com.au/3d-renders/architectural-modelling (viewed January 11, 2011)
6. Bodker, K., Kensing, F., Simonsen, J.: Participatory IT design - Designing for business and workplaces realities. The MIT Press, Cambridge (2004)
7. TUIO (2005), http://www.tuio.org
8. Quarles, J., Lampotang, S., Fischer, I., Fishwich, P., Lok, B.: Tangible User Interfaces Compensate for Low Spatial cognition. In: 3D User Interfaces - 3DUI 2008, Reno, NE, pp. 11–18 (2008)
9. Community Core Vision (2007), http://cv.nuigroup.com
10. Hong Kong Applied Science and Technology Research Institute Company Limited, ASTRI (2011), http://www.astri.org
11. Mackay, W.E., Ratzer, A., Janecek, P.: Video artifacts for design: Bridging the gap between abstraction and detail. In: DIS 2000. ACM Press, New York (2000)
12. ISO / TS 16982, Ergonomics of human-system interaction – Usability methods supporting human-centred design (2000)
13. Seichter, H., Schnabel, M.A.: Digital and Tangible Sensation: An Augmented Reality Urban Design Studio. In: Bhatt, A. (ed.) Proceedings of the 10th International Conference on Computer Aided Architectural Design Research in Asia CAADRIA 2005, CAADRIA, New Delhi, India, vol. 2, pp. 193–202 (2005)
14. Schnabel, M.A.: The Immersive Virtual Design Studio. In: Wang, X., Tsai, J.J.-H. (eds.) Collaborative Design in Virtual Environments. ISCA, vol. 48, pp. 177–191. Springer, Heidelberg (2011)
15. Seichter, H.: Augmented Reality and Tangible Interfaces. In: Dong, A., Vande Moere, A., Gero, J.S. (eds.) Collaborative Urban Design, CAADFutures 2007, pp. 3–16. Springer, Heidelberg (2007)
16. Marshall, P.: Do tangible interfaces enhance learning? In: TEI 2007: Proceedings of the 1st International Conference on Tangible and Embedded Interaction, New Orleans, 163170 (2007)
17. Dorta, T., Kalay, Y., Lesage, A., Pérez, A.: First steps of the Augmented Design Studio: The interconnected Hybrid Ideation Space and the CI Loop. In: Herr, C.M., Gu, N., Roudavski, S., Schnabel, M.A. (eds.) Circuit Bending, Breaking and Mending: Proceedings of the 16th International Conference on Computer-Aided Architectural Design Research in Asia CAADRIA 2011, CAADRIA, Newcastle, Australia, pp. 271–280 (2011)

Collaborative Learning through Cooperative Design Using a Multitouch Table

Tim Warnecke[1], Patrick Dohrmann[1], Alke Jürgens[2],
Andreas Rausch[1], and Niels Pinkwart[1]

[1] Clausthal University of Technology, Germany
[2] Primary School Goslar Hahndorf, Germany
{Tim.Warnecke,Patrick.Dohrmann,Andreas.Rausch,
Niels.Pinkwart}@tu-clausthal.de

Abstract. Today, typical classrooms are still equipped with blackboards, chalk and sometimes overhead projectors. Technology-enriched rooms can often only be found in school libraries or computer pools where students can research topics on the WWW or use other specific computer applications. In this paper, we present an educational game called "Parcours", developed for the interactive SMART table. This cooperative design game, installed on a tabletop that is located within a classroom, is intended to teach primary school children collaboration and coordination skills as well as logical thinking.

Keywords: Collaborative Learning, Cooperative Design, Multitouch table.

1 Introduction

Today, technology is getting increasingly ubiquitous for children even at younger ages. Many devices such as interactive cell phones (e.g., IPhone), game consoles (such as V-Tech, XBox360, Playstation 3, or Wii) or PCs are widespread and children often use them for a variety of purposes, including gaming. Device manufacturers as well as educational practitioners and researchers have tried to include *educational* games into their portfolio like Nintendo's Dr. Kawashima or V-Tech's V.Smile game series. Regrettably, many existing educational games for these systems can only be played in an unsupervised manner and are rather disconnected from education in schools yet. Also, many educational games such as Dr. Kawashima are not collaborative but either single-user based or competitive. Several studies, however, hve indicated that collaboration can promote children's learning [5, 11].

Interactive tabletops with multi touch input such as the SMART table bear the promise of providing opportunities for collaborative educational games [2]. They have a screen size large enough for several children to interact with it at the same time, thus increasing awareness [7], supporting a more balanced contribution of collaborators [6] and providing intuitive interaction methods [10].

The SMART Company regularly starts application contests in which ideas (and prototypes) for innovative collaborative educational games for tabletop devices are invited. In this paper, we present the design and implementation of the 2010 contest winner, the "Parcours" game. Exploiting the benefits of the table top device, this

Y. Luo (Ed.): CDVE 2011, LNCS 6874, pp. 22–29, 2011.

cooperative and co-constructive game is designed to teach primary school children coordination skills (many actions in the game can only be conducted by the group of players interacting in specific manners) as well as logical thinking skills.

2   State-of-Art: Cooperative Educational Tools on Large Displays

Educational tools that make use of large interactive displays have gained currency in recent years. The NIMIS project was one of the first applications of (single)touch large displays in primary schools. In this project, a special software application supported the acquisition of initial reading and writing skills embedded in a computer-integrated environment for young children [4]. The SIDES system employed multi touch displays to teach collaboration skills to adolescents with Asperger's Syndrome in a task that involved the joint construction of pathways [8]. Here, the players had to coordinate concerning "how does what" during the pathway construction in order to reach a common goal. Empirical studies with the SIDES system yielded that SIDES provided adolescents with Asperger's Syndrome with a positive experience through which they could develop effective group work skills and build confidence in social interaction. The StoryTable application [1] enforced co-operation during story-telling activities, and studies conducted with this system showed that cooperative storytelling can increase the level of engagement of less motivated children without affecting the involvement of the more active ones. Harris and colleagues [3] have described a study with the OurSpace application, a groupware tool for solving seat assignment tasks. A result of this study was that multi touch displays reduced group conversations about turn-taking activities and increased task-focused discussions (as compared to single touch interfaces). Recently, also projects that involve the research and development of frameworks (curricular and technological) for using multi touch applications in education have been proposed. This includes the SynergyNet project[1] with an emphasis on pedagogical strategies for designing multi touch applications across multiple stages of formal educations, as well as the work of Schneider and colleagues [9] who present a development framework designed to facilitate the creation of educational multi touch applications. The 2009 winner application of the SMART multi touch contest is an educational game named Laser Lights Challenge. The aim of this game is to direct a laser light through a labyrinth of different walls and obstacles into a goal using mirrors and prisms to direct the laser around corners. The main educational goal of this game is to teach the law of nature of laser lights and their reactions to mirrors and prisms.

In summary, research results both from the education sector and from the field of Human-Computer Interaction indicate that multi touch applications specifically targeted for collaborative learning are not only technically feasible but also potentially valuable, since they combine intuitive interaction concepts with new face-to-face cooperation mechanisms, leading to novel application areas, particularly within classrooms. In this paper, we describe the design and implementation of "Parcours", a co-constructive application which, compared to the existing research results as discussed in this section, is unique in its combination of target group (primary school), learning goals (coordination and logical thinking) and group activity type (collaborative game).

---

[1] http://tel.dur.ac.uk/synergynet/

3 Parcours: Purpose and Design

While many educational games focus on specific cognitive educational objectives like improving mathematical, language or memorizing skills, a discussion with a pedagogue spawned the idea to design a collaborative educational game that focuses on teaching logical thinking and coordination skills. These skills are important for everyday life and child development, yet there is typically no dedicated school subject for them: Physical education classes typically train coordination of one's body parts, but rarely the coordination among children. Mathematics classes, on the other hand, can teach logical thinking, but very often students will stick to their learned "cookbook" formulas and simply apply them to solve problems (without real logical reasoning).

The design goals of Parcours include that the children of the age group 5-10 should be able to intuitively understand the game, coordinate themselves to win, and enjoy the game. In the remainder of this section, we will first introduce the game itself with an overview about its functionalities. Next, the specific design choices (and how they meet the learning targets) will be described.

3.1 Basic Game Concepts

Parcours is a bridge builder game. It provides a rasterized gaming area where the players have to build a path from a starting point to a goal point by using certain tiles, located outside the gaming area, in order to help a playing figure across the map. The game comes with several user interface themes (including spaceships, pirates, animals) to motivate pupils with different interest areas. Figure 1, depicting the user interface of the game in the "car" theme (where the goal is to help a car reach the flag position), shows that the game can be operated from all sides of the tabletop display. The tiles are located on the complete border of the screen, and the "arrow" icons for the playing figure movement are also distributed on all edges of the table. There are two main actions that can be done in the game at the same time: building the path and moving the player. The small playing figure (the car visible in the lower left of the figure) can be moved across a built path by touching the arrow buttons, thus

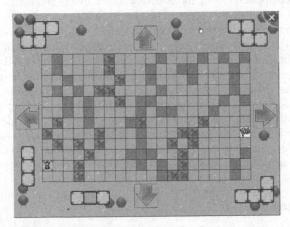

Fig. 1. The Parcours user interface in the "car" theme

maneuvering the figure in the direction the arrows are indicating. The path building process is complicated by different obstacles (visualized depending on the theme, here: rocks and ditches). The players have to build a path either around them or across them using special tiles. There are several tiles with different shapes and different features helping to cross obstacles. For instance, the "bridge" tile can be used to cross ditches by touching its two levers at the same time, lowering the bridge. The ladder tile can be used for crossing rocks. If the playing figure steps onto a ladder, the arrow buttons will change to four identical climb buttons. These buttons must be hit several times to cross the ladder, simulating the effort required to climb up.

All tiles in the game can be added to the gaming area intuitively by touching and dragging them (the game makes motivating, theme-dependent sounds during these movements). They can also be rotated by using at least two fingers, making a rotation movement. All tiles are slightly larger than the raster of the playing field as long as they are still "floating" (i.e., not fixed within the raster yet). The players can drop them into the gaming area with a "minimizing" gesture, using at least two fingers. A dropped tile cannot be removed any more. If the playing figure has reached the goal field, the game will be over and the players win. If the figure does not reach the goal and all tiles are used up, the players have lost.

3.2 Facing the Learning Goals

Parcours is a bridge builder game. As already mentioned, Parcours faces learning goals related to logical thinking and coordination. The main opportunity to learn coordination skills is connected to the use of the tiles surrounding the gaming area. The players have to cooperate and to agree concerning which tiles to use next in order to jointly design the path, then choose them and pass them to other players around the table, who will then drop them down. Furthermore, they have to coordinate themselves and to cooperate while using the special tiles like the bridge tile. Another feature supporting coordination and cooperation is the movement of the figure because the arrow buttons are split up and distributed around the area. Therefore, the players will have to discuss the next movement steps and work together. If the playing figure reaches a ladder and steps onto it, all players will have to cooperate by hitting the "climb" buttons. The faster they hit, the faster the figure will move up the ladder.

The players are forced to think logically because they have to choose the tiles they will use wisely. If there are no tiles left to finish a path from the starting point to the goal point, they will lose the game. This requires some planning and logical thinking.

4 Implementation

The architecture of Parcours consists of five internal and one external component as seen in Figure 2. These components which will be described in more detail in the following subsections.

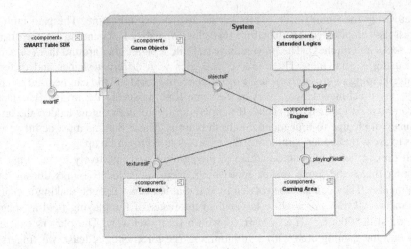

Fig. 2. System architecture

4.1 Smart Table SDK

The only external component is the SMART Table Software Development Kit (SDK)
which provides a multi touch enabled graphical user interface framework. The
SMART Table SDK contains classes and basic functionalities required by developers
to realize a multi touch enabled graphical user interface.

As described in section 3, players have to build a path from the starting point to the
goal using various tiles. To build the path, players have to drag, rotate, scale and drop
tiles. To implement graphical elements supporting these features in a multi touch
environment, the SMART Table SDK provides (among other features) a class called
DraggableBorder.

Developers implementing graphical elements that have to provide the mentioned
multi touch features only have to (re-)use the class DraggableBorder provided by
the SMART Table SDK. No further specific code is required to enable dragging,
rotating, scaling and dropping features for graphical elements. Based on this SMART
Table SDK, all tiles and functions of the "Parcours" game have been implemented.

4.2 Gaming Area

The Gaming Area component holds an abstract representation of what the players are
seeing as an array. The array contains information about the tile type of each square
of the gaming area as can be seen in Figure 3. The array is useful in two kinds of
manners: First, the array is used for collision detection. The players are not allowed to
drop tiles on a build path or on obstacles. The array can be used to check if a tile can
be dropped or not. Second, the information in the array is used by the engine to load
the corresponding textures from the Texture component for each element in the array
(e.g., the number 1 encodes a grass tile). This so-called tile engine is beneficial for
system performance because small graphics are reused as textures several times.

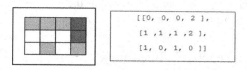

Fig. 3. Gaming area represented with an array

4.3 Textures

The Textures component provides all textures needed for the game visualization. The Engine component uses these textures to label all tiles like the grass, rock or ditch tiles (depending on the current theme). The textures are designed to provide the user with an intuitive understanding of which tiles are paths and which are obstacles.

4.4 Game Objects

This component realizes the visual appearance (i.e. the shape) of all usable tiles and the playing figure. Each tile is a 3x3 grid consisting essentially of a set of DraggableBorder objects, which are arranged in a way so that the tile has its desired shape. Furthermore, the Game Objects component holds information about the shapes of each tile in an array. Together with the array mentioned in the Gaming Area component, these arrays are useful for collision detection and to determine the needed textures for labeling the tiles. If a tile is rotated by the user, its representing array has to be rotated, too. This way, the tiles will always look correct (and have a correct system-internal representation).

4.5 Extended Logics Component

The Extended Logics component is very important because it implements the correct game behavior and the functionalities which force the players to cooperate.

Each tile is draggable, rotateable and scaleable, as already mentioned. Adding certain event handlers to each tile offers the possibility to increase the functionalities of the tiles, which are required by the special tiles in the game. Special tiles (cf. section 3) are used to enhance the coordination and cooperation among the players. Simple event handlers include, for instance, the counting the amount of touches on one tile or the calculation the distance of two touches.

Further functionalities of this component are collision detection, in order to forbid dropping tiles on paths or obstacles, switching the "arrow" buttons to "climb" buttons and backwards, and the correct movement of the playing figure.

4.6 Engine

The Engine is the main component of Parcours. It uses the other components to instantiate the gaming area, the playing figure and all tiles of the game. Furthermore, the engine connects the visual appearance of the tiles and the playing figure with their corresponding logics from the Extended Logics component and is controlling the game flow. The Engine component arranges the tiles and the arrow buttons always on the border of the gaming area and distributes them to engage the players in cooperation and coordination.

5   Pilot Tests and Teacher's Feedback

Very recently, the Parcours game has been installed on a SMART table and has been deployed in regular school usage in a primary school in Germany. The first feedback received from this field usage has been very positive: both teachers and pupils like (and use regularly) the tool. However, this field use period has been too short to draw meaningful conclusions. In this paper, we instead report on some tests conducted with a prototype of the system which has been shown to a primary school teacher and has been pilot tested by a group of approx. ten pupils to investigate if teachers and school children accept the educational game.

In the pilot tests, after a brief explanation of the game rules, the pupils began playing. An observation of the school children playing confirmed the simple and intuitive handling of the game. As expected, the children were discussing about the next steps they wanted to do and helped each other using the special tiles, which require cooperation and coordination (cf. Figure 4). We also interviewed the primary school teacher who observed the children playing the Parcours game. She was surprised by the good acceptance of the game by the children and stated that she believed that this kind of game can be very useful for multiple school subjects. While the cooperative design game was intended to teach coordination and logical thinking, the teacher also discovered other possible beneficial side effects like language skills (because of the coordination process) and geometry skills (because of the transformable tiles or the estimation of distances). The teacher also stated that she believes that generally, learning with a multitouch screen is very enjoyable and keeps the school children excited and motivated. So far, neither the pupils nor the teacher suggested specific improvements (we expect the field to reveal more in this regard).

In summary, while not constituting solid empirical evidence yet, first tests of Parcours in school suggest that this cooperative design game has the potential to help primary school children learn a set of diverse skills, including logical thinking and coordination. The next steps on our research agenda include an extended field study with the system.

Fig. 4. Parcours in a primary school

References

1. Cappelletti, A., Gelmini, G., Pianesi, F., Rossi, F., Zancanaro, M.: Enforcing Cooperative Storytelling: First Studies. In: Proceedings of ICALT, pp. 281–285. IEEE Computer Society, Washington, DC (2004)
2. Rick, J., Rogers, Y., Haig, C., Yuill, N.: Learning by doing with shareable interfaces. Children, Youth and Environments 19(1), 321–342 (2009)
3. Harris, A., Rick, J., Bonnett, V., Yuill, N., Fleck, R., Marshall, P., Rogers, Y.: Around the table: are multiple-touch surfaces better than single-touch for children's collaborative interactions? In: Proceedings of CSCL, pp. 335–344 (2009)
4. Hoppe, H.U., Lingnau, A., Machado, I., Paiva, A., Prada, R., Tewissen, F.: Supporting Collaborative Activities in Computer Integrated Classrooms - the NIMIS Approach. In: Proc. of CRIWG 2000, Madeira, Portugal, pp. 94–101 (2000)
5. Johnson, D.W., Johnson, R.T.: Co-operative learning and achievement. In: Sharan, S. (ed.) Co-operative Learning: Theory and Research, pp. 23–37. Praeger, New York (1990)
6. Marshall, P., Fleck, R., Harris, A., Rick, J., Hornecker, E., Rogers, Y., Yuill, N., Dalton, N.S.: Fighting for control: children's embodied interactions when using physical and digital representations. In: Proceedings of CHI, pp. 2149–2152. ACM, New York (2009)
7. Nacenta, M.A., Pinelle, D., Stuckel, D., Gutwin, C.: The effects of interaction technique on coordination in tabletop groupware. In: Proceedings of Graphics Interface 2007, pp. 191–198. ACM, New York (2007)
8. Piper, A.M., O'Brien, E., Morris, M.R., Winograd, T.: SIDES: a cooperative tabletop computer game for social skills development. In: Proceedings of CSCW, pp. 1–10. ACM, New York (2006)
9. Schneider, J., Derboven, J., Luyten, K., Vleugels, C., Bannier, S., De Roeck, D., Verstraete, M.: Multi-user Multi-touch Setups for Collaborative Learning in an Educational Setting. In: Luo, Y. (ed.) CDVE 2010. LNCS, vol. 6240, pp. 181–188. Springer, Heidelberg (2010)
10. Shen, C., Everitt, K., Ryall, K.: UbiTable: Impromptu Face-to-Face Collaboration on Horizontal Interactive Surfaces. In: Proceedings of the Fifth International Conference on Ubiquitous Computing, pp. 281–288 (2003)
11. Webb, N.M., Palincsar, A.S.: Group processes in the classroom. In: Berliner, D.C., Calfee, C. (eds.) Handbook of Educational Psychology, pp. 841–873. Simon & Schuster Macmillan, New York (1996)

The Use of 3D Optical Measurement Systems in Collaborative Ship Design

Marina Z. Solesvik

Stord/Haugesund University College, Bjørnsonsgate 45, 5528 Haugesund, Norway
mzs@hsh.no

Abstract. The paper presents three dimensional scanning tools elaborated by a Norwegian firm. This tool is applied by a number of Norwegian firms (ship designers, shipbuilders, suppliers of equipment, and classification societies) during their collaborating projects. This tool allows 3D scanning, making drawings and 3D hull models. This tool is also applied in other industries, for example, architecture, house construction, and mechanical production.

Keywords: cooperative design, shipbuilding, optical measurement system, 3D models.

1 Introduction

Ship construction is a complicated process where millions of parts should be assembled together. There are a significant number of partners collaborating in shipbuilding: designers, shipyard, shipping companies, authorities, and abundant suppliers. The role of collaboration is increasing each year in shipbuilding. Furthermore, shipbuilding is time consuming process and all participants are interested in shortening of lead time.

A number of CAD/CAM systems were adopted for the purposes of collaborative ship design and visualization of ship parts for easier production purposes. Three dimensional (3D) images make construction of ships and ship repair easier for workers than traditional drawings. Engineering solutions and models are also more convenient for customers and joint project discussions when they are presented in 3D form.

This paper presents 3D scanning tool developed by a Norwegian firm. This multi-purpose tool is successfully applied by ship designers, engineers, and specialist from shipyards during their collaborative work. This tool allows 3D scanning, making drawings and 3D hull models.

Ship design is a knowledge-intensive industry. Knowledge possessed by a firm's engineers is the main resource leading to a competitive advantage. Ship design firms widely use computer-aided design (CAD) tools in producing the detailed drawings, and advanced collaborative tools to share knowledge within a network. This gives a ship design firm an opportunity to dramatically shorten the duration of the design cycle. The internet and intranet allows for new forms of collaboration between contributors who may be geographically remote and operate in different time zones. Much time, effort, and resources are spent by all parties, especially by shipowners,

Y. Luo (Ed.): CDVE 2011, LNCS 6874, pp. 30–36, 2011.

shipyard engineers, and naval architects in coordinating all design details of the vessel under construction.

The paper is organized as follows. The next section presents theoretical issues related to cooperative design in shipbuilding. Then the proposed tool is presented with the illustration of applications in cooperative ship design. The paper terminates with conclusions.

2 Theoretical Background

2.1 The Role of ICTs in Cooperative Design

Information and communication technologies develop rapidly. Managers need to take into account breathtaking changes and to consider how to leverage new capabilities for their firms. Recent technological trends in ICT include minimization of computing resources, the rapid penetration of broadband network, the emergence of the internet as a communication backbone, the appearance of wireless technology, and development of mobile devices [1]. In the same time, the rapid development of interfirm collaboration has been documented. Business-process redesign is important when firms engage into alliances and develop inter-organizational relationships. It has been argued that IT and business-process redesigns are natural partners [2].

Boland et al. [3] have suggested that use of ICT in organizations leads to four types of changes: gaining large scale efficiencies, enhancing decision making and communication, changing the basis for competition and industry structure, and exploiting new business models. Gaining large scale efficiencies is related to introduction of different ICT tools (like enterprise resource planning, computer-aided design, computer-aided manufacturing, etc.) which allowed to shorten the processing time from several days to several minutes [9]. Enhancing decision making and communication supports communication and collaboration processes in firms. Introduction of group support systems (GSS), such as e-mail, computer conferencing systems, videoconferencing, and electronic meeting tools, in organizations added value to these organizations [4]. There are three ways how GSS add value: (1) reduction of time and distance barriers related to face-to-face interactions, (2) increasing the scope of available information, and (3) improving interaction processes in groups [1]. Emergence and development of ICT enabled communication tools lead to the appearance of the novel organization forms, notably virtual teams which referred as "temporary, geographically dispersed, culturally diverse, and electronically communicating working groups" [1: 600-601]. In shipbuilding context, virtual teams are a viable form of work. The use of ICT changes industry structure in a number of ways. ICT might aggregate previously fragmented markets; bundle productive resources more effectively; change the nature of interfirm relations; and replace existing channels [1].

Collaborative management systems (which are also called groupware technologies) can add firm's value in three ways: (1) significant cost savings, (2) faster cycle times [2], and (3) enhance flexibility and responsiveness to customer requirements [8]. Collaborative management systems, such as Groove [15] assist collaboration by helping to ease communication, share knowledge, and manage projects. The success or failure of ICT tools applications depend on competences of people who use them [14].

The significant research is done regarding how ICT can facilitate collaboration. However, there is still a lacuna in our knowledge base. Notably, the research on ICT application facilitating collaboration inside and outside shipbuilding firms is scarce [5]. The research in emerging collaborative ICT technologies also important because they "can help employees build in other's ideas, ease connections between people and develop shared knowledge. The result will be an organization with greater velocity and greater capacity to adapt to changing environs" [15: 222].

2.2 Cooperative Approach to Vessel Design

An increasing body of literature focuses on cooperative design issues [10, 12, 13, 16]. Cheng [7] divides the collaboration design research into two main categories. She argues that one set of studies concentrates on information technology issues assisting collaboration, such as information flow and data organization. The second set investigates the social issues of cooperative work.

Kvan [12] defines two modes of collaborative design. The first is the close coupled design process, when parties interface tightly on design. Second is the loosely coupled design process, when each participant contributes within his/her scope and expertise. Examples of both close and loosely coupled design processes in collaborative design can be found in the area of shipbuilding. The researchers of collaborative design in shipbuilding mostly explore possibilities of computer-supported collaborative work [5, 6, 18, 19].

A number of research papers stress the importance of different software and hardware interoperability [5, 17] since producers of different CAD tools are reluctant to create software compatible with competitors' products. Tann and Shaw [17] suggest that one of the most challenging tasks in collaborative ship design is to create a system which will be compatible with all existing CAD tools which will allow better knowledge sharing amongst stakeholders.

2.3 Main Stages in Collaborative Vessel Design

There are five main phases in ship design: (1) conceptual design; (2) preliminary design; (3) functional design; (4) transitional design; and (5) detail design. Different software tools are used in each stage. In the first stage, IT instruments are applied marginally [17]. At the same time some studies find it useful to apply software in the early design stages. For example, Krömker and Thoben [11] proposed a computerized system for the ship pre-design process. Furthermore, AutoCAD is widely employed in shipbuilding to create 2D drawings of classification projects (preliminary and functional stages). For detail design TRIBON, FORAN, NUPAS, and AutoCAD are utilized.

3   3D Software in Shipbuilding

The elaborated tool combines CAD-software and optical measurement systems. This 3D tool is developed for several purposes: making 'as-is' drawings, 3D modeling, technical drawing.

Making 'as-is' drawings

The life cycle of modern vessels is rather long. Usually, they are used during 25-30 years or even longer. In other words, some of the vessels which are operated nowadays were built using paper-and-pencil drawings. In some cases, the package of drawings is missing at all. During modernizations and repairs, there is a need in CAD drawings. The 3D scanning tool allows making 'as-is' drawings of the ship's hull. Optical measurement systems transfer images into software and as a result the software produces drawings suitable for further use (Fig.1).

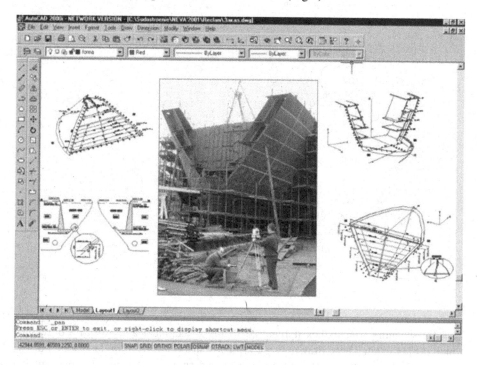

Fig. 1. Control of hull

These drawings are subsequently transferred from a shipyard to ship designers which are often situated in the other part of the world for further proceeding, e.g., repair, calculations, production of drawings for modernization, enlargement of a vessel, conversion to another type and so on.

Ships are not mass production goods. They are often unique and production of spare parts for older vessels might represent a problem, since necessary spare parts might be out of stock and/or out of production. 3D scanning tool enables rapid manufacturing.

3D modeling

This tool allows also to produce 3D models of objects and spaces. Virtual representations are very helpful in ship production. Making 3D drawings in ship design offices is more expensive and time-consuming. It is cheaper to make them when the parts of the vessels are constructed. And then make them with the help of 3D scanning tool developed by a Norwegian firm (Fig. 2). This has practical importance for ship production. In some cases, a prototype vessel is produced by a sophisticated and more expensive shipyard. The sister vessels might be subsequently produced by shipyards in countries which are newcomers in the world shipbuilding market.

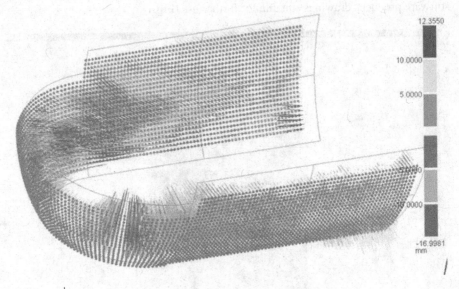

Fig. 2. Creating a model of hull

Technical drawing
The 3D scanning tool makes it possible to make technical and working drawings which do not exist. These drawings are typically made not by ship designers, but by shipyards for the needs of construction. Furthermore, often shipbuilders make changes during the construction. Thus, real shapes of the ships are sometimes different from theoretical drawings.

The 3D scanning tool is a useful instrument for ship breaking enterprises which can be used during disassembly of structures and the whole ship. Additionally, ship designers can get necessary volume calculations with the help of 3D scanning tool.

Norwegian shipbuilding firms used 3D scanning tool for control and overview of repair works. This enables to shorten a project period, speed up the design process, and allows to cooperate remotely.

Finally, as has been discussed in Chpater 2, the problem of compatibility is widely recognized. What is very important is that data produced is fully compatible with widely used software in shipbuilding and ship design, such as AutoCAD, Inventor, and Cyclon C (Fig. 3).

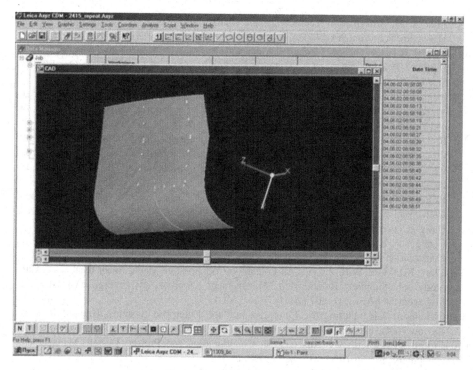

Fig. 3. Hull model

4 Conclusions

This paper presented a 3D scanning system developed by a Norwegian firm and its practical applications. This tool is used in the Norwegian shipbuilding to support collaborative design and production. This tool allows better collaboration between parties, enhances precision and improves cost efficiency during the collaborative design and production. This tool also enforces rapid manufacturing of ship's parts. The tool provides high accuracy and might be used inside the boat and outside. The whole measurement system is mobile and easily transported to ship construction spots. Time saving, objective information, high accuracy, and minimized risks of design faults are the main advantages of 3D laser scanning.

This tool is applied mainly in shipbuilding. However, there were trials to use the tool in other industries as well. For example, in architecture, house construction, and mechanical factories.

References

1. Alavi, M., Yoo, Y.: Use Information Technology for Organizational Change. In: Locke, E.A. (ed.) Handbook of Principles of Organizational Behavior, pp. 595–614. Wiley, Chichester (2009)

2. Attaran, M.: Information Technology and Business-Process Redesign. Business Process Management Journal 9(4), 440–458 (2003)
3. Boland, R.J., Lyytinen, K., Yoo, Y.: Wakes of Innovation in Project Networks: The Case of Digital 3-D Representations in Architecture, Engineering and Construction. Organization Science 18(4), 631–647 (2007)
4. Briggs, R.O.: On Theory-Driven Design of Collaboration Technology and Process. In: de Vreede, G.-J., Guerrero, L.A., Raventos, G.M. (eds.) Groupware: Design, Implementation and Use, pp. 1–15. Springer, Heidelberg (2004)
5. Bronsart, R., Gau, S., Luckau, D., Sucharowski, W.: Enabling Distributed Ship Design and Production Processes by an Information Integration Platform. Paper Presented at 12th International Conference on Computer Applications in Shipbuilding (ICCAS). August 23-26, 2005 Busan, Korea (2005)
6. Bronsart, R., Koch, T., Grafe, W., Petkov, V.: An Infrastructure for Inter-Organizational Collaboration in Ship Design and Production. Paper Presented at 9th International Marine Design Conference, Ann Arbor, Michigan, USA, May 16-19 (2006)
7. Cheng, N.Y.: Approaches to Design Collaboration Research. Automation in Construction 12, 715–723 (2003)
8. Choy, K.L., Lee, W.B., Lo, V.: An Enterprise Collaborative Management System - A Case Study of Supplier Relationship Management. Journal of Enterprise Information Management 17(3), 191–207 (2004)
9. Davenport, T.H.: Putting the Enterprise into the Enterprise Systems. Harvard Business Review 76(4), 121–131 (1998)
10. Girard, P., Robin, V.: Analysis of Collaboration for Project Design Management. Computers in Industry 57, 817–826 (2006)
11. Krömker, M., Thoben, K.-D.: Re-engineering the Ship Pre-design Process. Computers in Industry 31, 143–153 (1996)
12. Kvan, T.: Collaborative design: what is it? Automation in Construction 11, 535–544 (2002)
13. Lee, Y., Gilleard, J.D.: Collaborative Design: A Process Model for Refurbishment. Automation in Construction 16, 37–44 (2007)
14. Massa, S., Testa, S.: ICTs Adoption and Knowledge Management: the Case of an E-Procurement System. Knowledge and Process Management 14(1), 26–36 (2007)
15. McKnight, B., Bontis, N.: E-Improvisation: Collaborative Groupware Technology Expands the Reach and Effectiveness of Organizational Improvisation. Knowledge and Process Management 9(4), 219–227 (2002)
16. Rosenman, M.A., Smith, G., Maher, M.L., Ding, L., Marchant, D.: Multidisciplinary Collaborative Design in Virtual Environments. Automation in Construction 9, 409–415 (2000)
17. Tann, W., Shaw, H.J.: The Collaboration Modeling Framework for Ship Structural Design. Ocean Engineering 34, 917–929 (2007)
18. Zimmermann, M., Bronsart, R., Stenzel, K.: Knowledge Based Engineering Methods for Ship Structural Design. Paper Presented at 12th International Conference on Computer Applications in Shipbuilding (ICCAS), Busan, Korea, August 23-26 (2005)
19. Zimmermann, M., Bronsart, R.: Application of Knowledge Based Engineering Methods for Standardization and Quality Assurance in Ship Structural Design. Paper Presented at 2006 World Maritime Technology Conference, London, UK, March 6-10 (2006)

Simulation of Collaborative Innovation System in Cluster Environment

Shuangxi Huang[1], Hua Bai[2], Jinsong Bao[3], and Aidan Li[4]

[1] Department of Automation, Tsinghua University, Beijing 100084, China
[2] Shenzhen Tourism College, Jinan University, Shenzhen 518053, China
[3] School of Mechanical Engineering, Shanghai Jiaotong University,
Shanghai 200240, China
[4] Beijing Zhongji Kehai Tech & Dev. LTD. Beijing 100048, China
huangsx@mail.tsinghua.edu.cn, wendybai16@gmail.com,
baojinsong@gmail.com, liaidan28@hotmail.com

Abstract. Cluster innovation system (CIS) is a kind of complex adaptive system. The system performance of CIS depends critically on the interactions between its parts. Because it is hard to formalize and define the system equation, the analytical or deductive method is unfitted with the high dynamics, uncertainty, and complex structure of CIS. In the paper, swarm principles are used to deal with the complexity of CIS. The multi-agent model is established to represent the interaction, collaboration, group behavior, and the emergence of higher order system structure. Based on this multi-agent model, the emergent behaviors and the key characteristics of the system are obtained using swarm simulation. The key parameters for system evolution can be identified and the attribute features and behavior rules of an individual enterprise (agent) can be set up. The objective of the research is to find out the key factors influencing the evolution of CIS and the proper innovation strategy for CIS.

Keywords: Cluster Innovation System, Swarm Simulation, Multi-agent.

1 Introduction

Cluster Innovation System (CIS) is a kind of collaborative organization. Usually CIS consists of thousands of enterprises. Unlike an enterprise, nobody is responsible for the management of the cluster directly. The cluster is really self-organized. In CIS, there exists an interesting phenomenon named cluster effect. The enterprises in cluster may have limited knowledge. But through the share of knowledge and productive elements, the clustering of these enterprises will emerge the unique innovative capacity, which will become the main source of cluster competitiveness [1].

There are lots of successful examples for CIS. Audretsch studies about 30 clusters in six groups of industries. The results showed that the average innovative capacity for small or medium enterprises (SMEs) in cluster even higher than the large companies [2].

Because cluster plays a more and more important role in technical and economic growth, lots of local governments have been planning to setup clusters. However it is

Y. Luo (Ed.): CDVE 2011, LNCS 6874, pp. 37–44, 2011.

not easy to manage CIS effectively. Many artificial clusters failed [3]. CIS is a dynamic, self-organizational, and open system. How to establish the system model and how to analyze the system using the model are two basic research questions according to the management of CIS.

In the paper, the swarm principles are used to deal with the complexity of CIS. The multi-agent model is established to reveal the dynamic evolution of CIS based on the collective behaviors of agents. Based on swarm simulation, we can get the emergent behaviors and properties of the system through the interaction between agents. The system characteristics can be obtained and the attribute features and behavior rules of individual enterprise (agent) can be setup. The objective of the research is to find out the key factors influencing the evolution of CIS and the proper innovation strategy for CIS.

2 Multi-agent Model of Cluster Innovation System

2.1 Agent Model

CIS can be characterized as networks of innovation encompass production enterprises and research institutes. Each of the actors in CIS can be seen as an agent. Considering innovation related factors, four critical attributes are defined in agent model: economic capacity, technological capability, production capacity, and innovation capacity.

The economic capacity is determined by the profitability and reserve fund of the enterprise, and also related with the production capacity and technological capability. Defining EA_i as the economic capacity of Agent i,

$EA_i = f_1 (PR_i, RF_i, TA_i, PA_i)$:
  PR_i: The total profits of Agent i in time t-1.
  RF_i: The reserve fund of Agent i in time t-1
  TA_i: The technological capacity of Agent i
  PA_i: The production capacity of Agent i
  F_1: the renew rule of EA for agent

The technological capability is relevant to the technical domain, the technical level, the stock of knowledge. The broad technical domain, the high standard in technical level, and the abundant knowledge stock will lead to the high technological capacity. Defining TAi as technological capacity of Agent i,

$TA_i = f_2 (KS_{ik}, TL_{ik}, EI_{ik})$:
  KS_{ik}: The knowledge stock of Agent i in domain k
  TL_{ik}: The technical level of Agent i in technical domain k
  EI_{ik}: The economic investment of Agent i in technical domain k
  F_2: the renew rule of TA for agent

The production capacity is represented as the output of the enterprise. We can use annual production to denote production capacity of the enterprise. Defining PA_i as the production capacity of Agent i,

$PA_i = AO_i$:
  AO_i: the annual production of Agent i

The innovation capacity can be evaluated according to the economic capacity, techno-logical capacity, as well as the learning ability of the enterprise. The more economic and technological capacity used in innovation, the more knowledge learned from the cluster, the more innovation capacity will be. Defining IA_i as the innovation capacity of Agent i,

$IA_i = f_3(EA_i, TA_i, LK_{it})$:
    EA_i: The economic capacity of Agent i
    TA_i: Technological capacity of Agent i
    LK_{it}: The knowledge accumulation of agent i in time t-1.
    F_3: the renew rule of IA for agent

Besides these critical elements of innovation, we also drew out some accidental fac-tors which can influence innovation. The attributes of innovation cost, production cost, collaboration cost, and return of innovation are defined in agent model.

Based on the attributes, the related methods of the agent are defined. These meth-ods are used to calculate economic, technological, production, and innovation capac-ity. The value of the attributes can be set or retrieved through these methods. The methods "Get/Set Coop ()" are defined in agent model. They are about the status of collaboration. According to the calculation of investment and return, the agent can compare the different collaborative strategy and decide if it should collaborate with the others to do the innovation collaboratively or independently.

2.2 Cluster Model

The innovation capacity is the core of cluster competitiveness. Two indicators can be used as the metrics of cluster innovation capacity. One is the output scale of cluster. The other is the cluster's technical level. The output scale can be the measurement of cluster volume. And the technical level can be the measurement of cluster quality. At the same time, the number of enterprise in cluster is another indicator of cluster. The change in the number of enterprise reflects the scale of the cluster.

The output and technological level keep changing continuously due to the uncer-tainty in environment and enterprise behaviors, which results in the evolution of clus-ter innovation capacity and the cluster scale. In the paper, we defined three attributes for cluster model. Cluster output, cluster technological level, and cluster scale. Defin-ing CE as the number of enterprise in cluster,

$CE = n \ (n \geq 0)$

Cluster output is the total output of all the enterprise in the cluster. Defining CO as the output of cluster, if the number of enterprise in cluster is n,

$CO = \sum PA_i \ (i = 1,--,n)$:
    PA_i: the production capacity of Agent i

Cluster technological level can be calculated by the average technological level of all the enterprises in cluster. Defining CT as cluster technological level,

$CT = \sum TA_i/n \ (i=1,--,n)$

Accompanied with these attributes, two methods are used to calculate the cluster out-put and technological. And another method is used to manage the agent. By the method, we can create or delete an agent according to its economic and technological capacity. If an agent has no capacity to do innovation independently or collaboratively, then the agent will be deleted from the system.

2.3 Environment Model

Two essential factors in environment influence the evolution of CIS significantly. One is technological requirement. Another is government policy in cluster.

Technological requirement from environment is the external drive of cluster innovation and development. Continuous improvement in technological requirement brings about the gap between enterprise technological level and environment technological requirement, which is the direction of cluster innovation. The emergence of new technologies implies high business value and can improve the productivity and product quality of the enterprise. The tremendous commercial value drives enterprises developing and utilizing new technologies, which promote the innovation of the cluster.

The technological requirement relates to the environment technical level and cluster technical level. Environment technical level is influenced by the technical institution in a particular field or region, such as universities and other institutions of higher education, private and public research labs, consultancy and technical service providers and regulatory bodies. Define TR as the technological requirement of the cluster in time t.

$TR_t = f_4(ETL_t, CT_t)$:
   ETL_t: Environment technical level in time t
   CT_t: Cluster technical level in time t
   F_4: the renew rule of TR

Another essential factor in environment is the government policy in cluster innovation. Government will setup specific strategies to stimulate the innovation in order to bring about economic or social benefits. The common stimulating policy is the investment in cluster to support the innovation activities. The invest amount is related to the tax revenue of the government. Define GI_t as government invest in time t,

$GI_t = f5(GT_t)$:
   GT_t: Tax revenue of the government in time t

2.4 Behavior Model

The behavior model defines the interaction rules between agent-agent and agent-environment. Two basic rules were used in behavior model: (1) the rules are simple, and (2) the rules use only local information. Based on simple rules of behavior and agent interaction which are completely described by simple deterministic rules based on only local information, the sustainable patterns can emerge in system level. The patterns to be developed can be extremely sensitive to the initial conditions. The system seemingly exhibits collective intelligence, or swarm intelligence, even without the existence of a central authority. The system is able to not only survive, but also to adapt and become better suited to their environment, effectively optimizing their behavior over time.

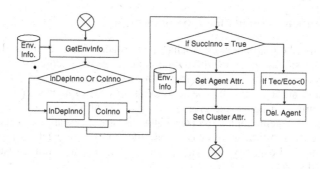

Fig. 1. The behavior model in CIS

In CIS, agents represent enterprises or institutes in cluster. The agents could emerge with a variety of characteristics and behaviors. The agent relationships represent processes of interaction. Figure 1 shows the behavior model of CIS. Firstly, the agent gets information from environment, such as the technological requirements. Next, the agent has to decide what kind of innovation strategy should be adopted. The innovation cost, return, and risk change dynamically according to different innovation strategies. In this paper, only two innovation strategies are considered in order to compare the different result of system evolution. One is collaborative innovation strategy. The other is independent innovation strategy. After that, the innovation process can be launched. The probability of success, the cost and profit of innovation will be calculated. The attributes of agent will be renewed. If the innovation is successful, then the economic and technological capacity of the agent will increase, and vice versa. If no technological or economic capacity left, the agent will be deleted from the system. As a result, the emergent processes can be observed, such as the fluctuation of population, total technologies, and total capital.

3   Swarm Simulation for CIS Evolution

3.1   Introduction to Simulation Case

The simulation case in the paper comes from the Anhui automobile cluster which is one of the six major automobile clusters in China. Through investigating about 500 organizations in Anhui automobile cluster, including manufacturing enterprises and the research institutes, we finished the survey about Anhui automobile cluster. The survey provided the information about the number of employees, the capital, the production capacity, the technical capacity, the innovative capacity, the R&D investment, and so on.

Based on the survey, the evolution of Anhui automobile cluster is analyzed by using swarm simulation. The swarm simulation platform has been established to setup the initial environment, the behavior rules, and the key parameters of the system. Through swarm simulation, we can reveal the relationship between individual behaviors of enterprises and the group/emergent behaviors of the cluster. The key features and parameters can be distinguished which is useful for the decision of cluster development strategy.

3.2 Configuration of Simulation Environment

Simulation is more often than not a stochastic approach. The swarm simulation model for CIS includes stochastic elements to model the range of outcomes for agent behaviors and interactions which are not known with certainty.

Based on the survey data, the basic simulation environment can be configured, such as the number of agent, the proportion of different agent. Here we just considered two kinds of agent: manufacturing enterprises and research institutes. We can also derive the distribution of stochastic variables in system, such as production capacity, technological capacity, innovation capacity, and innovation investment, innovative cost, and so on.

During simulation, the success rate of innovation, the return of innovation, the government investment, and the total simulation time need to setup as well.

In Anhui Automobile Cluster, by analyzing survey data, we can set the number of agent as 500. The rate for manufacturing enterprises in cluster is 60% and for institutes is 40%. The economic invest, innovation capacity, and innovation cost fit for normal distribution in parameter (200, 1), (100, 1) and (10, 1). The success rate of innovation can be calculated by TA_i / $Max[TA_i]$ (i= 1,--,500). The innovation return can be estimated by innovation profitability α, the rate of enterprise average technological level and cluster average technological level, and the innovation cost CC. The government investment is 5000 in every 20 times. The total simulation times are 500 steps. The detailed configuration of simulation environment for CIS is as follows:

Number of Agents: 500
Number of Manufactories: P (0.6)
Number of Institutes: P (0.4)
Economic Invest: EI: N(200,1)
Inno. Cap.: IA: N(100,1)
Inno. Succ: IS: TA_i / $Max[TA_i]$ (i= 1,--,500)
Inno. Cost: IC: N(10,1)
Coop. Cost: CC: 20
Inno. Return: $IR(IC)=\alpha\beta(1-s)IC$; α=2, β= TA_i /CT
GovInv: 5000 (every 20 times)
Total Sim. Times: 500

3.3 Analysis of Simulation Result

In order to analyze the evolution process of CIS, we defined three key performance indicators (KPIs) for CIS:

— Number of survival agents
— Total Capital
— Total Technological capacity

Via simulation, we can get the values of these KPIs. The change in the value of these KPIs can reflect the evolution process of CIS in population and quality.

Figure 2 shows the results of the simulation. We can further obtain some parameters for the system, such as the proportion of different agents, the reasonable investment, and the expected return. These will be helpful for the management of the cluster.

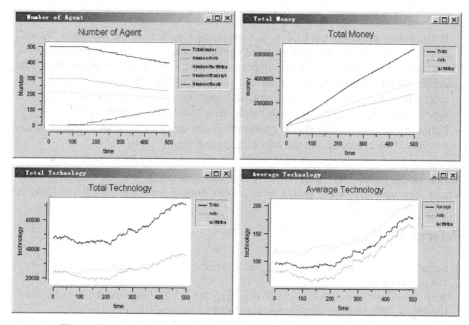

Fig. 2. Simulation of Anhui Automobile Cluster based on Swarm platform

We can also compare different innovation strategies and know which the best one is. For example, compared with independent innovation in non-cluster environment, the cluster innovation system shows higher output, capital, and technologies in general. And the survival rate for individual is also higher. In non-cluster environment, although the average technological capacity is higher, it is because the total number of survival enterprises is lower (in the same initial conditions). This shows that independent innovation is only better for the individuals who survived. It can not form synergy to achieve the maximal output.

4 Conclusion

Cluster innovation system (CIS) is a kind of complex adaptive system. The performance of CIS depends critically on the interactions between parts. The analytical or deductive method is hard to deal with the high dynamics, uncertainty, and complex structure of CIS. In the paper, swarm principles are used to deal with the complexity of CIS. The multi-agent model is established to reveal the dynamic evolution of CIS based on the collective behaviors of agents. Via swarm simulation, the emergent behaviors and the key characteristics of the system can be obtained through the interaction between agents. Based on the analysis, the system parameters can be distinguished and the attribute features and behavior rules of individual enterprise (agent) can be setup. The research results have been used in the analysis of Anhui automobile cluster in China. Through the simulation, we can get some key parameters for the system, such as the proportion of different agents, the reasonable investment, and the expected return, which will be helpful for the management of the cluster.

There are still some future works to be done about the research.

— In the paper, we did not consider the entry of new agents. In the next step, we will setup the entry policy to simulate the dynamic evolution of cluster population.
— Currently, we assume that the collaboration occurs between two enterprises. The collaborative strategy is based on cooperation game mechanism between two enterprises. However, it is more practical that the collaboration involves several enterprises. The multi-player game mechanism should be researched.
— Furthermore, only two kinds of organizations are set in the case study. More varieties should be considered in the future scenarios.

Acknowledgements. The work of the paper was granted by the National Key Technology Research and Development Program of China under Grant 2008BAF35B00.

References

1. Stamer (2000), http://www.meyer-stamer.de/2002/Intech-Cluster.pdf
2. DB Audretsch (2001),
   http://siteresources.worldbank.org/WBI/Resources/wbi37180.pdf
3. Rinaldi, A.: More than the sum of their parts? EMBO Reports 7(2), 133–136 (2006)

Implementation of a RIA Tool for Supporting a Collaborative Initiative of Software Process Improvement

I. Garcia[1], C. Pacheco[1], and D. Cruz[2]

[1] Postgraduate Department, Faculty of Computer Science,
Technological University of the Mixtec Region, Mexico
[2] Faculty of Computer Science,
Cañada University, Mexico
{Ivan,leninca}@mixteco.utm.mx, dago@naxoloxa.unca.edu.mx

Abstract. Under a Software Process Improvement (SPI) environment, all phases of a process improvement initiative involving establishing commitment, assessment or diagnosing, improvement plans generation, pilot implementation and improvements deployment, may be accomplished collaboratively by different groups inside an enterprise. Organizational, technical and process-based circumstances have an impact on process assessment and modeling practices. Based on a Model-based Collaborative Design, a strategy for collaborative process assessment and modeling is proposed. This collaborative support helps project managers in overcoming complexities and to create a common understanding of the process and products of a SPI initiative. Finally, a Rich Internet Application (RIA) is developed and applied to provide strong support for distributed project managers, to collaboratively assess and model their software process within a SPI project, the CEForSPI (Collaborative Environment For Software Process Improvement) prototype. This tool represents a collaborative strategy to support SPI teams in handling the different phases of a typical SPI lifecycle.

Keywords: Collaborative model, software process improvement, process modeling, process assessment, rich-internet applications.

1 Introduction

Over the last two decades, the Software Engineering (SE) community has expressed special interest in SPI in an effort to increase software product quality, as well as the productivity of software development. This means that in contrast to traditional production, the focus of quality assurance has to be set during the development process and not during the production process. Also worthy of note is the number of process assessment methods that have been developed (i.e., CBA-IPI [1], SCAMPI [2], ISO/IEC 15504:2004 [3]) and a large number of SPI approaches including the technologies. Nowadays, assessment methods are used to evaluate the maturity of the software development process of a software-producing organization; building a roadmap for process improvement. In order to ensure and facilitate the implementation of the assessment findings, an accepted process description reflecting

Y. Luo (Ed.): CDVE 2011, LNCS 6874, pp. 45–52, 2011.

the current status is needed. This means that an integration of process assessment and process modeling is vital to ensure successful and sustainable software process improvement activities.

However, and according to [4], the current problem with SPI is not a lack of a standard or model, but rather a lack of an effective strategy to successfully implement these standards and models. Much attention has been paid to *which SPI activities* to implement instead of *how to implement* these activities efficiently. This paper presents a lightweight tool prototype which integrates a cooperative approach for leading teams to implement the SPI activities. The rest of the paper is structured as follows: Section 2 discusses related work; Section 3 describes the cooperative approach related to SPI; Section 4 describes the implementation of the tool prototype including some models used to support the collaborative strategy, and finally; the conclusions are shown in Section 5.

2   Relevance of Collaborative Environments in SPI Initiatives

Understanding how to implement SPI successfully is a hard task. Malheiros et al. [5] have been identifying possible factors contributing to a diminished SPI process performance and compliance regarding quality and time. So far, they have found that many influences on the success of SPI programs are related to *coordination*, *communication* and *collaboration*, and mostly to the degree of stakeholders' motivation and participation in SPI initiatives. Bearing this in mind, a collaborative SPI approach should involve: (1) enhancing the communication and collaboration among SPI stakeholders; (2) increasing developers' participation in improving the software development process; and (3) allowing the coordination of SPI initiatives. However, the use of a collaborative environment for SPI is not a trivial task and it is becoming common both in local and international organizations. Different solutions have been proposed to deal with its complexity. For instance, some reports were found which related to the usage of Collaborative Development Environments (CDE) inside large organizations, and to the understanding of the network of communities around the development of software systems. However, their focus is on promoting an environment for developing the software itself, not for supporting the SPI endeavor.

Most Distributed Software Development (DSD) studies focus on developers and their activities, not in SPI professionals or SPI activities. Even so, the following experiences on using CDE or fostering software development communities in large organizations were considered and adapted to the SPI context. More recently, research by [5] presents an approach to support geographically distributed SPI initiatives: the ColabSPI strategy. ColabSPI is a distributed and collaborative strategy and infrastructure to support SPI teams and developers in handling the different phases of a typical SPI lifecycle. A prototype was presented together with some preliminary results and ongoing efforts.

In this context, our research is more strongly related to the SPI key success factors. Aside from this, we cannot find a similar proposal of collaborative and distributed SPI strategies for organizations. Nevertheless, an initial idea of applying a software tool for monitoring the level of the software process management model for distributed groups was introduced by Maindantchick et al. in [6]. Our previous literature review [7], evidences that existing SPI tools typically support assessors in collecting data during assessments. They provide reporting capabilities to aggregate the collected results. Some other works have focused their efforts on the content of distributed SPI work itself, for instance PIASS [8], in the context of a knowledgebase to support SPI activities, presented an approach to build a computational environment to make an assessment of targeted software processes, and a repository to store guidelines, experiences and know-how that were necessary to proceed with SPI activities for a particular organization. Our approach focuses on mechanisms to further improve software processes definition, assessment and support into a collaborative environment. The goal is to provide a strategy and a Web-based project workspace to support: (i) SPI teams in handling process improvement initiatives, (ii) process modeling and evolution; and (iii) doubt clarifications and experience exchange.

3 Model-Based Collaborative Design in SPI

SPI is a collaborative process with several interdependencies between tasks and participants. How to deal with the complexity of interdependent SPI tasks can be supported by several mechanisms. Such support for project managing activities can either be provided by integrated improvement environments, or by isolated tools like process appraisers, planners, resource editors, messaging and modeling tools, or common information spaces. Additionally, many standards, conventions, notations or rules can be established to unify SPI practices and help to communicate improvement principles and values within and improvement team. The impact of organizational settings like the way of work, the roles used by projects, structures for decision making, a common understanding of development activities, etc., are important issues to consider in introducing collaborative efforts into SPI. In the European STREP project called MAPPER [9] (Model-based Adaptive Product and Process Engineering) (IST-016527) it proposed technological and methodological possibilities to support designers in collaborative engineering, which involved participative engineering methodologies to enable joint product and process design, interdisciplinary, and inter-organizational collaboration throughout multiple product life cycles was investigated.

Our hypothesis is that SPI initiatives can benefit from a distributive and collaborative strategy and an infrastructure that not only creates a knowledgebase about a software development process and its improvements, but also allows SPI stakeholders to communicate and organize their work. Our focus is on any organizations that deal with distributed improvements and aim to apply a standard process to SPI. By providing structured support, our research may foster the emergence and progress of a cooperative environment for SPI. It can address major influences to the SPI success or failure such as *knowledge exchange and support*; *staff involvement and motivation*; and *communication and collaboration*. In [5] and [10] an organizational collaborative structure that would improve stakeholders' participation in SPI efforts was suggested. This structure corresponds to two groups of factors which directly affect the SPI's success. The first group of factors is related to their nature and relationship in five areas: (1) collaboration and communication; (2) organizational aspects; (3) compliance issues; (4) continuous improvement issues; and (5) staff motivation and participation. The second group is related to recurrent factors: (1) the need of staff motivation and involvement; (2) the benefits of feedback, support for discussions and clear establishment of goals; and (3) the availability of resources. This group of factors provides an invaluable set of requirements for any collaborative strategy focused on SPI.

Moreover, a mechanism of interaction must be established around common SPI models to facilitate collaborative initiatives, design and development. Active Knowledge Models (AKM) try to implement this requirement. According to [11], *"AKM are dynamic and reconfigurable, so tailorable for their users, and influence the behavior of the underlying computerized system"*. AKM can also be used as executable formal models to manage design workflows. This supports semi-automation of design processes when executed [12]. Research by Tellioğlu exposed that in collaborative engineering processes it is possible to identify and study four types of models. Their tailoring to our SPI context could be as follows:

- *Models to visualize several SPI issues* that are relevant for collaboration, like the organizational and temporal structure of a project, the collaborating partners and their suppliers, roles and responsibilities in these collaborations.
- *Models to support collaboration and coordination* between actors involved in the SPI process. These formal or informal models mainly created by an organization's employees (i.e. software development process) build the base of workflow systems established between distributed groups; and
- *Models to support software tools* which are created during the SPI process.

Figure 1 shows our approach to implement these models into a collaborative environment to support the adoption of an SPI initiative into an organization. In the following section a more detailed explanation about their implementation through a combination of the UWE [13] and RUX-Method [14] to develop an RIA (Rich Internet Application) [15] is provided.

4   A RIA Tool to Support a Collaborative Environment for SPI

To implement our collaborative environment for SPI a computational tool was developed, the CEForSPI (*C*ollaborative *E*nvironment *For* *S*oftware *P*rocess *I*mprovement) prototype. Models were integrated as follows:

4.1   A Model to Visualize Several SPI Issues

Before any organization can start modeling their cooperation in software development, they need to think about several other issues. First of all, they must try to model their own established software process with human and non-human resources to achieve a common understanding of their way to work.

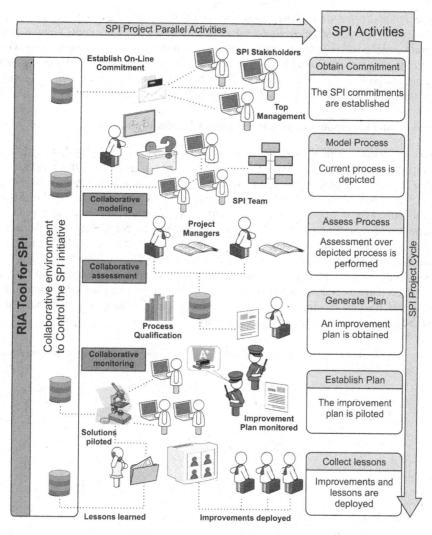

Fig. 1. Collaboration across the SPI lifecycle

The main tool the project managers at organization could use to model the organization's software process, is a collaborative diagram. The *collaborative modeling* component focuses on the current company's software development process. This component uses the Process Change Methodology proposed by [16] to depict the current software development process of the organization (see Figure 2, number 1). To accomplish this task, the mechanism introduces the use of a graphical notation to edit the current process of the company (see Figure 2, number 4). In this research, the UWE is used to specify the content, navigation, and business processes of the Web application; and the RUX method is used to add the typical capabilities of an enriched GUI. A second stage is responsible for generating the results from the modeling mechanism; this stage uses the collaborative model generated by the users in the *collaborative assessment* component, together with the ideal process kept previously in a database of assets (see Figure 2, number 2). The results show a new diagram enriched with activities not found in the current process and contrasting with the erroneous activities. In addition, the issues, detected in the current organization's process, are provided in the form of list. With this it provides the user with two forms for visualizing the issues of the modeling and assessment activities.

4.2 A Model to Support Collaboration and Coordination

After an initial, formal specification of the weakness and strengths of the organization' software development process, that is obtained through the cooperation of stakeholders and project managers, an improvement plan is generated to cover any identified issues. Besides showing the issues found in previous stages, the AKM records information about issues specification, verification activities, and product description for defining the improvement activities. Next, the *collaborative monitoring* component establishes actors responsible for particular activities, schedules, technologies and tools to be used in pilots (see Figure 2, numbers 5 and 6).

The improvement plan can be monitored by any project managers through a workspace. This workspace is a collaborative module where the plan's content can be edited and tracked by anyone who has access to it, provided that they have the required access levels (see Figure 2, number 6).

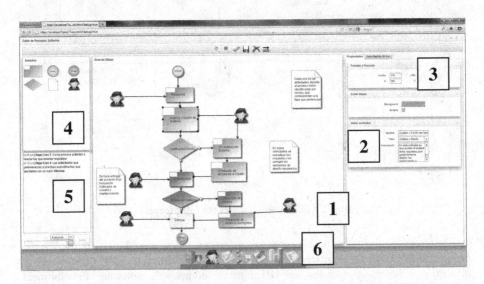

Fig. 2. A RIA implementation for the modeling-based assessment

4.3 A Model to Support Software Tools

Our collaborative approach classifies these kinds of mechanism into two major groups: (i) technical support and (ii) SPI process documentation. A chat module is configured to provide technical support about SPI issues. Once in the workspace, all communication and collaboration mechanisms are available to maintain and evolve the SPI initiative: forums; news; reports; files from the software development process description itself; and historical data about it. Also, information about all SPI contributors is available. Similarly, establishing commitment and deploying improvements use "mailing lists" which are useful for small groups with a common purpose. "Message boards" are used for asking and answering questions, encouraging in-depth conversations, and providing a context for the SPI initiative (see Figure 2, number 5). Regarding SPI support, any stakeholder may answer requests and the workflow status of support requests is limited to *"submitted"*, *"need information"* and *"answered"*. Thus, through CEForSPI it is possible to collaboratively define and control a SPI initiative in many ways. In a previous work, a free software tool to assess organizations' software processes using Web-based approach was developed [17]. CEForSPI is another tool that can be applied to enhance control in SPI initiatives within organizations.

5 Conclusions

In order to present an approach that supports collaboratively SPI initiatives, the CEForSPI tool was introduced. The tool requirements were defined using the Tellioğlu' types of models. This work presents the implementation of three of these models. The *models to trigger automated actions* are under research, to include them into a mechanism to reduce errors in pilots and simulations (after the improvement solutions have been identified).

Thus, by enabling collaborative access, the articulation and coordination of SPI work is supported. In this work we have combined and applied collaborative models, modeling and assessment techniques into a collaborative strategy for SPI as follows:

- First phase: *Model the current software process with a collaborative technique; Analyze the information gathered and define the issues and points for improvement; Create a standard process with the collected model; Inspect and approve this standard process (according to a reference model); and Analyze and enhance the approved model.*
- Second phase: *Identify and prioritize issues in process; Establish a collaborative improvement plan; and Pilot and inspect the results and plan a follow-up.*

The discussion of collaborative SPI in any future research context may open new directions for CEForSPI, for instance the maintenance and administration of an integrated Process Assets Library (PAL) to extend the control of software processes and reference models.

References

1. Dunaway, D.K., Masters, S.: CMM-based appraisal for internal process improvement (CBA-IPI). Method description. Technical Report. CMU/SEI-96-TR-007, Carnegie Mellon University, Software Engineering Institute, Pittsburgh (1996)

2. Members of the Assessment Method Integrated Team.: Standard CMMI® Appraisal Method for Process Improvement (SCAMPI), Version 1.1. CMU/SEI 2001-HB-001. Software Engineering Institute, Carnegie Mellon University. Pittsburgh, PA (2001)
3. ISO/IEC 15504:2003/Cor.1:2004(E): Information Technology – Process Assessment. Parts 1-5. International Organization for Standardization: Geneva (2004)
4. Niazi, M., Wilson, D., Zowghi, D.: A framework for assisting the design of effective software process improvement implementation strategies. Journal of Systems and Software 78(2), 204–222 (2005)
5. Malheiros, V., Seaman, C., Maldonado, J.: An Approach for Collaborative and Distributed Software Process Improvement (SPI). Presented in 3rd Brazilian Workshop on Distributed Software Development, WDDS 2009 (2009)
6. Maindantchick, C., Rocha, A., Xexeo, G.: Software process standardization for distributed working groups. In: Proc. of the 4th IEEE International Symposium and Forum on Software Engineering Standards, pp. 153–156. IEEE Computer Society, Los Alamitos (1999)
7. Garcia, I., Pacheco, C., Calvo-Manzano, J.: Using a web-based tool to define and implement software process improvement initiatives in a small industrial setting. IET Software 4(4), 237–251 (2010)
8. Nakakoji, K.: PIASS: process-improvement activity support system. Technical report SRA-SEL-97081, Software Engineering Lab., SRA Inc., Tokio, Japan (1997)
9. Model-based Adaptive Product and Process Engineering – MAPPER (2010), http://mapper.eu.org
10. Malheiros, V., Paim, F., Mendonça, M.: Continuous Process Improvement at a Large Software Organization. Software Process: Improvement and Practice 14(2), 65–83 (2009)
11. Fras, P.: Deliverable D15. Report on Collaborative Design Process Model, Analysis, and Evaluation. Version 1., April 3 (2008)
12. Tellioğlu, H.: Model-based Collaborative Design in Engineering. In: Luo, Y. (ed.) CDVE 2009. LNCS, vol. 5738, pp. 85–92. Springer, Heidelberg (2009)
13. Koch, N., Knapp, A., Zhang, G., Baumeister, H.: UML-Based Web Engineering: An Approach Based on Standards. In: Web Engineering: Modeling and Implementing Web Applications. HCI Series, vol. 12, pp. 157–191. Springer, Heidelberg (2007)
14. Linaje, M., Preciado, J.C., Sánchez-Figueroa, F.: Engineering Rich Internet Application User Interfaces over Legacy Web Models. Internet Computing Magazine IEEE 11(6), 53–59 (2007)
15. Preciado, J.C., Linaje, M., Morales-Chaparro, R., Sanchez-Figueroa, F., Zhang, G., Kroiß, C., Koch, N.: Designing Rich Internet Applications Combining UWE and RUX-Method. In: Proc. of the Eighth International Conference on Web Engineering (ICWE 2008), pp. 148–154. IEEE Computer Society, Los Alamitos (2008)
16. Fowler, P., Middlecoat, B., Yo, S.: Lessons Learned Collaborating on a Process for SPI at Xerox (CMU/SEI-99-TR-006, ADA373332). Software Engineering Institute, Carnegie Mellon University, Pittsburgh, PA (1999)
17. Garcia, I., Pacheco, C., Calvo-Manzano, J., Cuevas, G., San Feliu, T., Mendoza, E.: Managing the Software Process with a Software Process Improvement Tool in a Small Enterprise. Journal of Software Maintenance and Evolution: Research and Practice 23(3), 297–382 (2011)

On the Development of a Sensor Network-Based System for Wildfire Prevention

Luis Vicente-Charlesworth and Sebastià Galmés

Dept. of Mathematics and Computer Science, Universitat de les Illes Balears,
Cra. de Valldemossa, km. 7.5, 07122 Palma, Spain
lvcharlesworth@gmail.com, sebastia.galmes@uib.es

Abstract. In this paper, we show the process of designing a wildfire prevention system based on a time-driven wireless sensor and actuator network. The description highlights the architectural and cooperative aspects of the proposed system, as well as key design issues related with the deployment of nodes and the construction of a data-gathering tree that optimizes system lifetime and reduces the number of relay nodes necessary to create a connected network.

Keywords: Sensor network, data-gathering tree, Time-Division Multiple Access (TDMA), Minimum Spanning Tree (MST).

1 Introduction and Related Work

In fight against wildfires, ICT (*Information and Communication Technologies*) play nowadays an invaluable role. For instance, satellites provide the means to monitor big wildfires and deliver real time information to fire management services. In addition, satellites can also support reliable fire early warning systems, providing precise data on the location of incipient fires and their propagation. More recent technologies, such as (event-driven) sensor networks or unmanned airplanes (UAV - *Unmanned Air Vehicles*), which are able to explore wide forest areas and send images and environmental data in real time, greatly contribute to the fast detection of fires. Examples in the case of sensor networks, which are the concern of this paper, are [1-5].

The common denominator to these previous works is that their focus is on reacting against fire once it has ignited. However, the biggest expectations are put on the use of advanced technologies as the support of preventive rather than reactive or early-detection systems. In particular, this paper addresses the development process of a (time-driven) wireless sensor (and actuator) network for the support of a highly-cooperative system devoted to forest fire prevention. This work complements a previous contribution [6], which focused on the design of an intelligent interface for forest fire prevention based on a fuzzy model.

The main advantages of sensor and actuator networks (WSAN) in this domain is that they provide a cost-effective, real-time and high resolution means to monitor and react to the environmental conditions that can lead to fire ignition. However, in order to effectively exploit these benefits, it is necessary to carefully address some design aspects related to the weakest component of the system, which is the set of networked

Y. Luo (Ed.): CDVE 2011, LNCS 6874, pp. 53–60, 2011.

low-powered sensor nodes. Accordingly, the paper describes the application of advanced techniques aimed at maximizing the life expectancy of the system with no detriment of its functional and non-functional requirements. More specifically, the paper is organized as follows. In Section 2, we focus on some architectural issues and describe the different levels of cooperation in a WSAN-based wildfire preventive system. In Section 3, we assess the benefits of cooperation in terms of network lifetime. In Section 4, we describe the development process of a time-driven sensor network intended to monitoring a specific region. Finally, in Section 5, we draw the main conclusions and suggestions for further research.

2 Architectural Issues and Levels of Cooperation in Time-Driven WSAN

In *time-driven*, *continuous monitoring* or *proactive* sensor networks, communication is triggered by nodes, which regularly deliver sensed data to the user [7]. A common application of these networks is environmental monitoring, where some ambient condition is periodically sampled, coded and transmitted in order to be reconstructed both in time and space at a data management centre (a user PC in its simplest form). The reconstructed information can take the form of a multicolored map and can then be used for scientific purposes and/or preventive control. In the latter case, the map becomes a valuable repository of real-time data that can support appropriate control decisions or trigger preventive alarms in due course. However, even a more complete preventive scenario can be created by deploying actuator nodes in addition to sensor nodes. In the context of wildfire prevention, these actuator nodes could consist of electronic devices (with processing and transceiver units) attached to sprinklers or irrigation systems. Their action would be triggered by a decision-making process when the environmental conditions detected by the sensors revealed a risk situation.

Figure 1 describes the two basic architectures for a wireless sensor and actuator network. In both cases, it is supposed that actuator nodes have stronger capabilities than sensor nodes in terms of data processing, wireless communication, action range, and power supply [7]. For this reason, usually the number of actuators is lower than that of sensors. In the semi-automated architecture shown in Figure 1(a), all data collected by the sensor nodes are transferred to the base station, which is assumed to be locally or remotely connected to a decision-making application that diagnoses the level of fire risk. Depending on the diagnosis, this application entity may issue a command to activate some or all actuators in order to increase the indexes of air and soil humidity and correspondingly decrease the risk estimate. The transmission of this command is supported by an independent network that connects the base station with the actuators. Contrarily to the sensor counterpart, the actuator segment is not subject to severe limitations in terms of transmission range and energy capacity. Therefore, the semi-automated architecture is very similar to the architecture of time-driven wireless sensor networks, and in fact current protocols and algorithms developed for the latter can be easily extended to the scenario represented in Figure 1(a). An alternative architecture is shown in Figure 1(b), which corresponds to a fully automated scenario. In this case, sensed data flow directly from sensor to actuator nodes, with no intervention of any central device. Rather, the base station plays a secondary role, which basically consists of sporadically sending control and configuration messages to the sensor-actuator field (usually this is done by sending these messages to the actuators, which then forward them to the sensor nodes if necessary).

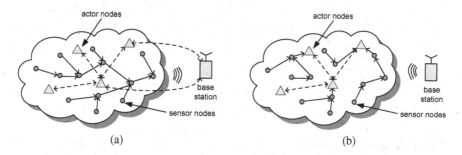

Fig. 1. Basic architectures for a WSAN: (a) semi-automated; (b) automated

This paper deals with the semi-automated case, in spite of the advantages exhibited by the fully automated architecture. The reason is that in many cases, especially those related to disaster prevention, the situation management requires that different actions are performed in a cooperative human-machine environment, among which the activation of actuators would coexist with other tasks such as central monitoring, alarm generation, etc.

In addition to the cooperation at the application level, the implementation of the proposed system requires other levels of cooperation derived from the intrinsic nature of sensor nodes. The fact that these devices are low-powered with small batteries converts the sensor segment into the weak component of the overall system. This can only be addressed by introducing additional mechanisms of cooperation with regard to conventional networks. Among these mechanisms, the most significant ones are located at the MAC and network layers of the protocol stack:

- MAC level synchronization. The limited energy capacity of sensor nodes recommends that they are switched to sleep mode whenever they are not committed to transmit or receive. However, this duty-cycle reduction can only be achieved by ensuring that a receiver node wakes up on time to capture a packet issued by a transmitter node. This uses to be done in a distributed way.
- Load-balanced routing. As it is shown in Figure 1(a), usually the topology of time-driven sensor networks takes the form of a data-gathering tree. This implies that every node is entrusted with conveying the traffic generated by all its descendents to the base station. Unless special care is taken with regard to the construction of such tree, the resulting workload distribution may cause fast energy depletion of some nodes. Therefore, the routing scheme should be aware of the distribution of the traffic. Then, if a distributed approach is adopted for the implementation of this routing scheme, an additional level of cooperation is introduced among nodes, which is again aimed at reducing energy consumption.

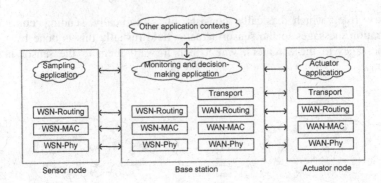

Fig. 2. Levels of cooperation in the semi-automated architecture of a WSAN.

Figure 2 summarizes the different levels of cooperation in the semi-automated architecture of a wireless sensor and actuator network.

3   Evaluation of Energy Costs and Lifetime

In principle, the traffic generated by time-driven sensor networks is periodic, and therefore the use of TDMA-based access mechanisms becomes appropriate [8]. In addition, these mechanisms allow for minimizing the duty-cycle in communication, since nodes can switch to sleep mode whenever they are not scheduled to transmit or receive. Obviously, this leads to significant energy savings.

In order to formalize the analysis of energy consumption, let the sensor nodes be denoted as $i = 0 \ldots N$, with node 0 corresponding to the base station and N the total number of nodes. These are supposed to take readings of the environment regularly or periodically in rounds of communication (time unit), whose duration is specified by the monitoring application and is typically much larger than the duration of packets. Besides, the workload supported by every node can be easily characterized via the following two parameters: $g(i)$, defined as the number of packets to be generated by node i in every communication round (*source intensity*), and $\sigma(i)$, defined as the number of packets to be forwarded by node i during every communication round (*forwarding parameter*). Note that the latter may encompass usual patterns of data aggregation (see [9] as an example). On the basis of these magnitudes, the following mathematical model describes the energy consumed by a sensor node in a round of communication (as usual, the energy consumption associated with the sensing and processing activities is neglected) [10]:

$$E(i) = (g(i) + 2\sigma(i)) \cdot E_{elec} \cdot m + (g(i) + \sigma(i)) \cdot E_w \cdot m \cdot d^f(i), \forall i . \tag{1}$$

Here, E_{elec} stands for the energy dissipated by the transceiver circuitry to transmit or receive a single bit, $E_w \cdot d^f(i)$ is the energy radiated to the wireless medium to transmit a single bit over a link of distance $d(i)$ (assuming the more generic scenario where sensor nodes are enabled with power control), f is the path-loss exponent and m is the packet size in bits. Next, network lifetime is commonly defined as the time until first node death (B stands for the battery):

$$L = \frac{B}{\max\{E(i)\,,\, i = 1\ldots N\}} = \frac{B}{E(i)\big|_{max}} \,. \tag{2}$$

4 Application Scenario

In this section, we illustrate the process of designing a sensor/actuator network-based system for wildfire prevention, by considering a scenario in Majorca (Balearic Islands, Spain) that has been categorized as of high fire risk in summer time. The description of this process is at theoretical level only, and has been decomposed into two stages: network deployment and network configuration. Next, these stages are described in more detail.

4.1 Network Deployment

The deployment of a WSAN encompasses both the sensor and the actuator segments. However, at least in the case of wildfire prevention, whereas the deployment of the sensor network is driven by application requirements, the location of irrigators is guided by structural conditions that are beyond the technical tradeoffs addressed in this paper. In essence, the number and distribution of irrigators would depend on the availability and location of water tanks, which are usually deployed at topographically-feasible locations for further use by helicopters from emergency services. For this reason, the subsequent analysis will focus on the sensor network component of the overall system.

A common assumption in literature is that sensor nodes are dense and randomly deployed over the sensor field. However, whereas this is true in the case of event-driven applications for coverage reasons, it does not usually correspond to reality in the case of time-driven sensor networks. Rather, the latter are typically deployed in a structured manner, either by selecting strategic locations or by adopting some regular pattern. More specifically, in wildfire prevention, the deployment of sensor nodes results from a decision process that takes into account all relevant factors in fire ignition and propagation. These factors are listed in Table 1. Among the triggering agents, experience all over the world shows that in most cases it is the human carelessness the main cause of fires: agricultural and shepherding-related burnings, forest works, smokers, electrical lines, machines and even arsonists. In fact, with no detriment of other factors (like density of vegetation and topographical features), the deployment proposed for the target region paid special attention to locations that were particularly vulnerable because of their proximity to human activity: forest tracks, crops, inner and peripheral roads, etc. This deployment is described in Figure 3, and the corresponding coordinates are shown in Table 2.

Table 1. Fire ignition and fire propagation factors in wildfires

Fire ignition factors			Fire propagation factors	
Meteorology	**Agents**	**Combustibles**	**Meteorology**	**Topography**
Temperature	Natural (bolts)	Biomass (wood, carbon)	Wind (speed, direction)	Height
Air humidity	Human	Plants in general		Orientation
Soil moisture				Slope

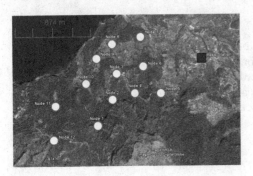

Fig. 3. Image of the sensor field. The base station is located in the village of Estellencs, in the northeast side of the map. The total area monitored is about 111 hectares.

Table 2. Location of nodes as provided by Google Earth

Node	Latitude (N)	Longitude (E)
1	39°38'48.80"	2°28'1.94"
2	39°38'57.77"	2°28'9.33"
3	39°39'7.41"	2°28'11.35"
4	39°39'0.24"	2°28'20.58"
5	39°39'0.09"	2°28'33.58"
6	39°39'9.62"	2°28'24.78"
7	39°39'21.41"	2°28'23.33"
8	39°39'18.69"	2°28'9.16"
9	39°39'13.16"	2°28'0.91"
10	39°39'3.73"	2°27'56.23"
11	39°38'55.21"	2°27'41.33"
12	39°38'43.04"	2°27'41.10"
Base station	39°39'12.67"	2°28'54.08"

Regarding the sampling process, every node is assumed to sense all meteorological variables that come into play: temperature, air humidity, soil moisture and speed and direction of wind. Despite the latter has been ignored in many proposals, it is the less predictable and more chaotic variable at the local scale, and the one that best justifies the use of a sensor network instead of conventional meteorological stations.

4.2 Network Configuration

As in the case of deployment, network configuration can also be decomposed into the sensor and actuator segments. However, given the fact that the actuator segment is not subject to severe limitations in terms of power, conventional wireless solutions can be adopted depending on other factors such as area coverage and budget: WLAN, WiMAX, GPRS, satellite. So, again the critical subsystem is the sensor network. Its configuration spans both the MAC and network layers of the protocol stack:

- MAC layer. Although the ZigBee protocol [11] is widely used at present for communication in sensor networks, other solutions tailored to time-driven sensor networks lead to better lifetime expectancies. Among them, TDMA-based protocols provide optimal lifetimes, although at the expense of tight synchronization among nodes, which is difficult to implement with supposedly inexpensive devices. Thus, in [12] we proposed RDG-UNI, which yields lifetime results very close to those of TDMA-based schemes, but under less strict requirements on synchronization.

Regarding the present paper, any protocol (TDMA, RDG) can be assumed, since the energy model developed in Section 3 is valid for both.

- Network layer. Here, the main design goal is to construct a connected network that yields optimal lifetime. Since the distances between nodes in Figure 3 (from about 300 m to almost 2 km) exceed usual transmission ranges, the insertion of relay nodes becomes necessary. Here, only 2-degree (at most 2 incident links) relay nodes are considered. On the other hand, expression (1) reveals that both traffic load and transmission distance are key factors in the evaluation of energy consumption. However, most contributions regarding the construction of data-gathering trees do not take all such factors into consideration. Either they only focus on transmission distance, by applying some variant of the well-known Minimum Spanning Tree (MST) algorithm, or at most consider the two factors in a limited way by upper bounding the degree of regular nodes. Thus, in [10] we proposed a heuristic algorithm based on the technique of *simulated annealing*, which undertakes a computationally-feasible tree exploration that accounts for both transmission distance and workload (without restrictions). This algorithm was completed with another module that allows for reducing the number of relay nodes to be inserted as long as the resulting lifetime is not degraded. The combined algorithm was called SA+LDR (Simulated Annealing + Link Distance Reduction).

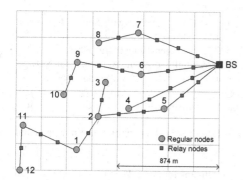

Node	XY coordinates	Node	XY coordinates
1	(-1237, -738)	7	(-730, 271)
2	(-1062, -461)	8	(-1066, 186)
3	(-1014, -163)	9	(-1262, 15)
4	(-795, -384)	10	(-1373, -276)
5	(-486, -389)	11	(-1726, -540)
6	(-695, -94)	12	(-1732, -916)
BS	(0, 0)		

Fig. 4. Data-gathering tree for the Estellencs network as a result of the SA+LDR algorithm

By applying this SA-based approach, the data-gathering tree shown in Figure 4 was obtained (coordinates are in meters). In this theoretical analysis, the parameters of the energy consumption model were taken from a realistic radio module previously introduced in [13]: $E_{elec} = 50$ nJ/bit, $E_w = 10$ pJ/bit/m^2 and $f = 2$ if the transmission distance is below 75 m (reference distance), $E_w = 0.0013$ pJ/bit/m^4 and $f = 4$ if the transmission distance is above 75 m, and $B = 15$ kJ. The maximum transmission range was set to 250 m. We also set the packet size to 32B (this packet size allows for embedding five data measurements – temperature, air and soil humidity, wind speed and direction, as well as for using a long preamble as required by the LPL (Low Power Listening) technique in order to reduce the energy consumed during the listening periods of RDG. The resulting lifetime was 3891599 rounds. For instance, if the round duration is set to 1 minute, this lifetime is around 7 years, which is quite satisfactory. As it can be noticed from Figure 4, the total number of inserted relay nodes is 21.

5 Conclusions

In this paper we have proposed a wildfire prevention system based on a wireless sensor and actuator network. We have assumed a semi-automated architecture that involves different levels of cooperation. The main differences with regard to other fire control systems supported by sensor networks is its fully preventive nature, which takes into account wind speed and direction and includes an actuator network based on irrigators. The analysis has focused on several design aspects such as network deployment and MAC and routing schemes. Further work includes the development of a distributed and adaptive version of the routing algorithm, which takes link qualities into consideration, and the implementation of a system prototype.

Acknowledgments. This work is supported by the Spanish Ministry of Science and Technology under contract TIN2010-16345.

References

1. Angayarkkani, K., Radakrishnan, N.: An Intelligent System for Effective Forest Fire Detection Using Spatial Data. International Journal of Computer Science and Information Security 7, 202–205 (2010)
2. Pripuzic, K., Belani, H., Vukovic, M.: Early Forest Fire Detection with Sensor Networks: Sliding Window Skylines Approach. In: Lovrek, I., Howlett, R.J., Jain, L.C. (eds.) KES 2008, Part I. LNCS (LNAI), vol. 5177, pp. 725–732. Springer, Heidelberg (2008)
3. Ramachandran, C., Misra, S., Obaidat, M.S.: A Probabilistic Zonal Approach for Swarm-Inspired Wildfire Detection Using Sensor Networks. International Journal of Communication Systems 21, 1047–1073 (2008)
4. Sahin, Y.G.: Animals as Mobile Biological Sensors for Forest Fire Detection. Sensors 7(12), 3084–3099 (2007)
5. García, M., Lloret, J.: A Cooperative Group-Based Sensor Network for Environmental Monitoring. In: Luo, Y. (ed.) CDVE 2009. LNCS, vol. 5738, pp. 276–279. Springer, Heidelberg (2009)
6. Fuster-Parra, P., Galmés, S., Ligeza, A.: An Intelligent Interface Using a Fuzzy Model in Prevention of Forest Fire. In: European Simulation and Modelling Conference, pp. 434–438. EUROSIS-ETI (2010)
7. Nayak, A., Stojmenovic, I.: Wireless Sensor and Actuator Networks. Wiley, Chichester (2010)
8. Krishnamachari, B.: Networking Wireless Sensors. Cambridge University Press, Cambridge (2005)
9. Wu, Y., Fahmy, S., Shroff, N.B.: On the Construction of a Maximum-Lifetime Data Gathering Tree in Sensor Networks: NP-Completeness and Approximation Algorithm. In: IEEE INFOCOM 2008, pp. 356–360. IEEE, Los Alamitos (2008)
10. Santamaría, M.L., Galmés, S., Puigjaner, R.: Resource Optimization Algorithm for Sparse Time-Driven Sensor Networks. In: Crovella, M., Feeney, L.M., Rubenstein, D., Raghavan, S.V. (eds.) NETWORKING 2010. LNCS, vol. 6091, pp. 277–290. Springer, Heidelberg (2010)
11. ZigBee Alliance,
    http://www.zigbee.org/About/AboutAlliance/TheAlliance.aspx
12. Galmés, S., Puigjaner, R.: Randomized Data-Gathering Protocol for Time-Driven Sensor Networks. Sumitted to Computer Networks Journal (currently under moderate review)
13. Heinzelman, W.B., Chandrakasan, A.P., Balakrishnan, H.: An Application-Specific Protocol Architecture for Wireless Microsensor Networks. IEEE Trans. on Wireless Communications 1(4), 660–670 (2002)

Taking Cooperative Decisions in Group-Based Wireless Sensor Networks

Miguel Garcia[1], Jaime Lloret[1], Sandra Sendra[1], and Joel J.P.C. Rodrigues[2]

[1] Integrated Management Coastal Research Institute
Universitat Politècnica de Valencia, Camino de Vera s/n, 46022 Valencia, Spain
[2] Instituto de Telecomunicações, University of Beira Interior,
Av. Marquês D'Ávila e Bolama, 6201-001 Covilhã, Portugal
{migarpi,sansenco}@posgrado.upv.es, jlloret@dcom.upv.es,
joeljr@ieee.org

Abstract. Several studies have demonstrated that communications are more efficient when cooperative group-based architectures are used in wireless sensor networks (WSN). This type of architecture allows increasing sensor nodes' lifetime by decreasing the number of messages in network. But, the main gap is to know how to take cooperative decisions in order to make the right communication. In this paper, we analyze the main aspects related to collaborative decisions in WSNs. A mathematical analysis will be presented in order to take the correct decision. Finally, the simulations will show the efficiency of the method used to make cooperative decisions in WSNs.

Keywords: cooperative decisions, cooperative WSN, group-based WSN.

1 Introduction and Related Work

Nowadays, there are a lot applications based on WSNs [1]. Most of them are based on centralized or distributed architectures, but we proved in a previous work that group-based architectures are more efficient in terms of performance and energy [2]. Moreover, we proved the benefits of a cooperative group-based WSN for environmental monitoring in [3]. In this case, when a group detects an event, it warns the alert, jointly with the parameters measured, to its neighboring groups. Cooperation with other groups could change the direction of the alert propagation and the level of the alert. According to this cooperation, the sensor network was efficient and the sensors had a longer lifetime [4]. But, how the sensor nodes take the cooperative decisions? There are some works, where the authors talk about the process to take the correct cooperative decision. For example, in [5], the authors propose a new approach to estimate the credibility of decision makers in a knowledge grid environment. They developed a new fuzzy operator, which aggregates decisions made inside the decision makers' community and considering the credibility of the decision makers.

In [6], there is another work where authors explain how to make distributed decisions in cooperative systems. They define cooperation processes and a set of models that are able to support designers of cooperative decisions. These models come from a more general architecture of a Cooperative Knowledge Based System

Y. Luo (Ed.): CDVE 2011, LNCS 6874, pp. 61–65, 2011.

and are based on the knowledge acquisition field. Finally, a paper which revises the group decision over cooperative work is shown in [7]. The authors review the group decision support systems (GDSSs) that have been configured to meet the needs of groups at work, and they evaluate the experience to date with such systems.

There are more papers with systems taking collaborative decisions, but none of them are designed for WSNs. Moreover, there is not any system for cooperative group-based WSNs where the decision is agreed with their neighbors based on their sensed parameters. In this paper, we assume that the energy consumed by processing tasks is lower than the power consumed in transmission [4], so a collaborative decision system will allow saving energy in the WSN.

The rest of the paper is organized as follows. In section 2, the mathematical analysis used for taking cooperative decisions in group-based WSNs is described. In Section 3, the simulation that shows the efficiency of the decision system is provided. Finally, in Section 4, we draw the conclusion.

2   Cooperative Decision

The cooperative decision system described in this section has been designed for the cooperative group-based WSN for environmental monitoring presented in [3]. In this system, the network is divided into groups, in which each group is formed by several sensor nodes. All sensor nodes sense several parameters. The parameters sensed by each node and the cooperation between groups make an efficient monitoring network. During the observation time, each sensor node gathers 4 parameters: temperature of the environment $T = \{t_0, t_1, t_2, t_3, ..., t_n\}$, humidity is $H = \{h_0, h_1, h_2, h_3, ..., h_{10}\}$, wind $W = \{speed, x, y, z\}$ and fire $F = \{f_{yes}, f_{no}\}$. Where T can be in Celsius, H is humidity in %, the wind variable, formed by its speed and the direction, and, finally, the fire variable, which gives the presence of fire. According to these parameters we define 6 network states (see Table 1).

Table 1. Possible states of our cooperative group-based WSN

State	Definition
S0	No fire + No wind + High humidity $\geq h_5$ + Low temperature
S1	No fire + No wind + Low humidity $\leq h_5$ + High temperature
S2	No fire + Wind + Low/high humidity + High temperature
S3	Fire + No wind + High humidity $\geq h_5$ + Low temperature
S4	Fire + No wind + Low humidity $\leq h_5$ + High temperature
S5	Fire + Wind + Low/high humidity + High temperature

We have also defined 6 actions that can be performed by the network in each state. When the network is idle, action *A0* happens (no alert). When there is low humidity and high temperature (*A1*), level 1 alert is sent to the same group. Action *A2* will send the level 1 alert to the same group and to neighboring groups in the same direction of the wind. *A3* sends the level 2 alert to the same group and this action is taken when there is a fire. *A4* sends the level 3 alert to the same group and this action is taken when there is a fire, wind, low humidity, and high temperature. Finally, *A5* sends the level 3 alert to the same group and to all neighboring groups, and this action happens when is there is a fire, wind, low humidity and high temperature.

Each state has an adequate action. The network must be able to choose the most appropriate action according to its state and on what is happening. In order to do this process, we used a decision system which is based on the uncertainty. The decision maker knows the possible states, but it does not have any information about which of them is the best state to be changed to. Not only it is unable to predict the next state, but also it cannot quantify in any way this uncertainty. In particular, this excludes the knowledge of probabilistic information on the possibilities of occurrence of each state. In order to develop the decision criterion it has to know the matrix of criteria (see Fig. 1a), where in each box is defined by the probability of performing an action for a state. It will be performed by each node, e.g. brown node in Fig. 1b.

		States					
		S0	S1	S2	S3	S4	S5
	A0	$x_{0,0}$	$_{0,1}$	$_{0,2}$	$_{0,3}$	$_{0,4}$	$_{0,5}$
	A1	$x_{1,0}$	$_{1,1}$	$_{,2}$	$_{1,3}$	$_{1,4}$	$_{1,5}$
Actions	A2	$x_{2,0}$	$_{2,1}$	$_{2,2}$	$_{2,3}$	$_{2,4}$	$_{2,5}$
	A3	$x_{3,0}$	$_{3,1}$	$_{3,2}$	$_{3,3}$	$_{3,4}$	$_{3,5}$
	A4	$x_{4,0}$	$_{4,1}$	$_{4,2}$	$_{4,3}$	$_{4,4}$	$_{4,5}$
	A5	$x_{5,0}$	$_{5,1}$	$_{5,2}$	$_{5,3}$	$_{5,4}$	$_{5,5}$

Fig. 1a. Matrix of criteria   **Fig. 1b.** A group of our proposed WSN

The matrix of criteria is based on the criterion of Savage [8], which indicates that the decision maker compares the result of an action under a state with all other outcomes, regardless of the state under which they occur. However, the state is not controllable by the decision maker, so that the result of an action should only be compared with the results of the other alternatives under the same state of nature. For this purpose, Savage defines relative loss or loss of opportunity $r_{i,j}$ (see equation 1) associated with a result $x_{i,j}$ as the difference between the result of the best alternative because Si is the true state and outcome of the action A_i under the state S_i.

$$r_{i,j} = \max_{1 \leq k \leq m}\{x_{k,j}\} - x_{i,j} \tag{1}$$

But the Savage criterion propose to select the action that provides the smallest of the major losses suffered (ρ_i), i.e., if r_i is defined as the greatest loss that can be obtained by selecting the action A_i (see equation 2).

$$\rho_i = \max_{1 \leq j \leq n}\{r_{i,j}\} \tag{2}$$

For the application of this criterion, the node calculates the matrix of relative losses which consists of the $r_{i,j}$ elements. Each column of this matrix is obtained by calculating the difference between the maximum value of that column and each one of the values listed. For selecting the best action in each state we use the equation 3.

$$r(A_i, S_j) = \begin{cases} max_{a_k}\{x(A_k, S_j) - x(A_i, S_j)\} & \textit{Good decision} \\ x(A_i, S_j) - min\{x(A_k, S_j)\} & \textit{Bad decision} \end{cases} \tag{3}$$

3 Simulation of the Cooperative Decision System

In order to evaluate the accuracy of our cooperative decision system we simulated it. We took the example provided in Fig 1b. This simulation has been done using Matlab. In each case when an event happens in a sensor node, it will send an information request to its neighbors, which will reply with their information and, after taking a decision based on the information received, it will reply with the decided action. Figure 2a shows the protocol procedure. We have defined 20 possible cases making a matrix of criteria. Then, we applied our decision system based on the Savage criterion during 100 times. Fig. 2b shows the estimated average for each case. In this figure we can see the action selected by each state. The best solution in each state is the action with the same subscript, i.e., $S_n \rightarrow A_n$. We can see in this Fig 2b that our system is not perfect, but it only has an error of 3.52%.

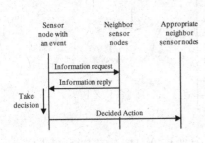

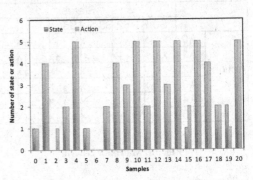

Fig. 2a. Protocol procedure   **Fig. 2b.** Cooperative decision system simulation

4 Conclusion

In this paper we propose a cooperative decision system based on several parameters for selecting the better action in a group-based WSN for environmental monitoring. According to this decision, the sensor node sends the appropriate level alert to its group or to the appropriate neighboring groups. Simulation shows that the accuracy of the criterion is quite good because the system only has an error of 3.52%.

References

1. Garcia, M., Bri, D., Sendra, S., Lloret, J.: Practical Deployments of Wireless Sensor Networks: a Survey. Int. Journal on Advances in Networks and Services 3(3-4), 170–185 (2010)
2. Lloret, J., Garcia, M., Tomas, J.: Improving Mobile and Ad-hoc Networks performance using Group-Based Topologies. In: Wireless Sensor and Actor Networks II. IFIP, vol. 264, pp. 209–220 (2008)

3. Garcia, M., Lloret, J.: A Cooperative Group-Based Sensor Network for Environmental Monitoring. In: Luo, Y. (ed.) CDVE 2009. LNCS, vol. 5738, pp. 276–279. Springer, Heidelberg (2009)
4. Garcia, M., Sendra, S., Lloret, J., Lacuesta, R.: Saving Energy with Cooperative Group-Based Wireless Sensor Networks. In: Luo, Y. (ed.) CDVE 2010. LNCS, vol. 6240, pp. 73–76. Springer, Heidelberg (2010)
5. Parsa, S., Parand, F.-A.: Cooperative decision making in a knowledge grid environment. Future Generation Computer Systems 23, 932–938 (2007)
6. Soubie, J.-L., Zaraté, P.: Distributed Decision Making: A Proposal of Support Through Cooperative Systems. J. Group Decisions and Negotiation 14(2), 147–158 (2005)
7. Kraemer, K.L., King, J.L.: Computer-based systems for cooperative work and group decision making. ACM Computer Survey 20(2), 115–146 (1988)
8. Kernan, J.B.: Choice Criteria, Decision Behavior, and Personality. Journal of Marketing Research 5(2), 155–164 (1968)

Cooperative Operating Control for Induction or Elimination of Self-sustained Oscillations in CSTB

Piotr Skupin and Mieczyslaw Metzger

Faculty of Automatic Control, Electronics and Computer Science,
Silesian University of Technology,
ul. Akademicka 16, 44-100 Gliwice, Poland
{piotr.skupin,mieczyslaw.metzger}@polsl.pl

Abstract. The problem of cooperative control is especially important in the case of selection of an appropriate mode of operation for a wide class of bioprocesses. In classical approach, this can be achieved via SCADA systems used by process operators. However, due to the nonlinear nature of bioprocesses, the operators usually are not able to assess the efficiency of a bioprocess, especially in the presence of self-sustained oscillations (SSO) of the biomass concentration. Hence, they must cooperate with experts who are usually geographically dispersed. This paper presents the solution of the above-stated problems using an additional server application in the layer of supervisory control. The main tasks of the application are to provide the process data (collected by the SCADA system) to a group of experts and allow them to discuss possibilities of enhancing the efficiency of the bioprocess. The taken decisions are then sent to the operator.

Keywords: cooperative operating control, agent-based cooperation, self-sustained oscillations.

1 Introduction

The Supervisory Control And Data Acquisition (SCADA) systems, whose main tasks are monitoring and supervising a process, play a key role in the modern industrial processes [1], [2]. The modern SCADA systems allow for processing of large quantities of data (even up to several thousands of input/output channels), creating both historical and real-time trends, and owing to embedded servers, for simple integration and data communication between many devices from different vendors. Moreover, the modern SCADA systems also allow for archiving and processing of measurement data, and properly defined alarms, which are automatically triggered in the system, notify process operators of the occurrence of emergency situations. Thus, it is possible to make appropriate decisions by users (process operators). All stored data can be sent and shared in the form of reports to the upper layer, which includes highly qualified experts. Their main goal is first of all to make decisions related to the efficiency of the process based on the collected measurement data. The role of experts is particularly important when the considered processes are strongly nonlinear, which is a typical property of many bioprocesses that involve microorganisms in very

Y. Luo (Ed.): CDVE 2011, LNCS 6874, pp. 66–73, 2011.
© Springer-Verlag Berlin Heidelberg 2011

complex chemical reactions [3-5]. Then, the process operators are not able to make decisions concerning the selection of a more advantageous control strategy and must based on the knowledge of experts. Moreover, in such processes, common phenomena are multiplicity of steady states [6] or stable limit cycles [7], manifested as oscillations of key process variables, which make it more difficult to decide what is the best strategy. In such cases, an assessment of the process efficiency may be a quite complex task, especially when the performance significantly depends on the assumed mode of operation [8-10] (e.g. operation in steady state regime or in the range of sustained oscillations). However, due to high inertia of the bioprocesses, any responses to changes in manipulated variables occur relatively slowly [5], [11]. Hence, there is sufficient time to discuss different strategies and to choose the best option by a group of experts. It should also be pointed out that experts are often geographically dispersed. Hence, they should be provided with appropriate communication services, as well as be allowed to access the process data and to cooperate with each other and with the process operator. Problems occurring among cooperating experts and engineers that are geographically dispersed are well-known and widely described in the literature and exemplary papers in the field are [12]-[17]. Although the main problem is the geographical distribution of the cooperating experts and engineers, there are also other relevant problems such as: conflict between cooperating users [17] (every user or a group of users has its own objectives and agenda), misunderstanding, lack of information, differing interests and personal values [14].

This paper presents a solution to overcome the aforementioned difficulties and to meet the set objectives based on a typical SCADA system aided by agent applications. Details of the proposed solution will be presented based on the example of a classical bioprocess taking place in a continuous stirred tank bioreactor (CSTB). The detail description of the bioprocess and the proposed solution will be given in the next sections.

2 Description of the Bioprocess under Consideration

In most bioprocesses, there takes place an increase in the concentration of microorganisms (biomass concentration) and secretion of a product, as a result of consumption of one or more of the available substrates [4], [5]. In the case of the optimization of the bioreactor performance, a biomass productivity DX is the most common performance index to be maximized [8], [18], where X is the concentration of microorganisms (biomass concentration), D is the dilution rate and D=F/V, where F is the flow rate of a medium flowing through the CSTB, V is the volume of the medium in the CSTB (V=const). The biomass productivity DX tells us how many grams of biomass is produced per unit volume of the medium in the CSTB and per unit time. Since the function DX(D) is characterized by a maximum in a narrow range of dilution rates, as shown in Figure 1, therefore there exist an optimal value of dilution rate D maximizing the biomass productivity DX [10], [18], [19]. However, due to the nonlinear nature of such processes, a frequent phenomenon is the occurrence of the self-sustained oscillations (SSO) of biomass concentration [7], [20]. Figure 1 presents a typical dependence of the biomass productivity on the dilution rate

D with characteristic ranges of steady states and oscillatory regimes. It can also be seen that if the dilution rates D are too high then the whole culture of microorganisms is washout from the reactor and the biomass productivity drops to zero [8]. Further analysis of such bioprocesses reveals that the operation of the CSTB in the range of SSO may lead to higher or lower average values of biomass productivity in comparison to the results obtained in steady state regime [8], [9]. This depends mainly on the process under consideration (a strain of microorganisms, a type of substrates), as well as environmental parameters (temperature, pH level, inlet substrate concentrations) [21], [22].

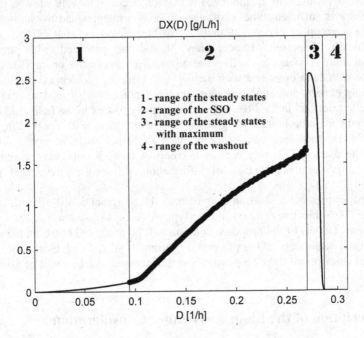

Fig. 1. The average biomass productivity versus dilution rate D in the case of the occurrence of the SSO of biomass concentration. The black thick line denotes the range of SSO

Hence, in such cases, the evaluation of the bioreactor productivity is not an easy task, thus the operation of the CSTB in the range of SSO is usually avoided in practice by changing some process parameters [8]. In such cases, the choice of the more suitable mode of operation (steady state or SSO) is usually made by changing manipulated variables (e.g. dilution rate D, inlet substrate concentration or the agitation speed of the reactor content that changes dissolved oxygen levels [21], [22]). In this paper, it is assumed that the choice of an appropriate mode of operation of the CSTB is made by adding an extra substrate which will attenuate or even eliminate the SSO of biomass concentration [23]. Moreover, it is assumed that the additional substrate is fed at the expense of the original substrate, in order to minimize the cost of such an approach. Figure 2 explains the idea of control of the SSO by increasing the percentage contribution of the additional substrate (which damps oscillations) to the mixture. Moreover, in the case of the occurrence of SSO, the measurement of the biomass concentration on-line is not sufficient. Therefore, some extra applications (e.g. agent applications [24]-[27]) for calculating the average biomass concentration (as an average value for the period), for detection of the oscillatory behavior and for choosing a desired mode of operation of the CSTB are necessary to apply. Collecting this information will help the group of experts to assess the bioreactor productivity and to take appropriate decisions concerning the choice of the operating point and desired mode of operation of the bioreactor.

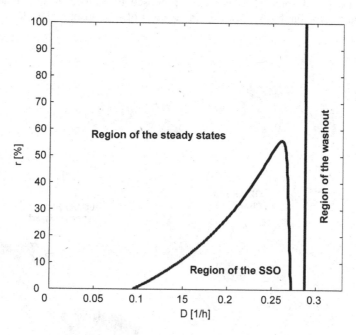

Fig. 2. The percentage contribution (r) of the additional substrate and its influence on the size of the region of the SSO

However, this requires the provision of certain mechanisms, which allow for sharing the data between all experts and also for their mutual cooperation. The details of the proposed solution have been given in the next section.

3 Description of the Environment for Cooperating Experts

The general scheme of the whole system has been presented in Figure 3. According to the presented scheme, three typical and well-known layers for the industrial processes can be distinguished: the layer of direct control (controlled plants, measurement devices, control systems (Programmable Logic Controllers (PLCs) or Programmable Automatic Controllers (PACs))), the layer of supervisory control (SCADA systems) and the layer of management and optimization (a team of experts). Each of these layers is responsible for fulfilling certain functions in a process. The process operator located in the layer of supervisory control monitors the process and has a possibility to influence its course through the SCADA system. In some cases, the operator can also have access to a simulator of the process [28]-[30] where equations governing the process dynamics are numerically solved [31], [32]. In turn, the measurement data are transmitted via a specific network interface and stored in a database which is one of the components of the SCADA system. Moreover, owing to (OLE for Process Control) OPC servers, it is possible to integrate measurement and control devices from different vendors [33].

In the presented solution, it has been proposed to include an additional server application located on the WEB Server in the layer of supervisory control.

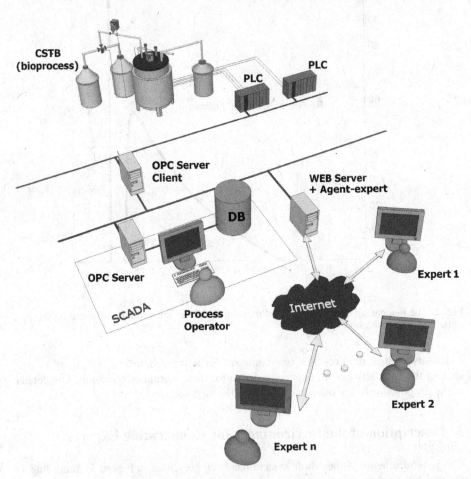

Fig. 3. The general scheme of the system including all the main components in each layer

The WEB Server has access to the database of the SCADA system and can send the data via the Internet. One of the main tasks of the proposed server application is to provide the process data (collected by the SCADA system), which are then needed to assess the bioreactor productivity and to choose the most suitable mode of operation of the CSTB. In turn, the group of a number of geographically dispersed experts can connect with the server application via the Internet, and based on the available process data, they can discuss the possibility of increasing of the biomass productivity DX. Furthermore, it is assumed the existence of an additional agent-expert, i.e. an agent application running within the framework of the server application and communicating with experts. The agent-expert, based on the simulation runs of a mathematical model calibrated to the process, can aid the decision made by experts. Each expert can also require the agent-expert to carry out some simulations for better assessment of the bioreactor productivity. This can be especially important, in the case of choosing the appropriate mode of operation of the CSTB (operation in steady state or in the range of SSO). Depending on the process under consideration, it may turn out that the oscillatory regime is more advantageous and it is possible to obtain higher values of the biomass productivity DX in comparison to the values of DX obtained in steady state operating regime. In addition, the agent-expert can also suggest some changes based on the simulation results of the same mathematical model of the bioprocess. For example, the following situation may be considered. After increasing the percentage contribution of the additional substrate to eliminate oscillations, there can be such a change in dilution rate D that the contribution of the additional substrate is too large. Then, the agent-expert can suggest to decrease the contribution of the substrate still providing steady state regime for the CSTB.

The decisions taken by the group of experts are sent to the process operator (in supervisory layer), who can influence the process by changing the dilution rate D (to operate close to the maximum of DX) and by setting the appropriate contribution of the both substrates in the mixture (to choose a desired mode of operation of the CSTB).

4 Concluding Remarks

The proposed solution, based on the cooperation of the geographically dispersed experts, allows for making appropriate decisions related to the bioreactor productivity. It is particularly important in the case of highly nonlinear processes for which the assessment of their performance is not an easy task. With the additional server application, in the layer of supervisory control, the selected process data can be shared on demand among several geographically dispersed experts through the Internet. Moreover, owing to the slow response of the bioprocess to changes in manipulated variables (e.g. dilution rate D), it is possible to carry out some simulation runs of the model calibrated to the process. Then, the simulation results, as well as discussion and analysis of the measurement data can help to choose the most advantageous control strategy to maximize the biomass productivity DX. In turn, by increasing the percentage contribution of the additional substrate (which damps oscillations) it is possible to choose an appropriate mode of operation of the CSTB. This is of great importance in practice, because the operating regime is usually chosen by setting small values of the dilution rate D. However, this is not always advantageous, because the small values of D give the small values of biomass productivity DX [8].

The proposed approach can also be applied for other processes that also require the cooperation of highly qualified experts, especially if it is difficult to assess the process performance.

Acknowledgements. This work was supported by the Polish Ministry of Science and Higher Education, grants no. N N514 471539 and no. BK-274/RAu1/2011.

References

1. Bailey, D., Wright, E.: Practical SCADA for industry. Elsevier, Oxford (2003)
2. Qiu, B., Gooi, H.B., Liu, Y., Chan, E.K.: Internet-based SCADA Display System. IEEE Comput. Appl. Pow. 15, 14–19 (2002)
3. Xiu, Z.L., Song, B.H., Sun, L.H., Zeng, A.P.: Theoretical analysis of effects of metabolic overflow and time delay on the performance and dynamic behavior of a two-stage fermentation process. Biochem. Eng. J. 11, 101–109 (2002)
4. Smith, H.L., Waltman, P.: The Theory of the Chemostat. Cambridge University Press, Cambridge (1996)
5. Dunn, I.J., Heinzle, E., Ingham, J., Prenosil, J.E.: Biological Reaction Engineering. In: Dynamic Modelling Fundamentals with Simulation Examples. Wiley-VCH Verlag (2003)
6. Follstad, B.D., Balcarcel, R.R., Stephanopoulos, G., Wang, D.I.C.: Metabolic flux analysis of hybridoma continuous culture steady state multiplicity. Biotechnol. Bioeng. 63, 675–683 (1999)
7. Chen, C.I., McDonald, K.A., Bisson, L.: Oscillatory behavior of Saccharomyces cerevisiae in continuous culture: I. Effects of pH and nitrogen levels. Biotechnol. Bioeng. 36, 19–27 (1990)
8. Balakrishnan, A., Yang, R.Y.K.: Self-forcing of a chemostat with self-sustained oscillations for productivity enhancement. Chem. Eng. Commun. 189, 1569–1585 (2002)
9. Nelson, M.I., Sidhu, H.S.: Analysis of a chemostat model with variable yield coefficient. J. Math. Chem. 38, 605–615 (2005)
10. Silveston, P.L., Budman, H., Jervis, E.: Forced modulation of biological processes: A review. Chem. Eng. Sci. 63, 5089–5105 (2008)
11. Khanal, S.K., Chen, W.H., Li, L., Sung, S.: Biohydrogen production in continuous flow reactor using mixed microbial culture. Water Environ. Res. 78, 110–117 (2006)
12. Korba, L., Song, R., Yee, G., Patrick, A.: Automated Social Network Analysis for Collaborative Work1. In: Luo, Y. (ed.) CDVE 2006. LNCS, vol. 4101, pp. 1–8. Springer, Heidelberg (2006)
13. Hanmin, L., Seong-Whan, P., Jai-Kyung, L., Je-Sung, B., Jaeho, L.: A Study on BDI Agent for the Integration of Engineering Processes. In: Luo, Y. (ed.) CDVE 2006. LNCS, vol. 4101, pp. 149–155. Springer, Heidelberg (2006)
14. Rasmussen, G.A., Brunson, M.W.: Strategies to manage conflicts among multiple users. Weed Technol. 10, 447–450 (1996)
15. Luo, Y., Dias, J.M.: Development of a Cooperative Integration System for AEC Design. In: Luo, Y. (ed.) CDVE 2004. LNCS, vol. 3190, pp. 1–11. Springer, Heidelberg (2004)
16. Choinski, D., Metzger, M., Nocon, W., Polakow, G.: Cooperative Validation in Distributed Control Systems Design. In: Luo, Y. (ed.) CDVE 2007. LNCS, vol. 4674, pp. 280–289. Springer, Heidelberg (2007)

17. Metzger, M., Polaków, G.: Cooperative internet-based experimentation on semi-industrial pilot plants. In: Luo, Y. (ed.) CDVE 2008. LNCS, vol. 5220, pp. 265–272. Springer, Heidelberg (2008)
18. Harmon, J.L., Svoronos, S.A., Gerasimos, L.: Adaptive steady-state optimization of biomass productivity in continuous fermentors. Biotechnol. Bioeng. 30, 335–344 (1987)
19. Chen, C.C., Hwang, C., Yang, R.Y.K.: Performance enhancement and optimization of chemostat cascades. Chem. Eng. Sci. 50, 485–494 (1995)
20. Satroutdinov, A.D., Kuriyama, H., Kobayashi, H.: Oscillatory metabolism of Saccharomyces cerevisiae in continuous culture. FEMS Microbiol. Lett. 98, 261–268 (1992)
21. Parulekar, S.J., Semones, G.B., Rolf, M.J., Lievense, J.C., Lim, H.C.: Induction and elimination of oscillations in continuous cultures of Saccharomyces Cerevisiae. Biotechnol. Bioeng. 28, 700–710 (1986)
22. Harrison, D.E.F., Topiwala, H.H.: Transient and oscillatory states of continuous culture. Adv. Biochem. Eng. 3, 167–219 (1974)
23. Metzger, M., Skupin, P.: Model-based operating control of the CSTB in order to improve its productivity. In: Proceedings of the 14th IEEE MMAR Conference (CD-Edition), Miedzyzdroje (2009)
24. Wooldridge, M., Jennings, N.R.: Intelligent agents: theory and practice. Knowl. Eng. Rev. 10, 115–152 (1995)
25. Jennings, N.R., Sycara, K., Wooldridge, M.: A Roadmap of Agent Research and Development. Auton. Agent. and Multi–Ag. 1, 7–38 (1998)
26. Van Dyke Parunak, H.: A practitioners' review of industrial agent applications. Auton. Agent. and Multi-Ag. 3, 389–407 (2000)
27. Weiss, G. (ed.): Multiagent Systems: A Modern Approach to Distributed Artificial Intelligence. MIT Press, Cambridge (1999)
28. Metzger, M.: Fast-mode real-time simulator for the wastewater treatment process. Water Science and Technology 30, 191–197 (1994)
29. Czeczot, J., Metzger, M., Babary, J.P., Nihtila, M.R.: Filtering in adaptive control of distributed parameter bioreactors in the presence of noisy measurements. Simul. Pract. Theory 8, 39–56 (2000)
30. Nocon, W., Metzger, M.: Predictive Control of Decantation in Batch Sedimentation Process. AICHE J. 56, 3279–3283 (2010)
31. Metzger, M.: A comparative evaluation of DRE integration algorithms for real-time simula-tion of biologically activated sludge process. Sim. Pract. Theory 7, 629–643 (2000)
32. Metzger, M.: Comparison of the RK4M4 RK4LIN and RK4M1 methods for systems with time-delays. Simul. 52, 189–193 (1989)
33. Zheng, L., Nakagawa, H.: OPC (OLE for process control) specification and its developments. In: Proceedings of the 41st SICE Conference, vol. 2, pp. 917–920 (2002)

Handling Different Format Initial Data in a Cooperative Decision Making Process

Sylvia Encheva

Stord/Haugesund University College,
Bjørnsonsg. 45, 5528 Haugesund, Norway
sbe@hsh.no

Abstract. Many-valued Galois connection reflects on the similarity between attribute values in a many-valued context. In this work we apply many-valued formal concept analysis for answering queries when some of the initial data is available in text form and another part in with crisp values.

Keywords: Many-valued Galois connections, intelligent systems.

1 Introduction

A cooperative decision making usually focusses on providing more information about the uncertain total payoff resulting from the final decision and at the same time improving on the individual welfare of each participant. Most available models and tools facilitating cooperative decision making are functional when initial data is presented in the same format. Real life situations however often require incorporation of initial data in crisp values, interval values, text, etc..

Many-valued Galois connections are defined with respect to similarity between attribute values in a many-valued context, [7]. In this paper we are further extending this method with respect to working with both numerical and linguistic initial data. The last due to real life occurrences where some human evaluators prefer text form for expressing their opinion and others are more comfortable with numerical values.

The rest of the paper is organised as follows. Section 2 contains definitions of terms used later on. Section 3 explains how to rank help functions according to personal responses. Section 4 contains the conclusion of this work.

2 Many-Valued Galois Connections

Many-valued Galois connections are discussed in [5] and [7]. Many-valued context has been recently applied in [6] for handling incomplete information. In [1] many-valued context has been applied for knowledge elicitation in case based reasoning processes. Various methods for data analysis can be found in [2] and [3].

Definition 1. [7] Consider an MV context (G, M, W, I) and a threshold θ.

Y. Luo (Ed.): CDVE 2011, LNCS 6874, pp. 74–77, 2011.

1. *If* (A_1, B_1) *and* (A_2, B_2) *are MV concepts,* (A_1, B_1) *is a subconcept of* (A_2, B_2) *when* $A_1 \subseteq_\theta A_2$ *(which is equivalent to* $B_2 \subseteq_\theta B_1$*). In this case* (A_2, B_2) *is superconcept of* (A_1, B_1) *and we write* $(A_1, B_1) \leq_\theta (A_2, B_2)$*. The relation* $\leq_\theta$ *is the hierarchical order of MV concept.*
2. *The set of all MV concepts of* (G, M, W, I) *ordered in this way is denoted by* $\mathcal{B}\theta(G, M, W, I)$ *and called the many-valued concept lattice of* (G, M, W, I)*.*

3   Combining Information in Text Format and Numerical Interval Data

One of the challenges in a shipbuilding process is related to issues of building of environmental friendly transport systems while improving on customers satisfaction. A holistic approach can be achieved by applying a decision support system incorporating different levels preliminary evaluations.

In this scenario six designer firms $F1, F2, F3, F4, F5, F6$ are evaluated by three experts where each expert is expressing his opinion related to a single criterion only. They submit their evaluations in different text formats. An additional criterion involving interval data is also included. The involved criteria are - regular practice in the maritime business (RP), quality of design of modern vessels (DM), experience with platform supply vessels in years (EV), and focus on green ship technology (FG). The goal is not only to rank the listed firms but to be able to provide answers to some queries.

Table 1 summarizes both numerical and linguistic form of evaluation. Empty cells indicate lack of data. Table 2 shows which firms have received the highest and second highest evaluation with respect to the four criteria (RP), (DM), (EV), and (FG).

Table 1. Mixed evaluation of the six firms

	RP	DM	EV	FG
F 1		moderate	$EV \geq 10$	high
F 2	regular	very good	$EV < 5$	medium
F 3	not that regular	very good	$5 \leq EV < 10$	
F 4	regular		$EV \geq 10$	medium
F 5	somewhat regular	good	$5 \leq EV < 10$	high
F 6	regular	good	$EV \geq 10$	

Table 2. Firms with the highest and second highest evaluation

	RP	DM	EV	FG
F 1			×	×
F 2	×	×		×
F 3		×	×	
F 4	×		×	×
F 5	×	×		×
F 6	×	×	×	

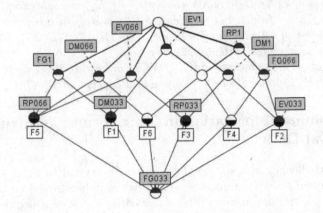

Fig. 1. Lattice of the context in Table 3

Table 3. Numerical results for the six firms

	RP	DM	EV	FG
F 1		0.33	1	1
F 2	1	1	0.33	0.66
F 3	0.33	1	0.66	
F 4	1		1	0.66
F 5	0.66	0.66	0.66	1
F 6	1	0.66	1	

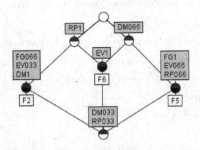

Fig. 2. Firms with good evaluations on criteria RP and DM

Information presented in Table 2 does not indicate to which degree an object satisfies a criterion. The initial information provided in Table 1 is normalized as in [4] and presented in Table 3. In particular we first divide the available data in three levels. Each number in a cell is afterwards divided by the highest level in the respective column. The corresponding lattice can be seen in Fig 1.

The lattice in Fig. 1 can be used to find answers to queries like 'Which firms have obtained evaluation values on criteria RP and DM that are not more than $\theta = 0.4$ less than the best available?'. The answer is firms F2, F5 and F6, Fig. 2.

Such information is very useful when a ship owner has constrains on resources and time, i.e. the best services might not be available for a long period of time and or they can be far too costly.

4   Conclusion

Application of many-valued Galois connections in contrast to formal concept analysis allows more flexible evaluations and provides inside information with respect to the degrees to which a particular object possess a particular attribute.

References

1. Daz-Agudo, B., Gonzlez-Calero, P.A.: Formal concept analysis as a support technique for CBR. Knowledge-Based Systems 14(3-4), 163–171 (2001)
2. Carpineto, C., Romano, G.: Concept Data Analysis: Theory and Applications. John Wiley and Sons, Ltd., Chichester (2004)
3. Davey, B.A., Priestley, H.A.: Introduction to lattices and order. Cambridge University Press, Cambridge (2005)
4. Djouadi, Y., Henri Prade, H.: Interval-Valued Fuzzy Galois Connections: Algebraic Requirements and Concept Lattice Construction. Fundamenta Informaticae 99(2), 169–186 (2010)
5. Ganter, B., Wille, R.: Formal Concept Analysis. Springer, Heidelberg (1999)
6. Liu, J., Yao, X.: Formal concept analysis of incomplete information system. In: Seventh International Conference on Fuzzy Systems and Knowledge Discovery (FSKD), pp. 2016–2020 (2010)
7. Messai, N., Devignes, M., Napoli, A., Smail-Tabbone, M.: Many-Valued Concept Lattices for Conceptual Clustering and Information Retrieval. In: Proceeding of the 2008 Conference on ECAI 2008: 18th European Conference on Artificial Intelligence. IOS Press, Amsterdam (2008)

Modeling Decisional Knowledge
with the Help of Data Quality Information

Jérôme Wax, Benoît Otjacques, Thomas Tamisier,
Olivier Parisot, Yoann Didry, and Fernand Feltz

Centre de Rercherche Public,
Gabriel Lippmann,
41, rue du Brill, L-4422 Belvaux, Luxembourg
{wax,otjacque,tamisier,parisot,didry,feltz}@lippmann.lu

Abstract. The success of the deployment of decision support systems heavily relies on the design of knowledge bases. In particular, assessing the quality of instanced data helps ensure an appropriate use of the knowledge. We present a collaborative editor for procedural knowledge that manages specific information about the quality of the data called into the procedures. Experimentations by a panel of users notably show that information being correctly interpreted and necessary to draw optimal procedures.

Keywords: Data quality, Knowledge models, Decision support.

1 Introduction

The benefit of decision support systems (DSS) is in practice frequently impaired by the processing of unsure and erratic data [1]. Data involved in decision rules are indeed frequently heterogeneous (qualitative vs. quantitative, unstructured or manually handled vs. retrieved from information systems...), which makes their processing challenging [2]. Moreover, data integration is provided by IT specialists whereas knowledge modeling is primarily the role of experts in the application domain [3], who are not necessarily aware of this problematic [4].

We present an experience of using Cadral, a business DSS developed at our department, for processing applications received by the administration of Family Benefits in Luxembourg. Cadral is a collaborative DSS: it consists of a Knowledge Editor (KE) and a Knowledge Simulator (KS), both supporting teamwork [5]. Knowledge in Cadral is a set of interconnected administrative procedures organized in a hierarchy of decision trees as follows: we start from a unique root node; every non-terminal node denote a test on specific data; according to the result of the test one arc leaving the node is univocally selected; terminal nodes denote an intermediate (for sub-trees) or final decision state. A display algorithm inspired from Sugiyama's [6] allows visualizing the trees.

Y. Luo (Ed.): CDVE 2011, LNCS 6874, pp. 78–81, 2011.

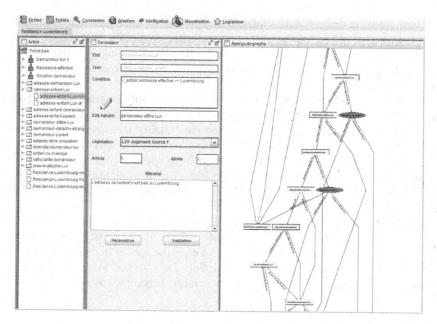

Fig. 1. Knowledge Editor with a decision tree

2 Managing Data Quality

From operational feedback we know that the correctness of the decisions suggested by Cadral is directly correlated with the place of the tests within the tree and the quality of tested data: in other words, there is a room for improvement provided we reorder the trees according to some strategy of data invocation. Similar optimization is presented in the literature: see notably [7,8]. As a matter of fact data originate from diversified sources that do not have the same level of accuracy, and in particular are not all in digital format. Optimal decisions trees should therefore make the most of reliable data, localize hazardous items as well as limit and postpone manual handling [9]. Following such guidelines is nonetheless by no means obvious to business experts, in particular due to their lack of consciousness about the quality of the data [10], which are all retrieved in the same transparent way from an Enterprise Service Bus.

Hence, we have defined some metrics for evaluating data with respect to business requirements and supplemented the graphical representation of the trees by attaching to the nodes and to the arcs information based on these metrics. We use 4 metrics that evaluate an independent data item as follows. *Availability*: one must minimize the impact of a possibly missing or manually handled item. *Trust*: an item loses trust due to different factors, in particular if not regularly updated. An untrustworthy item (e.g. and address) can directly lead to a false answer of the DSS. *Accuracy*: if the item is not accurate enough for a test (e.g. threshold detection), all subsequent processing can be irrelevant. *Cost*: cost concerns the resources (CPU, time, human handling...) needed to retrieve an item. Cost impacts considerably mass-processing and batch execution.

IT specialists in charge of data integration characterize each data item retrieved by Cadral. In a first time, for the sake of simplicity, credibility only is set through numeric values; the other metrics use a two-levels scale (low-high). Some validation routines have also been implemented to help the characterization concerning the accuracy metric.

Visual indications are helpful means to ease the legibility of graphs of significant size [11]. Moreover, specific patterns should be dedicated to data quality [12,13]. In Cadral, we use 3 patterns to show details on data quality measured thanks to the 4 metrics: (1) specific color on nodes with low-quality data; (2) specific icons attached to the nodes for reporting quality data problems; (3) specific color on arcs to follow the propagation in the decision trees of the impact of low-quality data. In addition, relevant messages on data quality are displayed in help and modeling tools (e.g. when selecting variable in a test).

Figure 2 illustrates different informative patterns on decision trees. Colors point out errors or uncertainties about the results of the decision tree (see left part). Warnings about potentially inaccurate or unsure results appear in orange. Parts of the tree impossible to process (e.g. due to missing data) appear in red. Credibility is notified in a red gauge, with complementary numeric percentage available in a tool tip (see right part).

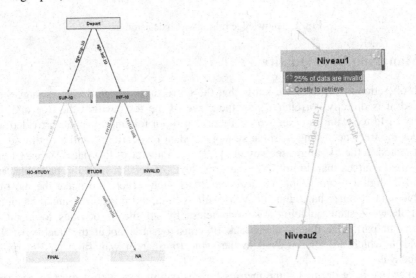

Fig. 2. details and impact of data quality

3 Experimental Tests

Before going into production, the modified Knowledge Editor has been proofed with a group of pilot users. We have designed a simplified test problem to be programmed in Cadral, that does not require any domain-related expertise: the problem is to decide whether a golf game must be played, according to weather conditions. We define 6 decision rules that imply problematic or missing data items. The goal was to find the optimal model, which delay as long as possible checks on unsure data.

Details of the example and the results will be discussed during the presentation. They highlight the following trends: (1) Most users are able (with some help) to find an optimal model; (2) Visual information has been correctly interpreted, and was necessary: the majority of the users mentioned that they should not have been able to optimize the model without. The main difficulty was as far as unsure data are concerned, to take into account the importance of the item in the model [14].

4 Conclusion and Perspectives

Decisional knowledge models can be made more efficient by enlightening application experts about data quality issues. A qualitative case study in the professional setting of Cadral will follow the preliminary user tests presented here. Further, we have in view 2 research directions. First is the automatic reordering of the decision trees to minimize the impact of low-quality data. In addition to processing application files, Cadral is also used for socio-economic prediction on projected demographic data or administrative and legal framework. The second research direction consists in evaluating the model on real data, in order to speed up prediction results by discarding as much as possible unsure data.

References

1. Redman, T.: Impact of Poor Data Quality on Typical Enterprise. Com. of ACM (1998)
2. Asproth, V.: Visualisation of Data Quality in Decision-Support Systems. International Journal of Applied Systemic Studies 1(3) (2007)
3. Shankaranarayanan, G., Cai, Y.: Supporting Data Quality Management in Decision-Making. Decision Support Systems 42(1) (2006)
4. Pipino, L., Lee, Y., Wang, R.: Data Quality Assessment. Com. of ACM 45(4) (2002)
5. Tamisier, T., Didry, Y., Parisot, O., Feltz, F.: A Collaborative Reasoning Maintenance System for a Reliable Application of Legislations. In: Luo, Y. (ed.) CDVE 2009. LNCS, vol. 5738, pp. 313–316. Springer, Heidelberg (2009)
6. Sugiyama, K., Tagawa, S., Toda, M.: Methods for Visual Understandings of Hierarchical System Structures. IEEE Trans. in Systems Man & Cybernetics 11(2) (1981)
7. Even, A., et al.: Utility-Driven Assessment of Data Quality. ACM SIGMIS Database (2007)
8. Wang, R., et al.: Beyond accuracy. Journal of Management Information Systems (1996)
9. Wang, R., et al.: Data Quality Requirements... In: Proc. of Intl. Conf. of Data Eng. (1993)
10. Hao, C., et al.: Business Process Impact Visualization... Information Visualization (2006)
11. Herman, I., Delest, M., Melancon, G.: Tree Visualisation and Navigation Clues for Information Visualisation. Computer Graphics Forum 17(2) (1998)
12. Xie, Z., et al.: Exploratory Visualization of Multivariate Data with Variable Quality. Computer Science Department, Worcester Polytechnic Institute, USA (2006)
13. Wittenbrink, C., Pang, A., Lodha, S.: Glyphs for Visualizing Uncertainty in Vector Field. IEEE Transactions on Visualization and Computer Graphics (1995)
14. Skeels, M., et al.: Revealing uncertainty for infor. vis. Information Visualization (2009)

Adapting Decision Support to Business Requirements through Data Interpretation

Thomas Tamisier, Olivier Parisot, Yoann Didry, Jérôme Wax, and Fernand Feltz

Centre de Rercherche Public - Gabriel Lippmann,
41, rue du Brill, L-4422 Belvaux, Luxembourg
{wax,otjacque,tamisier,parisot,didry,feltz}@lippmann.lu

Abstract. Decision support shows often a gap between the problems in terms of business knowledge and the answers restricted to a final decision result. We present a decisional framework for automating business procedures, developed through with the administration, that allows managing and formalizing extra information besides the mere decisional knowledge. This information can be useful to tune the knowledge model according to operational data, or to better exploit the decision result in the subsequent stages of a collaborative workflow.

Keywords: Decision support, Data interpretation, Information retrieval.

1 Introduction

Being popularized in diversified business areas, Decision Support Systems needs to manage, process, and produce daily information, i.e. knowledge merely empirical that can be heterogeneous, partially un-formalized, implicit, or diffuse [1]. However, the programming of such systems is normally done through formalisms that do not allow handling anything but structured information [2]. Through a well-established relationship with national administration, we develop a collaborative expert system, named Cadral, designed for the needs of the collaborative work in the organizations. The main application of Cadral is the processing the family benefits applications received by the Caisse Nationale des Prestations Familiales (National Family Benefits Fund) of the Grand-Duchy of Luxembourg. Handled administrative procedures are very complex due to the local open-economy where individual cases pertain to different national, supra-national and bilateral legal frameworks.

Cadral tackles the challenge of bridging this gap between the formal framework of Decision Support and the operational requirements by two means. First, it allows building its knowledge base from any kind of business procedures and information reference. Second, the reasoning engine of Cadral has been lately supplemented by data interpretation modules in order to refine the computed decisional output.

2 Cadral Architecture

Instead of the whole modeling of legal knowledge, Cadral is based on an explicit drawing of the mental procedures that governs the processing of the applications by

Y. Luo (Ed.): CDVE 2011, LNCS 6874, pp. 82–85, 2011.

interpreting operational data retrieved from the application files and centralized databases of the national administration [3]. When processing a benefit application, Cadral first validates the coherence of the rules applied in the particular case, and then ensures that an identical and consequently equitable answer is given whenever possible. Otherwise, the decision left to the discretionary intervention of a human operator is precisely circumscribed.

Cadral's main reasoning engine is implemented on top of the Soar architecture [4] for forward chaining application of "if... then..." decision rules. This choice is based on efficiency criteria, in order to process in parallel all legal grounds that can be relevant to grant a benefit. Links to a legal database, used in connection with the reasoning trace of the system, allows exhibiting a legal justification of the resulting decisions and therefore provides for possible complaints from the claimant against the administration. All the knowledge is thus organized into 3 kinds of data: procedural data (processing rules), reference data (law), and application data (individual cases). The procedural knowledge manages metadata to retrieve and interpret the two other datasets. In particular, individual parameters relevant to a demand, including the presence of required certificates, are dispatched on several tables, and special care must be taken in order to recombine the information.

The choice of data tables as the primary format to store this heterogeneous information is justified to ease cooperative works for running and updating Cadral. In fact, the legal-based knowledge data is subject to frequent evolution, dismissal, or addition, that must be dealt with by non-computer specialized users. Cadral includes a knowledge editor that offers 2 different views to the procedural knowledge. In the analytical view, the knowledge is modeled on elementary if-then rules, which are directly processed by the Soar a resolution engine [5]. The synthetic view offers a pictorial representation of all the knowledge, and in particular, shows the inter-dependence of the rules and their legal references. The editor allows checking the coherence of the procedural framework, which guarantees the equitability of individual decisions. To comply with the working infrastructure of the administration, Cadral is deployed as an aggregation of web services dedicated to ease collaborative work. The operators access them, according to specific rights depending on their pre-recorded user profiles, to share and manage their tasks, and to edit or update the knowledge base without the help of a computer specialist.

3 Perspectives: A Machine Learning Toolkit

With a view to better adapt the decision results to business requirements, we are now supplementing Cadral with a machine learning module. This module, defined and used as a toolkit, provides several machine learning techniques like clustering engine, classification engine and neural network engine, and uses well-known tools like Weka [6] and Encog [7]. An abstraction layer for machine learning is defined in the toolkit, in order to allow an easy use of the underlying concepts (like learning engine, dataset definition, algorithms for data encoding/decoding). Three different modes for using the toolkit have been implemented: cluster building, relation setting, and decisional intelligence.

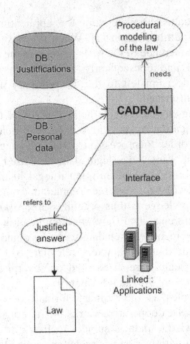

Fig. 1. Cadral Integration

As a method to extract information from bunches of data, clustering aims at discovering similarities to group the data into different sets [8]. It has been successfully applied in decision-support to structure the raw data and optimize the application of solving strategies [9]. In Cadral, clustering is based on similarities drawn from key criteria selected by experts when modeling the rules. It is used for two improvements. First, for adapting the processing workflow to specific profiles requiring special care. In addition to processing application files, Cadral is also used for socio-economic prediction on projected demographic data or administrative and legal framework. The second use of clustering allows interpolating or correcting missing or unreliable data in predictive mode: missing data is a classic issue, and machine learning is able to provide good results when dealing with missing data [10].

A variant of clustering, relation setting in Cadral adapts the processing workflow to input data based on pre-established criteria, calculated by the systems and hand-managed by the users. Relation setting is mainly used to refine the processing of specific input profiles (i.e. descriptive data relevant to benefit request files) requiring special care. For instance, Cadral manages a historisation module recording the previous computed results along with errors relevant to profiles' particulars. This historical information is then available to feed a relation base between profiles and possible processing errors.

Decisional intelligence is used by Cadral used to calculate the operational value of data not directly available (confidential, not recorded…). Manipulating this kind of data is quite different from manipulating missing data, because we never have values for them, so we can't use classical approximation or imputation, and we have to guess their values through mere "discovery" techniques. Among these techniques, neural networks have proven useful to derive an acceptation model from input and outputs datasets [11]. Hence, the machine learning toolkit allows building fictive data structures containing values of all available data, and uses neural networks to learn the particulars of data to discover. A good illustration is the income value when training Cadral for processing benefit applications: income being highly confidential data, we cannot be provided with, though it is taken into account into the acceptation procedures. A solution of the dilemma is to use the Decisional Intelligence mode and build a fictive data structure for the income and related available data. The neural network engine in Cadral draws relations between all these items, and so computes a value for the income from other available data values.

4 Conclusion

The architecture of Cadral, a collaborative knowledge builder and simulator for processing decisional workflow, has been presented. Additional solving techniques are being aggregated to the core reasoning engine. Emulated from historical data processed by Cadral, they provide useful assistance to write and exploit the decisional knowledge from an operational perspective. Owing to the flexibility of its reasoning scheme, of its deployment, and of its usability Cadral can be seen as a first step towards a generic professional reasoning assistant.

References

1. McCorduck, P.: Machines Who Think, 2nd edn. A. K. Peters, Wellesley (2008)
2. Redman, T.: The impact of poor data quality on the typical enterprise. Communications of the ACM (1998)
3. Tamisier, T., Didry, Y., Parisot, O., Feltz, F.: A Collaborative Reasoning Maintenance System for a Reliable Application of Legislations. In: Luo, Y. (ed.) CDVE 2009. LNCS, vol. 5738, pp. 313–316. Springer, Heidelberg (2009)
4. Laird, J., et al.: SOAR: an architecture for general intelligence. Artificial Intelligence 33(1) (1987)
5. Laird, J., et al.: The Soar User's Manual, http://ai.eecs.umich.edu/soar
6. Weka, http://www.cs.waikato.ac.nz/ml/weka
7. Encog, http://www.heatonresearch.com/encog
8. Kumar, V., et al.: Introduction to Data Mining, ch. 8. Addison-Wesley, Reading (2006)
9. Candillier, L.: Contextualisation, Visualisation et Evaluation en Apprentissage non Supervisé. PhD thesis, University of Lille-3, France (2006)
10. Lakshminarayan, K., Harp, S., Goldman, R., Samad, T.: Imputation of missing data using machine learning techniques,
    http://www.aaai.org/Library/KDD/1996/kdd96-023.php
11. Wang, Y., Xing, H.-J.: Knowledge Discovery & Integration Based on a Novel Neural Network Ensemble Model. In: Proc. of Int. Conf. on Semantics, Knowledge & Grid (2006)

Multilayer Automated Methods for the System Integration

Dariusz Choinski and Michal Senik

Silesian University of Technology,
ul. Akademicka 16, 44-100 Gliwice, Poland,
{dariusz.choinski,michal.senik}@polsl.pl

Abstract. Large distributed control systems present non trivial problems during integration. In order to successfully perform integration, MAS methodology has been widely incorporated. Multiple, distributed over the network, types of server objects can be treated as a good example of such dynamic systems. This paper describes multiple user cooperation problems during large system integration. The introduced MAS forms a top level interaction layer over the existing system which is composite of hierarchically organized internal sub layers. Each layer consists of multiple interacting agents which are indivisible functional entities that can form larger cooperating subsystems inside their parent layer. Concurrent user cooperation over the integrated system is performed by means of top level MAS layer which provides indirect access to all system resources possibly by the graphical interface. Concurrent user cooperation is possible through multiple agent interfaces and because agents are created in both Java and .Net no real obstacle currently exists. Possible user conflicts are solved in the real time automatically by the internal MAS system mechanisms because all system agents are independent to some extent.

Keywords: JADE, FIPA, OPC, Java, .Net, Multi-Agent Systems.

1 Introduction

Collaborative control is based on the data obtained during human to machine interaction processes. Concurrent cooperation over many different server entities in the dynamic, nondeterministic world is a non trivial, complex, hard to obtain and time consuming, yet very basic problem. Server object usually presents various kinds of different data to the end user. Those data can be organized into large reconfigurable, hierarchical structures and without prior knowledge about such complex structure it is hard to cooperate with it efficiently. Additionally, it is worth mentioning that the presented structures of data in most cases are dynamic, which means that unexpected reconfigurations are possible. Such nondeterministic behaviors inside the presented environment cause a lot of difficulties during fast data retrieval process because they directly impact quality and accuracy of the obtained results. Complete overcoming of such complex problems becomes a state of the art itself. Agent based system architecture however introduces completely different approach in the field of concurrent cooperation [1], [2], [3].

Y. Luo (Ed.): CDVE 2011, LNCS 6874, pp. 86–93, 2011.

Multi-Agent System (MAS) methodology for over a decade brought much attention as it provides a completely new and different approach of how complex and distributed systems should be structured and behave in order to achieve both peek quality and performance [4], [5]. Such an approach might also facilitate the predictive control and enable the use of the models as in [6]. However, even now it is hard to introduce a fully functional system composed of agent entities only [7]. It is because in the current situation agents are not used to integrate the whole environment from bottom to top rather then they are used to integrate existing systems creating top level coordination layer [7] [8]. This layer has two important tasks i.e.: to provide different parts of the existing system with data and provide cooperation mechanisms and interfaces to the end user. It is worth mentioning that existing systems are usually large, distributed, multi layered and composed of various different elements that have to be integrated and utilized [4]. Those different parts of the system are either software programs or hardware devices such PDAs or computer workstations. Each introduced system element can be frequently accessed by multiple users concurrently which can cause serious integration problems [5]. This also means that agents not only interact with themselves, and thus with the system, but with the end user as well and in order to cooperate with the user, agents must present some interfaces, possibly GUI. In such a case it is essential to understand that agent interfaces mechanisms are dual by their nature [9].

In the agent managed environment, reasoning capabilities are far more sophisticated than in the traditional object oriented solutions because in the agent world reasoning process is strongly supported by means of ontology [1], [2]. Conceptually, ontology itself is a static description of the surrounding, dynamic world. Technically, it is a set of terms, concepts, actions and predicates which can be created in many available environments such as Java, .Net or even in XML which perhaps is a better (the best?) solution. Agent's reasoning capabilities reuse those ontological structures during concurrent cooperation processes over many different system parts which assure high quality and accuracy of the retrieved data. Agent's ontology should be established prior to the MAS layer implementation. It is because ontology is used by agents to collaborate over existing system. Moreover, it is important to understand that agents can utilize more than just one ontological structure, which means that agent environment is by default open for the initially unknown modifications or even other functional elements such as a new agents.

Agent based cooperation over various kinds of system servers has been introduced in [10], [11]. Presented solution introduces a possibility of concurrent cooperation with different OPC (OLE for process control) Data Access Server (OPC DA Servers) entities asynchronously. OPC is an automation protocol which enables the end user to obtain various pieces of information from remote data sources (remote process controllers) [12]. OPC protocol provides an easy, secure and generic way in which each client application can connect with various types of OPC DA Servers which basically are a third party pieces of software that provide OPC protocol specific data from various types of controllers. Moreover, OPC DA Server can be accessed by a various number of OPC Client applications at the same moment, providing them with the needed information.

The presented concept is an evaluation of the work introduced in [10], [11] which describe fast and reliable cooperation with many different server entities distributed in the single network simultaneously. Robust agent cooperation is achieved by means of layered agent architecture. Agent's reasoning model is based on the subscription and notification mechanisms as well as on knowledge which is gathered from other agents which are located in different layers. That way only fresh and newest data is exchanged between separate layers which not only minimizes network workload but also improves agent performance.

In the following sections we describe distributed server system along with its requirements, structure, configuration and complexity (System architecture and configuration) (Fig. 1.). Next we present possibility of using MAS methodology to overcome system integration issues along with user participation and cooperation during system configuration (System integration). Moreover, we introduce MAS system structure as well as three main layers which generally characterize MAS system. In the last section (MAS multilayered automated integration scenario) we present different available MAS elements (agent types) which directly correspond to the particular cooperation layers. We present also how those different elements can be reused by the multiple users during concurrent system interaction.

2 System Architecture and Configuration

The introduced system consists of various OPC Data Access Server services distributed over the network and because of that it is completely decentralized. Those servers are located on various different workstations which can be considered as network nodes. A single network node can host a varying number of OPC DA Server entities. The number of both network nodes and OPC DA Servers is by default dynamic, which means that it can change during system lifetime unexpectedly. No prior restrictions as to the number of the OPC DA Servers as well as to the network nodes exist. The system itself presents unpredictable conditions for the integration problems.

OPC DA Server utilizes OPC Data Access interface and provides fast access to a various real time data points simultaneously. Physically, data points are located on various different PLC devices. Single OPC DA Server can provide access to all data points located on different PLC devices concurrently. OPC DA Server logically contains all real time data points inside hierarchical, tree like structures. Those structures are located in OPC DA Server namespace and usually are large and reconfigurable.

The user concurrent interaction depends on OPC DA Server configuration. The user, in order to obtain all needed data has to configure OPC DA Server which can be divided into two subtasks. The first task handles hierarchical namespace and data point configuration. It is always global, which means that the same configuration is visible for all connected client applications. This step is always performed by the user directly on the OPC DA Server. The second task handles OPC Groups and OPC Items creation and configuration and it is always performed by the user on the client side application which means that it is specific for the particular client application only. Separate instances of the client configurations can exist in the OPC DA Server configurable namespace. It is worth mentioning that a single OPC DA Server can be accessed and configured by many different client applications simultaneously. OPC

Groups are client application specific logical containers for the OPC Items which are client side application aliases for the physical, real time data points which on the other hand are located inside OPC DA Server namespace. In the real world OPC DA Server hierarchical namespace is rarely reconfigured whilst client side usually is reconfigured more often. It is a normal situation that two or more different client applications request the same set of data points simultaneously which introduces multiple concurrent interaction conflicts, not only for client side applications but for the integrated system itself.

Described configuration steps must be performed carefully and can not be omitted. To perform such configuration, prior deep domain knowledge about the system is required which sometimes can be very problematic even for the experienced personnel staff. This is the point in which MAS takes care of things that has been previously performed by the user, thus relieving him considerably from the complex, hard and time consuming analysis of the system.

3 System Integration

Dynamic conditions of the presented distributed system are challenging issues during integration. To handle them properly, MAS methodology has been successfully used. The presented system integration is based on a real time processing, hierarchical MAS capable of dynamical adjustment to existing conditions. It proves to be highly productive as it relives the user from both hard analysis and decision making processes. It is a less error prone, redundant, robust, durable and agile concept which is focused around ontology. It is important to mention that the environment from the MAS perspective over which MAS operates is defined by integrated system along with all its conditions, requirements and behaviors. In such a case, integrated system defines also a lower level interaction layer for the MAS layer purposes.

The presented MAS layer (AFIOPC - Agents for Integration of OPC) establishes efficient cooperation with OPC Servers through Java Native Interface (JNI) which bridges Java mechanisms into the native language world such as C/C++ or Delphi or through OPC Foundation .Net automation wrapper library. Both solutions present the same functionalities, however each one is different in the approach as the first solution is strictly Java based whilst the second one is based on Microsoft .Net framework. AFIOPC, along with its agents, represent dual characteristic as they can utilize Java or .Net technologies. Therefore, there are no physical limitations for the different AFIOPC agents to cooperate. Additionally, there are many possibilities to reuse those Java/.Net interfaces to cooperate with the multiple pieces of the integrated system and with the user side simultaneously.

The introduced MAS (Fig. 1.) in the current development stage consists of nine different types of agents: Management Agent (MA), Network Scanner Agent (NSA), Port Scanner Agent (PSA), Discovery Agent (DA), OPC Agent (OA), Lifecycle Supervisory Agent (LSA), Supervisory Agent (SA), Node Agent (NA) and DataBase Agent (DBA). It wraps over existing Java Agent Development framework (JADE) [2] using a set of newly implemented agents thus creating a complex, top level system. It can function on one or more remotely controlled hosts, which may vary in time. This also means that it can adapt to almost any existing situation. Presented agents have been specifically designed and implemented to automatically fulfill complex tasks on behalf of the user in the background. Moreover, because of the fact that we are dealing with distributed and dynamic environment, MAS itself follow the same characteristic pattern. It means that certain level of undependability from the user is required. That way the user can concentrate and focus on its own specific goals rather then executing each task manually and possibly solving multiple randomly encountered environmental problems. It is because all those problems are already automatically handled by the MAS layer internal mechanisms. Summary results of the MAS layer background activities are presented to the user affecting his decisions, thus adjusting the system itself. In the current development stage, MAS automatically handles processes of network resource locations discovery, OPC DA Server discovery, namespace browse, data points properties and server status, database interaction and OPC DA Server data analysis. All mentioned processes are executed concurrently in real time, immediately returning partial results. That way, the user does not have to wait until process execution finishes. Moreover, automatic processes execution can be reinforced by the user itself to speed up the work.

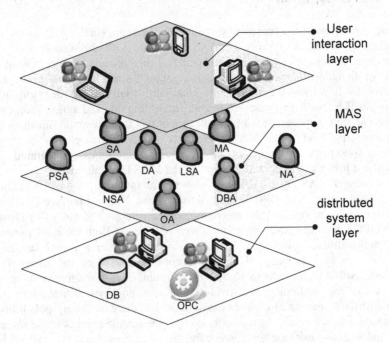

Fig. 1. Multilayered distributed system architecture

The presented MAS (Fig. 2) demonstrates multilayered structure. Each layer performs specifically designed tasks based on the lower level layer data for the purposes of the higher level layer. Starting from the top of the existing integrated system level, we can recognize three main interaction layers i.e.: direct cooperation layer, agent internal cooperation layer and user cooperation layer.

Direct cooperation layer is responsible for the low level system interaction. Its main task is fast data access and system elements state analysis. Each agent in this layer is tightly connected with the data resource. Because of that, such agent must own explicit knowledge of this particular system part over which it operates, so that it can withstand any problematic situation that may occur. Structure of this layer fits to the assumed system granulation model. Established granulation model shows how agents correspond to the system resources [4]. Agent internal cooperation layer is responsible for fast data analysis and independent agent cooperation processes which are results of both user and system cooperation activities. User cooperation layer is a top level layer which is responsible for fast, simultaneous user to system interaction and data analysis presentation and modification. User cooperation layer is dependant from the user's input as opposed to internal and direct cooperation layers. This is because both layers acts based on user input and on the system level layer behaviors. Each presented layer internally subdivides horizontally and vertically into smaller layers. Those sublayers cooperate with each other on a behalf of their parent layer.

4 MAS Multilayered Automated Integration Scenario

The proposed MAS consists of several different types of agents which form three main layers i.e.: direct cooperation layer, agent internal cooperation layer and user cooperation layer. Moreover, each presented agent can interact directly with agents located in the completely separated layer (Fig. 2.). Top level user cooperation layer is formed by the MA and SA. OA, DBA, NSA, PSA and NA correspond to direct cooperation layer. DA and LSA forms agent internal cooperation layer.

The most important agents from the user's perspective are MA and SA. By means of those two agents, the user has direct and indirect access to all lower level agent entities. MA and SA are the first type of agents that are created in the system. There can be many different MA and SA located in the single MAS. Each one can be accessed by many users simultaneously. The user, by means of SA mechanisms, is able to directly cooperate with each available MAS agent, whenever it is required. In that case, interaction with all those agents is restricted only to MAS system management activities such as agent kill or agent recreation. By means of single MA, the user can discover various different OPC DA Servers as well as configure, visualize and gather data from them. There can be many different MA created in the MAS that can be accessed simultaneously by other users. Each discovered OPC DA Server is accessed in the background by means of OA which is by default created by the DA. Single OA at the given time can maintain access only to a single OPC DA Server though it detects other servers as well. Both DA and OA agents are not accessible for the user directly. DA is the agent which is deployed directly to the newly discovered network node. Its task is to find all available OPC DA Servers that may reside on a single host and to deploy OA to each one. Every DA is created by the SA based on the data obtained from the NSA and PSA or NA. NSA is initialized by the SA and it is not accessible for the user. Its task is to discover available network host from the predefined IP addresses pool. Multiple instances of the PSA are created by the NSA to scan available host ports. NA is created by the user on the single network node. This agent requires MAS system to be already running because it tries to register its host in the MAS in order to be accessed by the DA for further processing. In the current development stage, the user, by means of MA, retrieves various OPC DA Server specific data from the multiple OA instances directly. This approach actually is slightly problematic because it can cause considerable delay in the system. It is because of the large server data structures that are sent through the network simultaneously. To overcome this problem DBA has been introduced. Each one OA will have access to its own DBA which will directly operate with the database server so the user will not only have access to the current real time data but to the historic data as well.

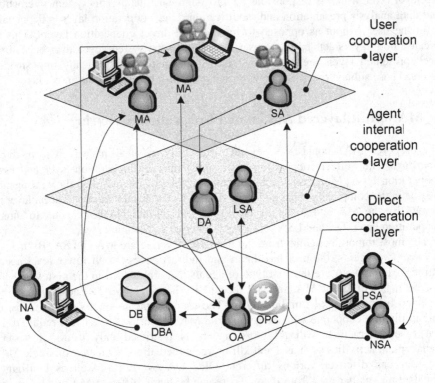

Fig. 2. MAS layer - multilayered system integration

5 Conclusions

User concurrent cooperation during large distributed system integration can be strongly reinforced by means of the MAS methodology. Large distributed systems generally present various complex difficulties during real time multiple user interaction. The presented dynamic distributed server system is composed of a various different OPC DA Servers. Each single OPC DA exposes large and dynamic, configurable and hierarchical structure. This structure can be accessed by many different end users and because of that it is almost impossible to ensure a conflicts free performance. Therefore, additional automated mechanisms for the user cooperation are required. MAS methodology however exposes the exact set of possibilities that can be utilized during multiple user concurrent cooperation. The presented MAS system enables different users to access and cooperate over the integrated system. It also relieves the user from the hard, complex and time consuming system data analysis which is a great advantage. MAS tasks automation is based on the ontology concept and is one of the key benefits of the whole methodology. Multilayered structure strongly supports MAS multiple tasks automation which can run on a behalf of the user in the background concurrently. MAS methodology basically demonstrates certain level of undependability which is a great advantage. Each presented layer subdivides internally into smaller functional subsystems which are composed of various different cooperating agents. Multiple user concurrent cooperation is strongly supported by the different agent interfaces. The presented MAS system is composed of agents that are written in both Java and .Net technologies. No visible restrictions to that exist.

Acknowledgments. This work was partially supported by the Polish Ministry of Scientific Research and Higher Education N N514 471539 and Silesian University of Technology BW/RGH-2/Rau0/2010.

References

1. Wooldridge, M.: An Introduction to Multiagent Systems. John Wiley & Sons Ltd., Chichester (2002)
2. Bellifemine, F., Caire, G., Greenwood, D.: Developing multi-agent systems with JADE. John Wiley & Sons, Chichester (2007)
3. Duffy, V.G., Salvendy, G.: Concurrent engineering and virtual reality for human resource planning. Computers in Industry 42, 9–125 (2000)
4. Buse, D.P., Wu, Q.H.: IP Network-based Multi-agent Systems for Industrial Automation. Springer, Heidelberg (2007)
5. Weyns, D.: Architecture-Based Design of Multi-Agent Systems. Springer, Heidelberg (2010)
6. Nocoń, W., Metzger, M.: Predictive Control of Decantation in Batch Sedimentation Process. AICHE Journal 56, 3279–3283 (2010)
7. Paolucci, M., Sacile, R.: Agent-Based Manufacturing and Control Systems. CRC Press, LLC (2005)
8. Botti, V., Giret, A.: ANEMONA – A Multi-Agent Methodology for Holonic Manufacturing Systems. Springer, Heidelberg (2008)
9. Leduc, R.J., Dai, P., Song, R.: Synthesis Method for Hierarchical Interface-Based Supervisory Control. IEEE Trans. on Automatic Control 54, 1548–1560 (2009)
10. Choinski, D., Senik, M.: Collaborative control of hierarchical system based on JADE. In: Luo, Y. (ed.) CDVE 2010. LNCS, vol. 6240, pp. 262–269. Springer, Heidelberg (2010)
11. Choinski, D., Senik, M.: Multi-Agent oriented integration in Distributed Control System. In: O'Shea, J., Nguyen, N.T., Crockett, K., Howlett, R.J., Jain, L.C. (eds.) KES-AMSTA 2011. LNCS (LNAI), vol. 6682, pp. 231–240. Springer, Heidelberg (2011)
12. Iwanitz, F., Lange, J.: OPC – Fundamentals, Implementation and Application. Huthig Verlag, Heidelberg (2006)

Active Citizenship in the Planning Process: Information Management vs. Creative Participation

Ursula Kirschner

Leuphana University Lüneburg, Faculty Culture Sciences,
Institute for City and Culture Environment Research,
Scharnhorststr. 1, 21335 Lüneburg, Germany
kirschner@uni.leuphana.de

Abstract. The significance of early and continuous involvement of the citizens in city development processes is clearly evident in the current critical reporting on Stuttgart 21 in Germany, a traffic and urban development project to relocate the Stuttgart railway junction. Stuttgart 21, a planning process for a new major train station that has gone on for over ten years, has been accompanied by a citizen protest movement across all party lines since 2009. Construction has been halted several times.

When citizens are consulted too late, not at all or only intermittently during the development process, the results are often the most varied protests and demonstrations.

This research project analyzes methods of citizen involvement in construction planning processes in Hamburg and attempts to identify new approaches to qualitative social research as expert research actions in function of deep drilling. The aim is the development and testing of a new methodology for active citizenship in terms of an expert research like deep drilling instead of working under the involvement of the majority.

Keywords: social networking, active citizenship, creative participation.

1 Introduction

Migration statistics assume that, by the year 2020 Hamburg's population will grow to over 1.8 million inhabitants. This translates to a demand for 5000 to 6000 more residences per year. To meet these new developments and demands of the residential, professional and leisure sectors, the district of Altona has designed a future plan intended to begin weighing the various development options.[1] The aim of the future plan for Altona is to provide all of the citizens and participants with a platform to inform about future developments. The intention is to ensure widespread participation of the citizens without citing specific goals.

An example: In 2009 there were demonstrations and public petitions protesting plans to build an Ikea home furnishing store. It would have meant tearing down an existing shopping center and redesigning the infrastructure. The Hamburg neighborhood Schanzenviertel in the district of Altona is considered a good example for the restructuring of a formerly alternative style to a classy "in" quarter, with fancy

Y. Luo (Ed.): CDVE 2011, LNCS 6874, pp. 94–101, 2011.

boutiques, stylish cafes and rapidly rising rents. The fear of gentrification, of excessive rent and "sterile" neighborhoods is growing, leading the citizens to step up and take notice as soon as urban planning projects are initiated. The street battles that have occurred regularly for many years in this area are one of the ways that the citizens express their discontent regarding developments that are happening without their consent and input.

2   Active Citizenship in the Context of Building Culture

Active citizenship in the context of the building culture is characterized by three traits: It is fragile in the sense that disappointments can quickly extinguish its emergence and drive. It also tends towards topical singularity. Unlike government bodies that at least strive to operate complexly, citizen involvement concentrates primarily on a certain issue – also referred to as "one issue movement" (e.g. relocation of bus stops). This behavior is commonly referred to as NIMBY – not in my backyard. [2] To overcome this attitude, in Holland projects have been initiated that emphasize WIMBY – welcome into my backyard. Citizens are encouraged to "open up" their yards to others, thus promoting social interaction.

2.1   Gentrification as a Motive for Citizen Protests at the Digital and Artistic Level

Continuously updated internet sites allow interested citizens to find out about urban planning developments, to get organized and to react spontaneously. A small selection of such forums that have cropped up in the last three years in Hamburg:

- Critical discussion regarding the IBA (international construction exhibition 2013) and other restructuring in Wilhelmsburg (isolated district of Hamburg, part of Hamburg Mitte (downtown): http://aku-wilhelmsburg.blog.de/
- To whom does the city belong? Discussions about the "right to city" issue and critical examination of restructuring and major projects such as the Empire Riverside in St. Pauli: http://www.rechtaufstadt.net/
- Action network against gentrification: http://www.esregnetkaviar.de/
- Interest group No-BNQ (no Bernhard Nocht quarter) directly adjacent to the Empire Riverside; fighting against the planned "renovation/improvement/modernization" of Bernhard-Nocht-Straße: http://www.no-bnq.org/

An alternative to verbal protests is the approach taken by artists: With temporary installations around the city, they attempt to effectively convey the feelings and ideas of the residents. One example is the *Park Fiction,* with its unusual origin: In the mid 1990's, a group of residents and artists from St. Pauli (adjacent district with red light scene) decided to design a public park – not in some dormant location, but in a very specific place for which the city had just approved a new zoning plan: the bank of the Elbe river. No one knowledgeable of the situation at the time would have thought it possible to prevent the sale of the property and construction of concrete behemoth costing millions.

In January, a cast member from the *Schauspielhaus* theater in Hamburg and activists belonging to the group *Lux and friends* shrouded the abandoned *Electrolux* building and then unfurled a gigantic safety vest.

Fig. 1. Lux_KirLoyal 001[3] „Lux and friends meets *Deutsches Schauspielhaus Hamburg*. An empty Building and a theatre in need. Both same results of failed politics in the City of Hamburg. Linking the protest up! While artists, players and friends take over the stage for a night of protest and fun, a live report of a symbolic squatting is transmitted on to stage."[4]

3 Current Parallel Planning Processes in the District of Hamburg Altona

In this context, this paper was examined the methods and media that can be applied to the communication between citizens, planners, administrators and investors to promote activation of the creative process. We will attempt to understand those people whose material, social and historic living conditions are affected by the plan, by applying the concept of democracy, internet-based communication, protest movements and participation in an ongoing process. The ultimate goal is to develop a new perspective on life in the city, which these people produce and reproduce through their daily actions.

In addition to two other major construction projects in *Hamburg – Hafencity* (harbor area)[1] and the *IBA Wilhelmsburg* (international building exhibition site 2013) – a third, very extensive construction project has been launched: *Mitte Altona*, development of the district center. By relocating the current Altona train station to the

---

[1] The European greatest building site at the moment.

Diebsteich station about 2 km north, a 75 ha area will be free for residential and commercial construction. The central Hamburg government agency for city development and environmental protection is responsible for planning and it takes place without the participation of citizens and without the assistance of the local district office Altona.

Parallel to the planning process, the district office of Altona, with input from citizens, is attempting to develop the surrounding areas to meet future needs. The goal is a future plan, "More Altona," for the next 10 – 20 years. The intention is to update the plan over the years and adapt it to evolving conditions. The future plan Altona is to be considered an open planning instrument, in regard to the methods as well as to the contents."[5] This method reveals city planning deficits and incorporates planning recommendations with citizen involvement. Because both planning procedures are occurring parallel and the citizens do not see an opportunity for their input in planning the area around the old station, there is resentment within the planning procedure "More Altona."

In addition to the citizen involvement procedure initiated by the city council with support from external moderator groups, we developed a qualitative procedure in the sense of citizen involvement as expert involvement.

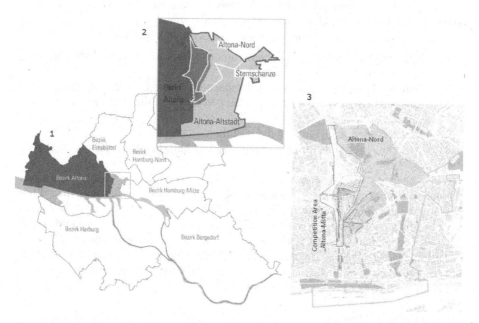

Fig. 2. *1)* Map of Hamburg; *2)* Plan Detail: Hamburg Altona with the districts of Altona North, Altona Altstadt and Sternschanze. The highlighted area marks the relocation of the station and the building site thus freed for "Altona center "; *3)* Altona map with the design for the first part of "Altona Mitte", 2010, André Poitier[6]; Altona Nord District, outline describes the area for the future plan "More Altona"[7]

3.1 Research Method for Qualitative Active Citizenship

The methodology of this research project is developed for the Civil-society involvement in the area of tension between the building culture and the gentrification debate.

The semi-structured or guided expert interview with subsequent experiments in the sense of action research[8] was chosen as the method for the survey. Seven citizens of the district were selected as experts. The selection is generated randomly, but with the aim that it reflect almost the cross section of the citizens of the district. The perceptive experiences of each individual are an essential component in being able to judge city quality and to establish paradigms for future plans designed for the long term. It appears that a qualitative procedure is most suitable for taking the ideas derived from their knowledge of local conditions and including it in the current planning process. Quantitative methods enable only the examination of previously presented hypotheses derived from theoretical models.

This work focuses on a culture-related, aesthetic consideration of the city. It concentrates on the everyday building culture, as this is a relevant factor for the quality of life of a normal citizen. Altona Nord, a section of Altona, is a good study subject, because it is so "ordinary" and it has not found much consideration within the current, parallel planning processes. Also, this is the area where there is the most potential to influence the plans for the future.

Following steps have been done during the expert research actions day:

1. Semi-structured interviews, focused on the quality of their own building, of the street and the district area.
2. Walking through the city - photo documentary for visual citizen portrait combined with experiments about the perception of the city and the everyday ways
3. Analysis of the geographical dates of the "Atlas Altona"
4. Designing proposals for uses of the new building site of the railway area.

Surveying experts – in this case, the citizens of Altona Nord – generates information that enriches work with the experiences gained from everyday occurrences and offers revelations regarding relevant criteria for the future plan. The results of the survey are a verified part of facts generated in the Altona Atlas. This is a method that is "intermeshed" in two directions, with an analytical and a creative thought part.

The knowledge gained from meeting with the "experts" is compiled to create citizen portraits and is intended to offer planners and government agencies impulses that confirm, revise or pose new questions. [9]

3.2 Summary of Results

Seven citizens of Altona Nord were questioned. They were: two small families with preschoolers, high school student with migration background, two university students, retired couple and single freelancer with physical handicaps. Our students generally spent 5 – 6 hours with their test subjects in Altona Nord, either all in one day or split between two days. Only the retired couple and the high school student considered Altona Nord to be the long-term center of their lives. The retirees are both from

Hamburg and have lived in Altona for many years. They chose Altona Nord as the place to grow old. The high school student strongly identifies with the district. She wants the current atmosphere to be maintained, and any changes should be implemented to stabilize the existing structure. She considers it important to avoid a gentrification process. She would like to see a city with a wide range of social services, offering shelter to the socially disadvantaged.

The parents with preschoolers, on the other hand, would like to move away from Altona Nord; they feel that their children cannot grow up to be healthy there. They cite reasons such as excessive pollution, traffic noise, danger posed by heavy traffic and neglected parks and playgrounds. All of the parents have lived in the district since they were at university. At the time, they considered the area attractive because of the public transportation and low rent. The popular *"Schanze"* area, as well as nature and recreation along the Elbe river, can be reached on foot and characterize the inner-city location enjoyed by students. Many of their university friends have moved away, so their friends are no longer close by. They have also noticed that the nearby infrastructure has deteriorated over the years. The area has lost dramatically in attractiveness for them. The 40-year old freelancer expressed similar sentiments. He considered the quality of life poor, even without a child. He misses all types of gathering places. He thinks that an urban neighborhood should be characterized by landscaped squares, parks, restaurants, cultural offerings and athletic facilities.

The two university students confirmed the current attractiveness of the district for them. However, the male student moved to Hamburg from a small town two years ago and misses well maintained athletic fields, and he perceives some areas, particularly in the northern part of Altona Nord, as dangerous. Although all of those surveyed said that they feel safe in the district, they were all able to name areas that they avoid after the dark and where they would take a longer route for safety reasons.

In regard to traffic, everyone expressed a wish for traffic reduction - however they all stated different through streets. Because of its three major four-lane road axes, the district has excessive traffic for a residential area. This is the reason that the female student emphasized that, in the event that the train station is moved, development should progress from the north or east to avoid even more traffic. All of those surveyed would like to see more parks and suggested different park concepts for the northern train station tract. Keywords that were used to describe the future visions for the district included:

Colorful Altona
Family-friendly ecological city
Parent-child neighborhood
Altona – a social city for everyone
Sports town Altona Nord
Multicultural neighborhood with nightlife and daylife.

4 Conclusion

From our perspective and considering feedback from the district office, the seven citizens of Altona Nord were able to provide representative statements on the quality of residence and life in the district. Two of them had heard about the plans for new construction and had participated to some extent in citizen involvement forums. The others were completely surprised to have heard nothing about the process, despite the many announcements. All of the participants welcomed the efforts of the students and were satisfied with the results.

To achieve a greater degree of agreement between government agencies and citizens, it is essential that citizens be included in the process early on. Looked at this way, it would be desirable that the suggestions of the citizens surveyed, which are in general agreement on the essential points, be taken into consideration for the ongoing plan for the northern section of Altona Mitte being redesigned.

The "city" intends to embrace this positive citizen involvement and is cooperating with other public agencies with its internet platform "nexthamburg."[10] The foundation of *nexthamburg* is the new understanding of urban planning: The agenda is no longer conceived in the background, it is devised together with the citizens of the city. The role model for this type of joint action: the open source movement, which the software industry has already revolutionized.

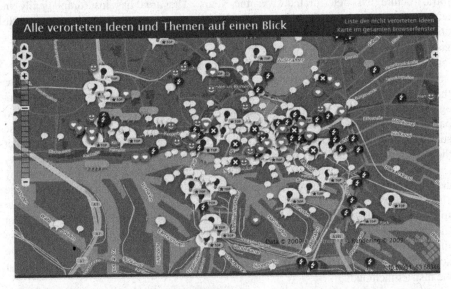

Fig. 3. Navigation Map from *nexthamburg* with ideas and further information about Hamburg. The input is done by the citizens of Hamburg.[11]

Digital communication should be viewed as an aid. It requires regular feedback . and has to be transported from the virtual realm back to the city. The city space of a civil society should offer temporary space for politically motivated cultural events, to be able to test ideas and discuss them in reality. Campaigns such as that of "Lux and Friends" are valuable contributions to the city and support peaceful disagreement and urban development.

Acknowledgements. The research described in this paper refers to the seminar I ran within the Department of cultural studies of the Leuphana University Lüneburg,

Germany. I greatly appreciate the enthusiasm of the students and of the photographer Dagmar Sommerfeld of the Leuphana University of Lüneburg, who participated in this course. I would like to extend our gratitude to the district office of Hamburg Altona for the support and cooperation. In this context I would like to extend my gratitude the responsible in town planning in the department of the district office Altona Mrs. Martina Nitzl and the seven citizens of Altona Nord, Hamburg.

References

1. Atlas Altona, Freie und Hansestadt Hamburg, Bezirksamt Altona, p. 9 (2010)
2. Enquete-Kommsission des Deutschen Bundestages "Zukunft des Bürgerschaftlichen Engagements" (Hrsg.): Bürgerschaftliches Engagement: auf dem Weg in eine zukunftsfähige Bürgergesellschaft (14/8900), p. 163 (2002), http://dipbt.bundestag.de/doc/btd/14/089/1408900.pdf (access on March 21, 2011)
3. Fig. 1: Lux_KirLoyal 001, Published with permission from the photographer G.W.; photographed at March 22 (2011)
4. G.W., http://www.flickr.com/photos/rasande/5380345799/in/photostream/ (access on March 27, 2011)
5. Atlas Altona, Freie und Hansestadt Hamburg, Bezirksamt Altona, p.12 (2010)
6. http://www.competitionline.de/beitraege/40371 (access on March 7, 2011)
7. Fig. 2. Illustration on my own
8. Freire, P.: Creating alternative research methods: Learning to do it by doing it. In: Hall, B., Gillette, A., Tandon, R. (eds.) Creating knowledge: A monopoly?, pp. 29–37. Society for Participatory Research in Asia, New Delhi (1982)
9. Refer to Bungard, W., Holling, H., Schultz-Gambard, J.: Methoden der Arbeits- und Organisationspsychologie, Weinheim, p. 78 (1996)
10. http://nexthamburg.de/navigator.php (access on March 24, 2011)
11. Fig. 3, Screen capture from http://nexthamburg.de/navigator.php (access on March 24, 2011)

A "Live" Interactive Tagging Interface for Collaborative Learning

Yang Ting Shen, Tay-Sheng Jeng, and Yen-Chia Hsu

IA lab, dept. of Architecture,
National Cheng Kung University, Taiwan
{N78941044,tsjeng,N76994017}@mail.ncku.edu.tw

Abstract. We present a real-time interactive tagging system called SynTag for collaborative learning in lectures. The system allows students accessing the web-based interface to tag an ongoing lecture. The collective tagging outcomes are instantly visualized with a dynamic timeline chart to illustrate the assessment of all students. With SynTag, students not only engage in a lecture by the interactive tagging function, but also cooperate with each other to contextualize the lecture. According to the outcomes of students' collaborative tagging activities, the critical spatio-temporal segments of a lecture video are automatically generated as the wave-shape timeline chart. Through the peaks of the wave-shape timeline chart, the valuable video chips of the lecture can be easily highlighted and recognized. In the end of this paper, we demonstrate how the SynTag system contributes to the collaborative learning in undergraduate classes through quantitative and qualitative studies. Finally, we conclude with a discussion based on our evaluation for the improvements and potentials of our system in future works.

Keywords: Collaborative learning, Collaborative tagging, synchronous, Timeline, Interface design, Interactive tagging system, Education, Lecture.

1 Introduction

There is growing evidence that collaborative learning procedures are more effective than traditional instructional methods in promoting student learning and academic achievement [1]. The collaborative learning, especially in terms of CSCL (Computer-Supported Collaborative Learning), is built in web-based and synchronous environments. The typical web-based learning system, GSS (Group Support Systems) or GDSS (Group Discussion Support Systems)[2, 3], which is designed for computer-mediated collaboration. The use of synchronous GSS within an actual educational environment has enabled more effective learning practices and improved group performance [2]. Furthermore, the collaborative learning conceptualizes collaboration as a process of shared meaning construction [5]. As Hodgson and McConnell pointed out, co-operative learning makes public our own learning, learning of others and learning of the group [6]. Instead of the limited one-way track from the teacher, the collaborative learning process has multiple tracks, which enables learning resources not only from the teacher but also from all participants.

Y. Luo (Ed.): CDVE 2011, LNCS 6874, pp. 102–109, 2011.

However, the collaborative learning is criticised by the lack of interpretations from participants' raw data. Some researches suggest that adding metadata (data about data) on raw data to facilitate some organization and access of information [13, 14, 15]. Generally, metadata are represents with the simple, short, and universal keyword style such as tags. Tagging represents an action of reflection, where the tagger sums up a series of words into summary tags. The tag stands on its own to describe consistent and collective aspect based on the tagger's experiences [13].

Collaborative tagging describes the process by which many users add metadata in the form of keywords to shared content [8]. A fine-grained tagged approach can be applicable to a broad set of content objects and has the advantages of providing search capability and quick access to material of interest within the body of the content [7]. In short conclusion, the collaborative learning integrating with tagging function could supports meaningful and interpretable learning materials.

This paper proposes an innovative system called SynTag for collaborative learning in a class lecture or presentation via the interactive tagging interface. There are two hypotheses of our research. First of all, the interactive tagging functions during the learning process increases students' learning will. Secondary, the real-time visualized feedbacks collected from all students enhances the cooperation between students. In this paper, we introduce the design of the SynTag system and its web-based interface. We report field experiment outcomes to examine the usability of the system interface. In addition, the effects in terms of collaborative learning through the assistance of the SynTag system are also demonstrated by qualitative interviews. Finally, we conclude with a discussion based on our evaluation for the improvements and potentials of our system in future works.

2 Related Work

Collaboration in educational settings supported by computer-mediated tools or ICT (Information Communication Technologies) facilitates data sharing based on the Internet environments. In the last decade, many researches and prototypes in terms of CSCL has been developed and applied in the learning context. The Classroom 2000 project at Georgia Tech [16, 17] integrates multiple media with web-based interface for the collaborative classroom environment. During the class, students could access the web-based interface to review the real-time collaborative notes. The Livenotes project [18] presents a system for cooperative and augmented note-taking in lectures. The Livenotes interface enables students to interact with one another by taking lecture notes cooperatively, as well as to augment student note-taking by providing instructor slides in the background to annotate over. Those two cases demonstrate an idea that collaborative learning can be benefited from the web-based platform due to the convenience of data exchange. However, we also can discover some cognitive problems and difficulties caused from un-contextualized data during the data sharing process, especially individual notes sharing. The cognitive gaps between different students' note-taking are apparent, even they are annotating the same lecture slide. It results that the collaborative learning may increase the redundancy rather than create learning efficiency.

Regarding to this issue in collaborative learnign, some researches propose a convicible solution by collaborative tagging. The OATS (Spen Annotation and Tagging System) [13, 19] project integrates content-tagging with note-taking to motivate students tagging learning contents. OATS' approach is to applying collaborative tagging in e-learning systems to supplement learner-centric metadata gathering. The research conducting by IBM T. J. Watson Research develops a system called InSight [7] for clooaborative editing with micro-tags. In "micro-tagging", users attach a tag to a subset of large media, such as a segment in a video. According to InSight system, the complicated video can be segmented into several significant fragments which are sorted by collaborative tagging.

Our work subscribes the notion of collaborative learning to support a platform for information sharing between students during a classs lecture. Relevant technologies and resources such as ICT, video/audio recording and broadcasting, and multiple media are integrated into the SynTag system and visualized with a web-based interface. In addition, the colleated information can be classified by students' collaborative tagging to enhance the effieiency of collaborative learning.

3   Synchronous Tagging Interface for Collaborative Learning

The collaboration between students can efficiently enhance the learning process due to the collective knowledge. In this paper, we propose a novel way to collect students' comments for the collaborative learning purpose. We develop the interactive system which is aimed to support the "live" collaborative tagging in one-to-many learning events such as lectures or presentations. The SynTag system allows students accessing the web-based interface to tag an ongoing lecture and share the outcomes. The collective tagging outcomes are instantly visualized with a dynamic timeline chart in real time to illustrate the result of collaboration between students. The SynTag system is implemented in the university classroom in 2010 fall and practically functions in some academic courses for usability experiments (Fig 1).

Fig. 1. Students listen a lecture and tag it via SynTag

The SynTag system is consisted of two parts: the streaming facility and the web-based interface. The streaming facility contains a camera and a streaming server to record a real-time lecture video and broadcast it to the website immediately. The end users access the web-based interface via Internet to watch the real-time video (Fig 2 left). Furthermore, the most important contribution of SynTag is the "live" collaborative tagging. The web-based interface proposes a instant tagging function that students can tag their feedbacks within the accurate time point of the video by clicking buttons. Due to the limited tagging time during an ongoing lecture, we argue the efficiency of textual tag input by users. In addition, the proliferation of incorrect or incomplete tags is often found in social networking systems [8]. Therefore, on the contracts, the SynTag system simply defines three kinds of tagging buttons instead of textual tag input: the positive tagging button "GOOD", the neutral tagging button "QUESTION", and the negative tagging button "DISAGREE" (Fig 2 right). The tag-generated method by toggling buttons allows students to pay their attentions on lecture itself rather than the labor of tag-making. Students can comment special temporal intervals within a video by quickly clicking the intended button. The collected tagging results marked in corresponding time point will instantly update to the system server and broadcast to all students who access the web-based interface. The collected tagging results broadcasted to all students are visualized as a dynamic timeline chart (Fig 3). With the visualized tagging results in the timeline chart, students can therefore take part in other participants' learning process during the lecture.

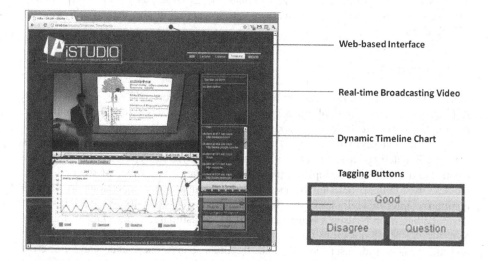

Fig. 2. Left: The web-based interface displays instant video and visualizes tagging results with dynamic timeline chart. Right: Three kinds of tagging buttons (Positive tag: GOOD, Neutral tag: QUESTION, Negative tag: DISAGREE).

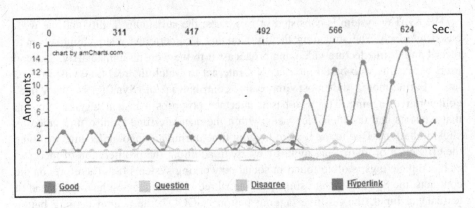

Fig. 3. The timeline chart visualizes the collected tagging results synchronously

The wave-shape timeline chart supports an innovative collaborative learning method during the class lecture. The spatio-temporal segments of a video are generated automatically from students' collaborative tagging activities. The points on the peaks and troughs represent the tagging amounts in the video. The valuable video chips of the lecture can be easily highlighted and recognized. In addition, for the purpose of video retrieving, students can quickly filter the lower troughs and pick up the higher peaks to replay the spatio-temporal segments. Therefore, the wave-shape timeline chart along with the synchronous video augments the value of raw video by visualizing collective tagging outcomes in real time. Furthermore, from the e-learning perspective, the SynTag system also extend the possibilities of the collaborative learning to not only the synchronous or on-site learning, but also the asynchronous or off-site learning.

4   Evaluation

SynTag located at iStudio Classroom, Dept. of Architecture, NCKU, Taiwan started running in the beginning of spring semester, 2011 and continued functioning for practical academic courses. We cooperated with class teachers to conduct several experimental classes with the SynTag system involved. 24 undergraduate students were participated and asked to access the web-based SynTag system via their personal electronic devices such as laptops, tablet PC, or smart phones etc. At the end of the classes, we collect the feedbacks through a quantitative questionnaire and a qualitative interview. In terms of the quantitative questionnaire, its contents were designed based on Nislsen's heuristics [9,10,11] to estimate the interface usability of SynTag. We asked questions about visibility of system status, match between system and the real world, user control and freedom, consistency and standard, error prevention, recognition rather than recall, flexibility and efficiency, aesthetic and minimalist design, help users recognize, diagnose and recover from errors, and help and documentation. Totally there were 34 questions associated with interface usability and each question was rated on 5 scales: 1 (strongly disagree); 2 (disagree); 3 (neutral); 4 (agree); and 5 (strongly agree). We analyzed the quantitative data and illustrated the result with the proportion chart (Fig 4).

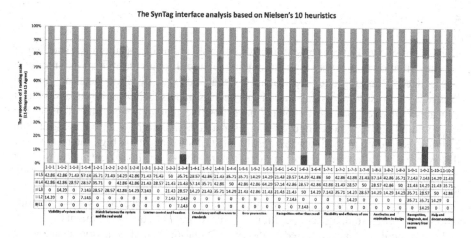

Fig. 4. The quantitative analysis of SynTag interface usability based on Nislsen's heuristic criteria

The overall result showed that most of students have positive reactions to the interface usability of SynTag. The quantitative analysis indicated 73% students give positive agree in our questionnaire (37% give 5 point, 36% give 4 point). Most of the students considered that the interface design was user friendly, easy to use, and consistency with their expectancy. Only 27% students had neutral or negative points (22% with 3 point, 4% with 2 point, 1% with 1 point). According to Fig 4, we identified that most of the negative points were located on question 1-9-2, 1-9-1, and 1-3-4. We tracked those problems back to Nislsen' heuristics criteria and indentify them. We concluded that those problems were caused from the lack of recognition, diagnosis, and recovery function from errors. Therefore, the top priority of further interface improvement was to develop the help documents or functions against to the error recovery.

Another critical issue we were interested is if the capability of collaborative learning between students was augmented through the assistance of the SynTag system. According to the interview, the result revealed that the design of timeline chart which could visualize all students' real-time tagging outcomes certainly increased their learning will as well. Students were strongly engaged in the class lecture because they could immediately assess the lecture by clicking the tagging buttons. Furthermore, the most import motivation for students keeping their eyes on the system was the instant dynamic outcome in the timeline. They were eager to know whether other participants had common agreements or not in the same lecture issue. The effect of "social behavior" stuck them together and cooperated with each other. In addition, several students also found that the archived tagging outcomes were very useful when they missed classes or didn't pay close enough attention to some sections during the lecture. The wave-shaped timeline chart (Fig 3) helped them to highlight the valuable key points. They could just re-play the video section around the peak to retrieve the lecture clips. In other words, the archived timeline from students' cooperation made the lecture video more accessible and retrievable.

5 Conclusion and Future Work

The system of SynTag presents an innovated application for collaborative learning in a lecture. It allows students to tag an ongoing lecture through the web-based interface. The collective tagging data are instantly visualized by a dynamic timeline chart to illustrate the result of collaboration between students. The usability assessment indicates that over two-third subjects have positive reactions in terms of using the SyTag interface for knowledge exchanges and understandings during a lecture. In addition, according to the interview result, most of students show high interests to use this system for collaborative learning in a lecture. Two significant contributions about why the SynTag system encourages students' learning will are addressed. First of all, the tagging buttons increase students' engagement during a lecture due to the interaction and participation. Second, the instant collective feedbacks by a timeline indeed encourage students' cooperation to achieve the consequent comments.

Furthermore, we are interested in the finding that the social behaviors occur when students are using the SynTag system. Students regard the outcomes of collaborative tagging as the valuable social event just like using some social media such as twitter, plurk, or facebook. They spontaneously turn the collective learning process into a social activity. This finding suggests a potential direction to improve our system as a social platform. We propose to integrate the SynTag system with some social media to increase the adherence and constancy of users. Armed with this insight, we will continue to explore the valuable researches for collective learning in the next version of SynTag.

References

1. Alavi, M.: Computer-mediated collaborative learning: An empirical evaluation. MIS Quarterly 18(2), 159–174 (1994)
2. Marjanovic, O.: Learning and teaching in a synchronous collaborative environment. Journal of Computer Assisted Learning 15, 129–138 (1999)
3. Trauth, E.M., Jessup, L.M.: Understanding computer-mediated discussions: positivist and interpretive analyses of group support system use. MIs Quarterly 24, 43–79 (2000)
4. Nielsen, J.: Finding usability problems through heuristic evaluation. In: Proceedings of the SIGCHI Conference on Human Factors in Computing Systems, pp. 373–380. ACM, New York (1992)
5. Schneider, J., et al.: Multi-user multi-touch setups for collaborative learning in an educational setting. Cooperative Design, Visualization, and Engineering, 181–188 (2010)
6. Hodgson, V., McConnell, D.: Co-operative learning and development networks. Journal of Computer Assisted Learning 11, 210–224 (1995)
7. Topkara, M., Rogowitz, B., Wood, S., Boston, J.: Collaborative editing of micro-tags. In: Proceedings of the 27th International Conference Extended Abstracts on Human Factors in Computing Systems, pp. 4297–4302. ACM, New York (2009)
8. Golder, S., Huberman, B.A.: The structure of collaborative tagging systems. Arxiv preprint cs/0508082 (2005)
9. Dix, A., Finlay, J., Abowd, G.D.: Human-computer interaction. Prentice Hall, Englewood Cliffs (2004)

10. Ssemugabi, S., de Villiers, R.: A comparative study of two usability evaluation methods using a web-based e-learning application. In: Proceedings of the 2007 Annual Research Conference of the South African Institute of Computer Scientists and Information Technologists on IT Research in Developing Countries, pp. 132–142. ACM, New York (2007)

11. Nielsen, J.: Finding usability problems through heuristic evaluation. In: Proceedings of the SIGCHI Conference on Human Factors in Computing Systems, pp. 373–380. ACM, New York (1992)

12. SynTag website, http://ialab.tw/istudio/main

13. Bateman, S., Brooks, C., McCalla, G., Brusilovsky, P.: Applying collaborative tagging to e-learning. In: Proc. of ACM WWW (2007)

14. Mathes, A.: Folksonomies-cooperative classification and communication through shared metadata. Computer Mediated Communication 47, 1–13 (2004)

15. Duval, E., Hodgins, W., Sutton, S., Weibel, S.L.: Metadata principles and practicalities. D-lib Magazine 8, 16 (2002)

16. Abowd, G.D., et al.: Teaching and learning as multimedia authoring: the classroom 2000 project. In: Proceedings of the Fourth ACM International Conference on Multimedia, pp. 187–198. ACM, New York (1997)

17. Abowd, G., et al.: Anchoring discussions in lecture: An approach to collaboratively extending classroom digital media. In: Proceedings of the 1999 Conference on Computer Support for Collaborative Learning, pp. 1–es. International Society of the Learning Sciences (1999)

18. Kam, M., et al.: Livenotes: a system for cooperative and augmented note-taking in lectures. In: Proceedings of the SIGCHI Conference on Human Factors in Computing Systems, pp. 531–540. ACM, New York (2005)

19. Bateman, S., Farzan, R., Brusilovsky, P., McCalla, G.: Oats: The open annotation and tagging system. In: The Proceedings of the Third Annual International Scientific Conference of the Learning Object Repository Research Network, Montreal, Citeseer (2006)

Ask Friends for Help: A Collaborative Query Answering System

Dominik Popowicz[1], Piotr Bródka[2],
Przemysław Kazienko[2], and Michał Kozielski[1]

[1] Silesian University of Technology, Akademicka 16, 44-100 Gliwice, Poland
[2] Wrocław University of Technology,
Wyb.Wyspiańskiego 27, 50-370 Wrocław, Poland
{dominik.popowicz,michal.kozielski}@polsl.pl,
{piotr.brodka,kazienko}@pwr.wroc.pl

Abstract. The probability that we get help is greater if we ask a friend, rather than a stranger. On the basis of this sociological phenomenon, the innovative SocLaKE recommender system for query propagation in the social network was invented. In this paper, a general concept of the system as well as a discussion on various issues and challenges related to its application are presented.

1 Introduction

During each day of life of the organization, employees are asking questions, some of which are new and some are not. The answers for some of them can be found in documentation, forum, web logs and other content widely available in the organization. However, there are questions where discovering the answer is not a simple task. In such cases employees usually communicate with help desk or office supervisors and wait for an answer. This so-called "official way" can take a lot of time and many of these problems stay unresolved. Therefore, it is a significant challenge for a medium-sized and large organisations to simplify and speedup the process of finding the right answer for the questions which arise during a daily work.

What the employees can do, when they can not find the solution for their problem? The most common advice which can be given is "ask your friend", maybe the friends know an answer? If not, maybe they know someone who had the same or similar problem in the past and solved it? Then they can contact you with this person and you will get the solution. If your friends are not able to help you, they can ask their friends for help. In this way the question is propagated through the friends of the friends until the satisfying answer is found. Why this approach can prove to be efficient? Because people are more eager to help someone they know than a stranger, even if their expertise is out of scope of the question.

Company's standard communication system has no explicit information about informal social relationship between the employees. However, it is possible to extract this information from existing data. IT systems in every organization

Y. Luo (Ed.): CDVE 2011, LNCS 6874, pp. 110–113, 2011.

contain information about e-mail or instant messenger conversations, employees common activities such as: the projects developed, the tasks solved, participation in meetings [1,2], etc. This data can be used to create multi-layered social network of the company employees [4].

In this paper, we present the concept of the recommender system SocLaKE - Social Latent Knowledge Explorator [5,6], which utilises this social network to propagate queries and to find reliable solutions in the fast way. Additionally, the discussion on various issues and challenges retaled to system application are presented.

2   General Concept of the System

The main goal of the system is to improve communication between organisation's employees. This improvement can be measured twofold: quantitatively, because more queries should be correctly answered and qualitatively, because the time needed to receive an answer should be shorter.

The query in the system is propagated through the social network of friends and colleagues. This process can be recognised in a real behaviour of people looking for an answer, when they do not know a competent expert directly. The system presented will support this process.

The basic concept of the system is presented in Figure 1. In the first step it is necessary to create a social network. Next, the system gathers information about the employees' knowledge. Several sources of information can be utilised in this step: any official or informal documents such as reports, notes, recruitment process information as well as e-mail or instant messenger contents, organisation structure, e.g., positions occupied and employees' responsibilities.

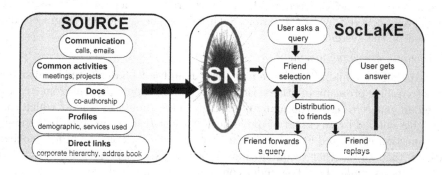

Fig. 1. Basic concept of the SocLaKE system

The following scenario can be realised by such a system. A user defines a question using e-mail or IM message. The system discovers domain of the question and returns to the user a list of the recommended users to whom the question can be addressed. The recipient of the message can send the solution back to the author of the question or using the same recommendation system and forward the question to someone else. This can be repeated until the correct answer is found.

3   Discussion on System Functionality

In this section, various issues and challenges related to system application are discussed.

Privacy related issues

The information resulting from collecting and processing the data from different sources provided by organisation should not be accessible by the users of the system due to privacy issues. The list of the recommended users who possibly can help in solving a problem should be the only rłesult of knowledge base analysis presented by the system. Therefore, it is required to properly secure the confidential content.

If both an expert and author of the question agree, the question and its solution can be stored in a local database. If a similar question is sent in the future, then the system returns the archive solution and relays the question directly to the recognized expert. Obviously, for the users who are concerned about the privacy of the messages, the system should provide possibility to turn this feature off for selected conversation.

Expert determination

The system has to decide who is an expert and what is the area of its expertise. Initially, the experts are identified utilising the knowledge derived from the company documentation as well as its organizational structure. During runtime, the system itself becomes additional valuable source of knowledge about experts. The employees continuously acquire the new knowledge and skills. Therefore, it is possible that a correct answer will be given to an author of a query by his colleague who was not recognised previously as an expert. Also each time the askers receives a correct response from an expert what increases their expertise in the area covered by this question. Such kownledge should be recognised and utilised by the system.

Expert and query management

An expert is a valuable employee and they should not be dedicated exclusively only to resolve problems of others. Hence, the system should prevent from a casen when an expert receives too many questions. There should be a limit which can be either defined by an expert or dynamically adjusted to the expert's behaviour. If a question is rejected by an expert due to a current lack of time or for another reason, then the further recommendation of this expert should be delayed and other experts should be taken under consideration. The further inspirations how to manage this problem can be searched in the field of active queue management (AQM), e.g. [3].

The questions covering the same topic should be managed by the system and aggregated also in order to respect the expert's time preferences. Also answers can be managed by the system. It is possible to enable several answers for the same question which remains active in the system although the first solution has already been provided. The author of a question should also have the possibility to assess the answer and rate it. It is possible to evaluate the expertise quality of experts in this way. Another approach is to introduce the methods of advanced feedback analysis as it was proposed for online auction systems, e.g. [7].

System dynamics management

Very important issue related to the operation of the system is the dynamics of the modelled organisation. The changes that will influence the system operation can be related e.g., to the structure of the organisation, informal social relations, knowledge of the users and their expertise, parameters of the query propagation model, etc. Therefore, the change management will be one of the significant challenges related to application of the system.

4   Conclusions

The general idea of the recommender system for query propagation based on the social network is presented in the paper. Several issues can be encountered while introducing the system of this kind. In particular, privacy related issues, expert determination, expert and query management and system dynamics management were are discussed in the paper.

Acknowledgement. The work was supported by The Polish Ministry of Science and Higher Education the research project, 2010-13, Fellowship co-financed by the European Union within the European Social Fund, and the training in the "Green Transfer" project co-financed by the European Union from the European Social Fund, the European Union from the European Social Fund.

References

1. Balog, K., Azzopardi, L., de Rijke, M.: Formal models for expert finding in enterprise corpora. In: Proceedings of the 29th Annual International ACM SIGIR Conference on Research and Development in Information Retrieval, p. 50. ACM, New York (2006)
2. Campbell, C.S., Maglio, P.P., Cozzi, A., Dom, B.: Expertise identification using email communications. Information and Knowledge Management, 528–531 (2003)
3. Floyd, S., Jacobson, V.: Random Early Detection gateways for Congestion Avoidance. IEEE/ACM Transactions on Networking 1(4), 397–413 (1993)
4. Kazienko, P., Bródka, P., Musial, K., Gaworecki, J.: Multi-layered Social Network Creation Based on Bibliographic Data. In: SocialCom 2010, Minneapolis, August 20-22, pp. 407–412. IEEE Computer Society Press, USA (2010)
5. Kukla, G., Kazienko, P., Bródka, P., Filipowski, T.: SocLaKE - Social Latent Knowledge Explorator. In: Proceedings of the Second International Conference on Social Informatics, SocInfo 2010, pp. 113–124 (2010)
6. Kukla, G., Kazienko, P., Bródka, P., Filipowski, T.: SocLaKE - Social Latent Knowledge Explorator. The Computer Journal (in review)
7. Morzy, M., Wierzbicki, A.: The Sound of Silence: Mining Implicit Feedbacks to Compute Reputation. In: Spirakis, P.G., Mavronicolas, M., Kontogiannis, S.C. (eds.) WINE 2006. LNCS, vol. 4286, pp. 365–376. Springer, Heidelberg (2006)

Extended Ontology-Based Process Management Architecture

Tingting Liu, Huifen Wang, and Linyan Liu

School of Mechanical Engineering,
Nanjing University of Science and Technology,
Nanjing, China
{liutingtingwy,8351121_whf,llylgy01}@163.com

Abstract. Process management is a technology used to design, enact, control, and analyze business processes. Today although workflow management systems are readily available and a large number of literatures present improvements in business process management, the reuse ratio of knowledge involved in process is low and most of organizations cannot reuse existing knowledge effectively. In this paper we propose an extended ontology-based process management architecture. Through analyzing the process characters, we identify six ontologies in the process management, including process ontology, organization ontology, resource ontology, knowledge ontology, object ontology and constraint ontology. OWL language has been used to describe each element in the ontology. Based on these six ontologies, a four-level process management architecture is presented and described in detail to show how it can work to reuse the context-related knowledge in process execution. The main contribution of this paper is to achieve knowledge reuse in process management.

Keywords: process management, ontology, knowledge reuse.

1 Introduction

Process is a set of activities related to customer value creation containing the input of resources, activities, output, customer, value, etc. In recent years, with the development and application of business process management and workflow management, manufacturing, R & D companies, service companies and government agencies have already invested heavily in business process.

However, although there has been a shift from "data-aware" to "process-aware" in recent information systems through applying ontology and semantics in process management, the reuse ratio of knowledge involved in process is low and most of organizations cannot reuse existing knowledge effectively because of the gap between the models from the management perspective (e.g. BPMN) and the actually deployed process models. The task undertaker usually needs to be a specialist and a novice should spend a long time to train himself/herself to be a specialist.

There is a number of information related to enterprise business process including specifications, engineering drawings, standard specifications, etc. Effective use of the

Y. Luo (Ed.): CDVE 2011, LNCS 6874, pp. 114–120, 2011.

knowledge will help to improve the efficiency of the process users. The aim of this paper is to develop an ontology-based process architecture considering knowledge reuse to make the process users use related knowledge easily while they are finishing their tasks.

2 Related Research and Requirements

Processes have emerged as one of the major developments to ease the understanding of, communication about, and evolution of enterprise IT systems. There has been a shift from "data-aware" information systems to "process-aware" information systems. To support business processes, an enterprise information system needs to be aware of these processes and their organizational context [1].

The topics about processes addressed cover areas like process modeling, analysis and verification of business processes, process mining, process translation, adaptivity, etc. workflow management, business process management and project management are prevalent techniques for process management. Today workflow management systems are readily available [2-3] and a large number of literatures present improvements in Business Process Management [4].

Semantic has been used in existing literatures to improve the automation and adaptivity of process management. A core challenge in business process management is the continuous, bi-directional translation between (1) a business requirements view on the process space of an enterprise and (2) the actual process space of this enterprise, constituted by the multiplicity of IT systems, resources, and human labor. Semantic Business Process Management is a novel approach of increasing the level of automation of BPM by representing the various spheres of an enterprise using ontology languages and Semantic Web Services frameworks. The goal is to be able to apply machine reasoning for the translation between these two spheres, in particular for the discovery of processes and process fragments and for process composition [5]. Adaptivity is important for the successful application of process management technology in practice and approaches have been developed to ensure system correctness after arbitrary process changes [6].

The term ontology originally stems from the field of philosophy where it is "the science of what is, of the kinds and structures of objects, properties, events, processes and relations in every area of reality" [7]. Dietz has provided a comprehensive ontological approach to enterprise modeling [8]. An ontology based extension for business process models is presented in literature [9]. Through defining semantic metadata for business processes modeled with Petri nets, the extension makes it easy to automate the communication among process-implementing software components.

3 Ontology for Process Management

In enterprises processes are used to regulate business processes and they are often characterized by the following features.

1) Processes involve a number of knowledge that has diversity. For instance, the knowledge involved in product design process includes design specifications, design wizards, design manuals, product models, design experience, simulation, testing, user feedback, etc while process specifications, technical drawings, business capacity and equipment information can be found in technology approval process. Some knowledge is fuzzy, implicit in the memory of those who complete the task; some knowledge is structured, such as drawings, equipment information and some other one is semi-structured, such as technology standards.

2) Process knowledge is closely related to the organization, the process itself, the process goals and the design objects which are relatively stable.

According to the above characteristics, we can identify six areas in the process management, including *Organization, Resources, Knowledge, Objects, Constraints*, and the *Process* itself (Fig.1).

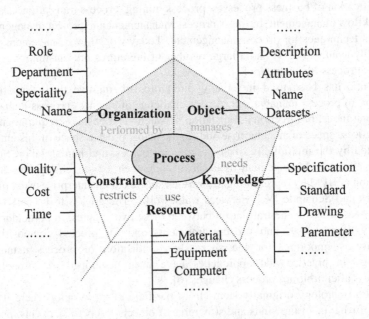

Fig. 1. Six areas in process management

1) *Organization* refers to the staff relation, topology and other related concepts formed by the process makers, executives and participants. In the process management, the staff usually has identity and is a member of some department. He acts as some role to perform the task under the constraints of specifications.

2) *Resource* refers to the equipment, materials, etc consumed in the implementation of processes. Effective resource management and scheduling can safeguard the smooth and effective implementation of processes while unbalanced use of resources means the upgrading cost and lack of resources results in the decline in the quality. Also, all tangible and intangible resources are part of the organization of an enterprise.

3) *Knowledge* refers to the specifications, engineering drawings, standard specifications, etc in an enterprise formed during the process.

4) *Object* refers to the specific objects implemented in the process, such as product in the product design process, processing draft in the approval process.

5) *Constraint* refers to the process goals, specifications, etc restricting the process.

6) *Process* refers to the chains of activities that are actually executed, e.g. explicitly designed processes as well as ad-hoc processes.

Based on the above analysis, we establish six ontologies including *process ontology, organization ontology, resource ontology, constraint ontology, knowledge ontology* and *object ontology*.

3.1 Process Ontology and Organization Ontology

From the view point of application, the *process ontology* and *organization ontology* are industry-independent while the other four ontologies are closely related to enterprise features.

Process ontology can be described as shown in Fig.2. It includes elements *Activity* and *Relation*. And *Relation* is further composed of *SEQUENCE, AND-SPLIT, XOR-SPLIT, AND-JOIN, XOR-JOIN* and *LOOP* activity-relation spaces.

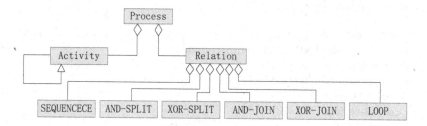

Fig. 2. Process ontology

Organization ontology defines common types of divisions, roles, and tasks to provide the basic vocabulary and structure for describing organizations. We depict *Organization ontology* as Fig.3. Elements of *Organization ontology* are the concepts *Role, Department, Employee* and relationships among them.

3.2 Other Ontolodges

Resource ontology, constraint ontology, knowledge ontology and *object ontology* are industry-independent. For example, automotive industry and chemical industry tend to have different product design, technology, production, and marketing knowledge. Enterprises of different backgrounds need inconsistent raw materials, components and processing methods. Currently, to express and integration ontologies of various industries has been concerned in some literatures.

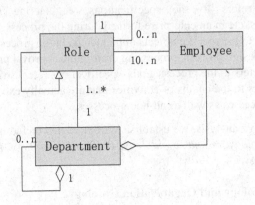

Fig. 3. Organization ontology

3.3 Ontology Realization

The OWL web ontology language can be used to describe each element in the ontology. The OWL Language is designed for use by applications that need to process the content of information instead of just presenting information to humans. We here only give out an example as following.

```
<owl:Ontology rdf:about="">
 <rdfs:comment>AND-SPLIT</rdfs:comment>
</owl:Ontology>
<rdfs:Class rdf:ID="AND-SPLIT">
 <rdfs:subClassOf>
  <owl:Restriction>
   <owl:onProperty rdf:resource="#INPUT"/>
        <rdf:Bag>
            <rdf:li>task-in-1</rdf:li>
            <rdf:li>task-in-2</rdf:li>
            ......
            <rdf:li>task-in-n</rdf:li>
        </rdf:Bag>
    <owl:allValuesFrom
        rdf:resource="http://www.w3.org/2001/XMLSchema#string"/>
   </owl:Restriction>
 </rdfs:subClassOf>
 <rdfs:subClassOf>
  <owl:Restriction>
   <owl:onProperty rdf:resource="OUTPUT"/>
        <rdf:Bag>
            <rdf:li>task-out-1</rdf:li>
            <rdf:li>task-out-2</rdf:li>
            ......
```

```
        <rdf:li>task-out-n</rdf:li>
      </rdf:Bag>
   <owl:allValuesFrom
         rdf:resource="http://www.w3.org/2001/XMLSchema#string"/>
   </owl:Restriction>
   </rdfs:subClassOf>
   ......
   </rdfs:Class>
```

4   Extended Ontology-Based Process Management Architecture

We have established an extended ontology-based process management architecture based on above six ontologies. There are four levels in the architecture including data level, model level, instance level and executing level.

Data level is composed of ontology base consisting of process ontology base, organization ontology base, resource ontology base, constraint ontology base, knowledge ontology base and object ontology base.

Based on the data layer, process models can be created applying ontology to achieve computer identifiable and readable. Moreover, process instances can be established in the third layer.

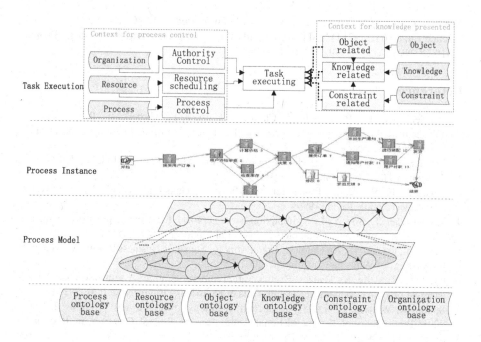

Fig. 4. Process management architecture

The most important layer is the task execution layer. In this layer, according to process ontology, resource ontology and organization ontology, tasks, authorizations, resources and process can be recognized automatically. We can decide whether a task should be executed based on whether resources needed are in place, whether the actor has permission to perform the task and whether all the input tasks have been completed.

While an employee is completing a task, he or she can obtain the object-related knowledge. The architecture will match context-related knowledge and present to the executor. For example, while an evaluator is reviewing a process document, context-related knowledge can be found through querying process knowledge. The object the process document refers to will be considered as the constraints to obtain effective knowledge and the semantic consistency of ontology can guarantee the presented knowledge correctness and validity.

5 Conclusion

We have proposed an extended ontology-based process management architecture. The main contribution of our study is that we take full account of the reusability of knowledge. Knowledge ontology is established to describe the knowledge involved in the process to guarantee the consistent semantic representation for knowledge acquisition. The next step is to study how to implement intelligent storage and accumulation of knowledge.

Acknowledgements. This work has in part been funded by the China National Natural Science Fund (61003211) and China National Major Science and Technology Projects (2010ZX04014-051, 2009ZX04014-036).

References

1. van der Aalst, W., Benatallah, B., Casati, F., Curbera, F., Verberk, E.: Business process management: Where business processes and web services meet. Int. Journal on Data and Knowledge Engineering 61(1), 1–5 (2007)
2. van der Aalst, W.M.P., van Hee, K.M.: Workflow Management: Models, Methods, and Systems. MIT Press, Cambridge (2004)
3. Leymann, F., Roller, D.: Production Workflow: Concepts and Techniques. Prentice-Hall PTR, Upper Saddle River (1999)
4. Madhusudan, T., Son, Y.-J.: A simulation-based approach for dynamic process management at web service platforms. Computers & Industrial Engineering 49, 287–317 (2005)
5. Hepp, M., Roman, D.: An Ontology Framework for Semantic Business Process Management. Proceedings of Wirtschaftsinformatik (2007)
6. Ly, L.T., Rinderle, S., Dadam, P.: Integration and verification of semantic constraints in adaptive process management systems. Data & Knowledge Engineering (64), 3–23 (2008)
7. Smith, B., Weltym, C.: FOIS introduction: Ontology-towards a new synthesis. In: FOIS 2001: Proceedings of the International Conference on Formal Ontology in Information Systems, pp. 3–9 (2001)
8. Dietz, J.L.G.: Enterprise Ontology. Springer, Heidelberg (2006)
9. Koschmider, A., Oberweis, A.: Ontology Based Business Process Description. In: Proceedings of the CAiSE 2005 Workshops. LNCS, pp. 321–333 (2005)

Information Model for Cooperative Disassembly Process Planning

Hanmin Lee[1], Seongwhan Park[1], and Shaw C. Feng[2]

[1] Korea Institute of Machinery and Materials,
Daejeon, Korea
{hmlee,swpark}@kimm.re.kr
[2] National Institute of Standards and Technology,
Gaithersburg, USA
shaw.feng@nist.gov

Abstract. Disassembly of end-of-service-life products is a key operation to separate a product into reusable and recyclable parts. This paper describes an information model for cooperative disassembly process planning. A description of the classes and their relationships on assembly structure, disassembly sequence and method, features, disassembly equipment, disassembly workflow, and operations of separations are included in the paper. A case study on a car suspension design is conducted to test the model.

Keywords: Information Modeling, Disassembly Process Planning, Disassembly Information Model.

1 Introduction

For reuse and recycle of a product at the end of its useful life, disassembly is the key operation to separate the product into reusable, recyclable, and disposable parts. Disassembly process planning requires information from design, such as disassembly operation, sequence, disassembly features, their relationships, and subassemblies. Disassembly plans need to be exchanged among disassembly process planning systems. This paper describes an information model for cooperative disassembly process planning.

2 Information for Cooperative Disassembly Process Planning

Information requirement analysis for disassembly process planning was accomplished by literature surveys, standards surveys, domain experts' interviews and industrial data reviews. Generally, disassembly process planning includes preliminary product analysis step, sequence generation step, disassembly tools and equipment selection step and economical evaluation step[1]. Table 1 shows the information requirement for each step of disassembly planning. The disassembly information model was developed to be able to represent all the information.

Y. Luo (Ed.): CDVE 2011, LNCS 6874, pp. 121–124, 2011.
© Springer-Verlag Berlin Heidelberg 2011

Table 1. Information required for disassembly process planning steps

Disassembly Planning Step	Information Requirement
1. Preliminary Product Analysis	- Assembly Hierarchy - Connection Relation Between Parts or Subassemblies - Connection Relation Between Assembly Features - Damage Level of Connection - Type of Connection and Connector
2. Sequence Generation	- All Feasible Sequences - Operation(Component Level) and Its Sub-Task(Feature Level) - Input and Output Components - Type of Disassembly Task - Target Connection
3. Selection of Disassembly Tools and Equipment	- Disassembly Time, Cost - Disassembly Tool, Jig/Fixture - Disassembly Direction, Force
4. Economical Evaluation	- Reuse Information (Type, Revenue, Cost) - Material Price, Toxicity - Optimal Sequence

3 Disassembly Information Model

We have developed an information model for disassembly process planning based on the information requirement analysis. The disassembly information model consists of assembly structure module, disassembly sequence and method module, and reusability module.

Assembly structure module was developed by extending Open Assembly Model(OAM)[2]. *AssemblyFeatureConnection* class was added to represent connection relationship between assembly features. Damage level of *AssemblyFeatureConnection* determines whether disassembly method should be destructive or non-destructive. Connection between assembly features can be established with or without a connector. *BoltNutConnection* has *Bolt* and *Nut* connector while *SnapFitConnection* between two assembly features needs no connector.

In the disassembly information model, there are separate classes representing sequences and individual disassembly actions as shown in Fig.1. *Process* and *ProcessElement* are responsible for the sequence representation. *ProcessElement* has zero or many *ProcessElement* as its successor. Using these classes, one could represent all possible sequences as well as one optimal sequence.

There are two levels of disassembly action: *DisassemblyOperation* for sub-assembly or part level and *DisassemblyTask* for assembly feature level. *ProcessElement* refers to *DisassemblyOperation*, and *DisassemblyOperation* has one

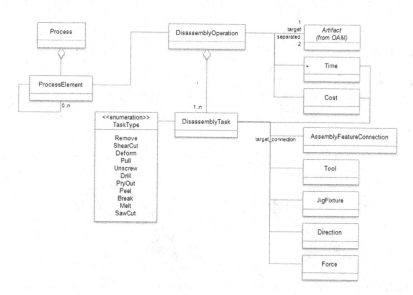

Fig. 1. Disassembly Information Model – Disassembly Sequence and Method

or more *DisassemblyTask*. Separating an assembly into two sub-assemblies requires breaking one or more connections between assembly features of the assembly. *DisassemblyOpearation* refers to an input assembly as its *target* property and two output sub-assemblies as its *separated* property. *DisassemblyTask* refers to a *AssemblyFeatureConnection* as its *target_connection* property. For the purpose of the economical evaluation, *DisassemblyOpearation* and *DisassemblyTask* have *Time* and *Cost* property. *DisassemblyTask* also has detailed disassembly information such as tool, jig/fixture, applied force and direction.

4 Case Study

A case study for a car suspension module was done to verify if the disassembly information model meets the information requirement as shown in Table.1. The disassembly of the suspension module is shown in the bottom of Fig.2. The module is separated into two sub-assemblies. To do this, one screw connection and two mating connections should be removed. The top of Fig.2 shows the instance diagram of the disassembly information model representing the disassembly tasks and corresponding assembly structures. A disassembly operation refers to its input assembly, output sub-assemblies, and three sub-tasks(one unscrew task, two remove task). Each task refers its target connection in the assembly structures. Through the case study, it was verified that the disassembly information model can represent all the information required for disassembly process planning systems.

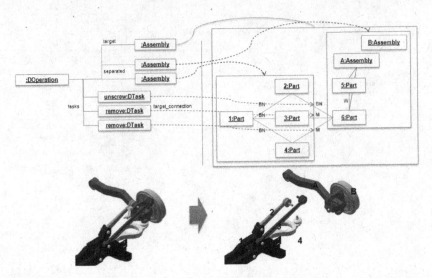

Fig. 2. Instance Diagram of Disassembly Information Model for Car Suspension Module

5   Conclusion

We have developed an information model for data exchange among cooperative disassembly process planning systems. Information required for disassembly planning steps was collected by requirement analysis and three module of disassembly information model such as assembly structure module, disassembly sequence and method module and reusability module were developed. A case study for a car suspension module was done to verify if the disassembly information model meets the information requirement. Since there has been no information model for disassembly, the proposed model could be used as a basis for data exchange of cooperative disassembly process planning systems. For the future work, it should be refined by applying it to the real disassembly process planning systems.

References

1. Santochia, M., Dinia, G., Faillia, F.: Computer Aided Disassembly Planning: State of the Art and Perspectives. In: CIRP Annals - Manufacturing Technology, pp. 507–529 (2002)
2. Sudarsan, R., Han, Y.H., Feng, S.C., Roy, U., Wang, F., Sriram, R.D., Lyons, K.: Object oriented representation of electro-mechanical assemblies using UML. NISTIR 7057, National Institute of Standards and Technology (2003)
3. Fenves, S.J.: A core product model for representing design information. NISTIR 6736, National Institute of Standards and Technology (2002)

RFID Supported Cooperation for Construction Waste Management

Jack C.P. Cheng and Lauren Y.H. Ma

Department of Civil and Environmental Engineering,
The Hong Kong University of Science and Technology
{cejcheng,yingzi}@ust.hk

Abstract. The severity of construction and demolition waste problem has been observed around the world in recent years. Therefore, management of construction waste is important worldwide. Currently, radio frequency identification (RFID) technology is a growing technology which has been applied in many areas including the construction industry. This paper discusses the application of RFID technology for construction waste management, which is lacking in research in the construction industry. This paper presents a proposed RFID-based approach to facilitate the cooperation among on-site contractors, pick-up truck companies, and recycling companies. Waste pick-up and recycling could therefore be enhanced. Some reusable construction wastes like high strength cables are valuable and prone to be stolen. The proposed system could help the inspection of these construction wastes by using the automatic tracking capability of RFID technology.

Keywords: RFID technology, construction waste management, waste recycling, pick-up schedule, construction cooperation.

1 Introduction

Construction waste refers to the waste arising from such activities as construction, renovation, demolition, land excavation, and road works [1]. Construction waste is a serious environmental problem in many large cities in the world. Construction and demolition (C&D) debris frequently makes up 10–30% of the solid waste received at many landfill sites around the world [2]. In Hong Kong, for example, the Environmental Protection Department (EPD) reported in 2010 that about 13,300 tons of solid waste is disposed at landfills in Hong Kong every day, of which about 3,200 tons (24%) is attributable to construction waste [3].

Contractors often take the greatest responsibility for waste management on site in construction projects. The contractors need to not only cooperate with the site inspectors and recycling companies for waste reuse and recycling, but also communicate frequently with the hauling companies for waste pick-up and removal. Radio frequency identification (RFID) technology, which supports automatic identification and detection, provides much potential for contractors to cooperate with other stakeholders for construction waste management.

Y. Luo (Ed.): CDVE 2011, LNCS 6874, pp. 125–128, 2011.

A RFID system enables RFID readers to capture the data from RFID tags and transmit the data to a computer system without line of sight or physical connection. Applications of RFID technology for safety and access control, facilities management, and asset management are being studied and tested in the construction industry. However, the research on the use of RFID technology for construction waste management is relatively lacking. Applications of RFID technology for planning and tracking of municipal solid waste have been proposed and investigated [4,5]. Construction waste management is different from municipal waste management in that waste removal at regular time interval is not practical for construction waste since the waste generation rate fluctuates throughout a project. In addition, on-site sorting is difficult for construction waste due to limited site space and dis-organized material storage on site. This paper presents our proposed RFID-based system which supports automated, cooperative waste recycling, reuse, and removal on construction site.

2 Waste Tracking and Identification for Cooperative Waste Recycling, Reuse, and Special Treatments

The 3Rs (Recycle, Reuse, and Reduce) are the three main strategies for waste management. Recycling and reuse of C&D waste require contractors to find the waste collection and recycling companies. Usually, contractors have identified the partner recycling companies at the beginning of a project, but cannot provide an accurate estimation of the amount of waste and the time that the waste will be generated. Therefore, contractors need to communicate seamlessly with the partner recycling companies to avoid accumulation of construction waste on site.

On-site auditing is crucial for effective recycling in a demolition project [6], because materials in demolition waste often have a wider variety of types and are less organized than new construction waste. A team that includes architectural salvage companies, contractors, demolition engineers, and recyclers should work together on the project site to assess material recyclability. Construction Specifications Institute provides a list of common demolition waste items that are suitable for recycling and reuse [6]. Examples are metal handrails and grab bars, elevator and escalator motors, wood and metal windows and doors, ceramic and glass tiles, carpet, and furniture. RFID tags could be attached to these waste items with high recycling and reuse value before demolition. Contractors can then easily locate those tagged items on the project site and group them together during and after demolition.

In addition, contractors can also upload the information of those RFID-tagged waste items on the Intranet to attract potential waste collection and recycling companies. Architectural salvage companies, contractor, and recyclers could obtain the specifications and location of the waste items and perform waste assessment and estimation remotely. Recyclers can select the waste items that they are interested in based on the information available online. In this way, contractors could save efforts in searching potential recyclers for the waste items generated from the site.

High-value waste such as high strength cables and hazardous waste such as asbestos waste materials need special attention and frequent inspection on site. By attaching active RFID tags to the high-value, hazardous waste items or their containers, continuous signals will be received by RFID readers on site, monitoring the location of the waste items. Missing items are avoided on site. Special routes of those waste items could also be controlled during pick-up and delivery.

3 Automated Monitoring for Cooperative Waste Pick-Up Scheduling

There are two approaches to construction waste recycling – single stream and source separated. Single stream recycling allows contractors to put recyclable waste items of various types in one container on project site. Sorting of the collected recyclable waste is then done externally in sorting facility. On the contrary, source separated recycling requires contractors to put multiple containers on site for recyclable waste of different types. The collected waste in different containers are then delivered to separate recycling companies, saving the cost of hiring external sorting facility, reducing double handling of the recyclable waste, and increasing the rate of recycling. Thus, source separated recycling is recommended [6], but it requires more spaces for the containers on site and/or more frequent waste pick-up. The generation rate of a particular type of waste may vary throughout the entire construction project. Therefore, for source separated recycling, the field waste management contractor needs to cooperate with the waste hauling and recycling companies to determine daily, or even hourly, the pick-up schedule for each type of waste.

Automated detection of waste container levels using an integrated RFID-sensor system is proposed in this paper. Arebey et al. [5] proposed a RFID-based system for solid waste container collection and tracking. The proposed system in this paper focuses on the real-time monitoring of waste containers and the automated hauling arrangement of the containers during construction waste generation process. Ultrasonic sensors are leveraged in the proposed RFID-based detection system for

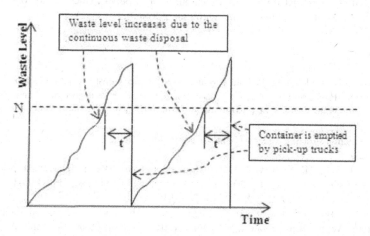

Fig. 1. Pick-up strategy of a waste container using the proposed RFID-sensor system. N represents the point when the hauling company is notified to send pick-up trucks to the construction site. t is the time between the notification and the arrival of pick-up trucks on site.

detecting the waste level of each container and sending the information through the integrated RFID system.

The system follows a waste pick-up strategy as illustrated in Fig. 1. When the waste level reaches a certain pre-defined amount (N), automated notification is sent to the recyclers. According to the given real-time information, the recyclers will send necessary amount of hauling trucks immediately. A vital part of this system is the determination of N. The value of N depends on the size of the container, the traveling time of the pick-up trucks, and the generation rate of the waste. Generation rate of the waste can be estimated by referring to the construction process schedules and by inserting RFID-sensor integrated tags at different levels of the waste container for prediction. The detection system can save the time of the field waste management engineer in coordinating containers and trucking services.

4 Summary and Future Works

This paper presents novel applications of RFID technology for cooperative construction waste recycling and management. Automatic tracking and identification of waste items supported by RFID technology facilitate the cooperation among contractors, waste recyclers, and architectural salvage companies. The integrated system of RFID active tags and ultrasonic sensors proposed in this paper enhances the cooperation between field waste management engineer and waste hauling companies for automated waste pick-up scheduling.

There have been rapid advancements of RFID technology in recent years. Metal is a strong reflector of radio waves and adversely affects the performance of nearby RFID tags. Special RFID tags designed for harsh environment and metal surfaces have been developed. Omni-ID Ultra, a passive tag that requires no battery and provides a read range of over 100 feet, is currently available on market. Chipless RFID tags such as the SAW (surface acoustic wave) one may have great potential in the construction industry due to their low cost and high reliability on thermal and mechanical behaviors. Further study on these new RFID technologies and their performance is needed for the proposed RFID-supported waste management approach.

References

1. Fishbein, B.K.: Building for the Future: Strategies to Reduce Construction and Demolition waste in municipal Projects (1998), http://www.informinc.org/cdreport.html
2. Poon, C.S.: Management of Construction and Demolition Waste. Waste Management 27(2), 159–160 (2007)
3. Environmental Protection Department (EPD) of Hong Kong, http://www.info.gov.hk/epd
4. Nielsen, I., Lim, M., Nielsen, P.: Optimizing Supply Chain Waste Management through the Use of RFID Technology. In: 2010 IEEE International Conference on RFID-Technology and Applications (RFID-TA), pp. 296–301 (2010)
5. Arebey, M., Hannan, M.A., Basri, H., Begum, R.A., Abdullah, H.: Integrated Technologies for Solid Waste Bin Monitoring System. Environmental Monitoring and Assessment 177(1), 399–408 (2011)
6. Winkler, G.: Recycling Construction & Demolition Waste: A LEED-Based Toolkit. McGraw-Hill Construction, United States (2010)

Planning for the Environmental Quality of Urban Microclimate: A Multiagent-Based Approach*

Dino Borri and Domenico Camarda

Dipartimento di Architettura e Urbanistica, Politecnico di Bari, Italy
d.camarda@poliba.it

Abstract. An increasing concern about urban environmental quality has grown in the last decades caused by urban production mechanisms. Now, policies and ICT models need to integrate traditional quantitative techniques with more complex multiagent tools to support effective recovery strategies.

Basing on a hybrid scenario approach, the present research links information and knowledge aspects to define sequences of events and processes for decisionmaking. An ICT-based model is set up, involving human agents, low-profile artificial (routinary) agents and/or high profile (intelligent) agents, as defined by computer-science and multi-agent studies.

Particularly, the paper focuses on the case study of Bari, Italy, addressing multi-agent-based relationships between urban microclimatic and social characters.

Keywords: Urban microclimate planning, multiple agents, urban pollution, scenario management, decision-support systems.

1 Introduction

Negative impacts are increasingly induced by processes of urban production on human health and socio-economic systems. Legislative and scientific efforts try to face such impacts, through analytical models and ad-hoc policy measures [1]. Data models adopt hybrid approaches, able to deal with complex urban environments. However, statistical georeferenced data management needs structural integration with distributed-agent management for effective decision making over time [2].

An appropriate ecological modelling approach should address some critical issues. First is the knowledge of urban environmental processes and its formalization, in order to keep the dynamics of urban systems. Then, such process trends and features are monitored to deal with urban microclimate impacts and changes. Built strategies need to be related to future scenarios that simulate the potentials of impact-reducing actions. Particularly, a multiagent inclusive approach should carried out, involving all environmental (human, artificial, hybrid) agents in the simulation [3][4].

ECOURB project is developed just in such framework, by involving research units to model data collections and generate hybrid scenarios for urban environmental quality decisions [5][6]. It is a Strategic Project financed by the 2006-2012 Framework

---

* The present study has been carried out by the authors as a joint research work. Nonetheless, section 3 has been written by D. Borri, sections 1 and 2 have been written by D. Camarda.

Y. Luo (Ed.): CDVE 2011, LNCS 6874, pp. 129–136, 2011.

Agreement between Italian State and Apulia Region to support scientific research. The project is supposed to generate guidelines to enhance the quality of urban microclimate and environment, by issuing strategies to challenge environmental decays at the urban level [7].

The multi-agent architecture relies on the work of two different research units: the Department of architecture and planning of Politecnico di Bari (DAU) and the Department of Computer Science of the University of Bari (DIB). DAU draws out the complex management model supporting the multi-dimensional, multi-scale, synchronous and asynchronous knowledge interactions among agents. DIB develops the IT architecture implementing the multi-agent management model. This paper discusses the setting up of the multi-agent model, by dealing with agent processes, roles, tasks, formal relations in the ECOURB case study of Bari (Italy) [8].

After this introduction, chapter 2 shows a model of multi-agent knowledge management, by first dealing with multi-agent literature on urban climate managing and then discussing the model used in the context of Bari. The paper ends up with remarks on results and follow-ups.

2 A Multiagent Model of Knowledge Management

2.1 Some Basic Literature

Recent case studies specifically deal with the roles, actions, contributions of distributed agents in an urbanized environment. Human agents, routinary and/or intelligent artificial agents are analyzed with typical computer-science approach [4].

Studies have mainly focused on the relations between urban microclimates and the social component of urban contexts, revealing interesting insights. For example, a first study is about monitoring and managing air quality in Athens (Greece). It is interesting because of the articulated multi-agent, AI-based information-management support system. However, its architecture has not been implemented in full [9]. Other studies of Mainz University (Germany) develop model research on building up virtual support environments to simulate urban climate management, with fair success [10]. In a number of works in Fukuoka (Japan) the environment-inhabitant relationship is analysed to investigate the microclimate management of residential housing, with behavioural models [11].

This brief survey confirms that a multi-agent approach to the interpretation and management of relevant processes of urban production and degradation is possible and can be carried out. Building on that, we will now synthetically discuss some results of ECOURB project, in terms of modelling approaches for urban microclimate planning and management support systems in the context of Bari.

2.2 A Multiagent-Based Model

The ECOURB urban quality management system (UQMS) model is based on a hybrid multi-agent architecture. It considers human (cognitive) and artificial (routinary) human agents, interacting *au paire*. Although routinary human agents are not involved, some routines are supposed to be performed by human agents when needed, by declassifying cognitive agents during their normal task time [12].

Different units of the organizational structure develop autonomous activities either indoor, or by exchanging elements with other units, with internal interaction processes enhancing such outward exchange. This dual interaction behaviour makes each unit an actual agency in the multiagent model, as occurring in complex societies [4].

That multi-unit model represents just a preliminary structure of agents in the model-building stage. In the operational stage, different units may be grouped in a unique collective agent, with intrinsically different roles and tasks. We will now discuss the operational architecture of the system, as a final evolution of the multi-unit preliminary structure. At the current intermediate stage of the project, a fine-grained architecture is not yet available. The complete structure of agent roles, relations and working algorithms will be ready in the next future. The current framework of the model architecture can be outlined in three modules (figure 1).

1. Multiagent System (MAS) to survey, collect, process and transmit data to the Knowledge Management System (KMS);
2. KMS to manage the cognitive base, to process and simulate scenarios. KMS is a collective agent and is part of MAS. It has not been fully developed yet.
3. Decision-making stage. The Decision agent is part of MAS.

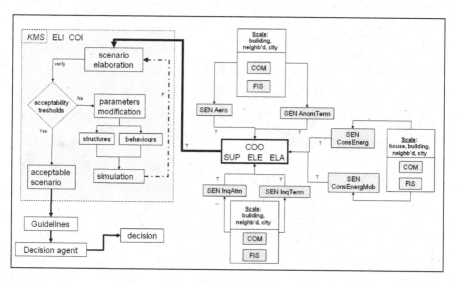

Fig. 1. The general model *(AnomTerm: Thermal anomalies; Aero: Aerosol optical thickness; ConsEnerg: Residential energetic consumption; ConsEnergMob: Energetic consumption of mobility; InqTerm: Thermal pollution; InqAtmo: Atmospheric pollution; Neighb'd: Neighbourhood)*

Involved agents are identified in relation to their types, roles and cognition levels (figure 2). The details of UQMS processes are drawn out from the mechanics of the model functioning in the Bari case study. A contingent availability of sensors and elaborating devices on some areas of the urban district has driven our testing attention on a satellite temperature survey (Figure 3) [13]. The KMS has not been fully developed yet, therefore this is a partial application.

name	agent type	cognition level	task/role
COM	Behavioural	cognitive	Human agent (consciously or unconsciously) interacting with the environment through her behaviour.
FIS	Physical	pseudo-routinary	Physical, non-cognitive feature of the environment.
SEN	Sensor	routinary	Device collecting either a physical characteristic of the environment or a given behaviour in the environment, transforming it in a datum that is qualitatively and/or quantitatively measurable
ELA	Analytical processor	routinary	Device processing and possibly normalizing data transmitted by sensors.
ELE	Expert processor	cognitive	Agent analysing and formally processing the causal chains of environmental processes.
SUP	Supervisor	cognitive	Agent controlling qualitatively the process of data acquisition, processing, transmission and updating.
T/F	Transmission and/or feedback algorithm	algorithm	Function or system that allows the setting up of a quali-quantitative relation among elements (e.g., through data transmission).
COO	Coordinator	cognitive	Agent controlling the quality of the processes of quali-quantitative exchange and coordination among agents.
ELI	Inferential processor	routinary	Expert-based (normative/causal) device processing multiple-source data & transforming them into output decision-support scenarios.
COI	Inferential controller	cognitive	Agent controlling the quality of the process of inferring scenarios

Fig. 2. Taxonomy of involved agents

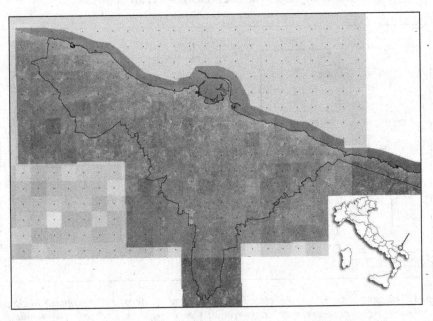

Fig. 3. Temperature survey of the greater Bari district (1000x1000m grid)

Temperature is intended as a physical feature of the environment (FIS) and a proxy for an environmental agent, so manageable in the MAS model architecture. A satellite temperature sensor (SEN), belonging to a general device collecting thermal anomalies (SEN *AnomTerm*), can transform FIS into quantitatively measurable data. The survey focuses on both city level (1000x1000m grid) and neighbourhood level (100x100m grid), with manageable data at different scales and with different hierarchical and cognitive levels of agents [14].

Data are then transmitted (T) to the processing collective agent (COO, ELA, SUP), relying on ad-hoc formal routines (see, e.g., [15]) for subsequent process uses in the system architecture. Routines draw coloured temperature maps highlighting thermal pollution at different urban scales, and red areas are most impacting in heating terms. In particular, some buildings of the industrial seem to be the most responsible for the local rise in temperature (Figure 4). Different scales allow the information fine-tuning and the preservation of knowledge complexity for subsequent scenario stages.

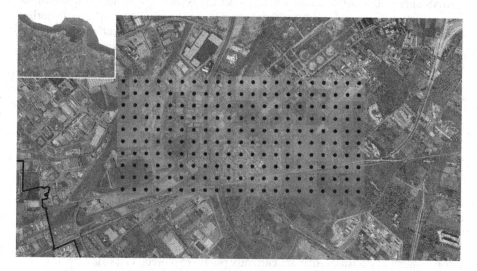

Fig. 4. Temperature survey, detail on a high-impacting area (100x100m grid)

In fact, data mapping is not only a transmission task, but rather a feature of the processing unit (ELA), elaborating data for successive scenario management. ELA normalizes temperature data, too, in order to homogenize measured values. The processing unit is also a coordinator (COO) of incoming information, to enhance the qualitative complexity of each datum by sharing additional significance. In our case, each temperature datum transmitted by SEN is normalized with the whole temperature dataset, compared and integrated with pressure, humidity, pollution, behaviours etc. datasets collected. It is also added with the technological memory of its development [3].

The knowledge elaborated by the processing unit is richer than the single datum collected by SEN. Such complex knowledge needs to be formalized in a complex protocol to be handled in the KMS. Therefore, the complex dataset is considered quantitatively but also qualitatively, in terms of features and concepts with mutual relations, so enhancing data significance in the process. The processing unit's ELE agent formalizes such causal chains of environmental features in the form of complex ontologies. Then concepts, relationships, issues and values are explicitly involved and can be managed by ad-hoc software platforms [16].

The ontology of the temperature survey works as formal data transmission pattern (T) after the processing unit's elaboration. The ontology enters the KMS and its scenario process with all ontologies originating throughout the whole MAS. At present, as mentioned, KMS architecture is not yet operational, and therefore the current case study cannot be tested thoroughly.

3 Short Discussion and Conclusions

A MAS approach to urban microclimate modelling is an awkward task because of the vast variety of natural and artificial agents acting and interacting in urban environments and ecosystems. Yet it acknowledges integrated evaluation of biotic and non-biotic environments and agents, so accessing the core dynamics and mechanics of urban ecosystems [3].

The decisions of human agents concerning building air conditioning, urban artificial materials, urban mobility and transportation, general urban supplies, industry and other productions in the city space have impact on microclimate pollution. Agents often take such micro-decisions basing either on reactive, tactical reasoning or even on strategic reasoning concerning investments and related returns. The physical architecture of such decision spaces is complex, insofar as it concerns well-structured, ill-structured, or non-structured problems and spaces. Yet, modelling is worthwhile because such tactical or strategic decisions influence environment sustainability [2]. Organization and decision theory focus on target-oriented structured environments, therefore they hardly help dealing with the multiple and conflicting goals of complex decisions in urban organizations and planning [17]. Socio-individual rational, emotional, perceptual culture and knowledge play an important role in framing such urban contextual decisions, that are currently poorly explored [17][18].

Artificial and natural entities and processes are the foundations of urban spaces and ecosystems. Therefore, technology and biology need to be integrated within a MAS-based approach, in order to achieve better understanding and modelling. Natural human and non-human agents together increasingly characterize urban spaces and ecosystems. For example, ECOURB project shows that geological (non-biotic) and biotic agents of urban creeks interact and counteract their surrounding built environment, affecting the dynamics of micro-climate and biodiversity. Proxy variables are used on order to understand and monitor such biotic/non-biotic interaction. Yet the important role of biodiversity dynamics in urban spaces and ecosystems will challenge KMS scenario analysis expectations in the next future, because of the difficulty of managing non-human biotic agents' behaviours and decisions in front of changes in urban environments.

The ECOURB MAS approach to analyze the environmental impacts of the behaviours of artificial and natural agents in urban spaces and ecosystems seem to show the need of manifold agents' organizations, roles, hierarchies and rationales to face the task complexity. A starting point in ECOURB for a MAS approach in dealing with urban spaces and ecosystems is represented by the Minsky paradigm of an agent society of distributed intelligence at any social, ecological or individual organizational level of system operation [19]. The use of ontology models has integrated such approach in order to grasp the complexity of this society of agents into manageable representation and operation systems [16]. Also, ecological mathematical modelling is used, in order to compact formal structures and synthesize a huge variety of system dynamics [15].

Finally, ECOURB confirms the convenience of using hybrid models to face the great complexity of urban spaces and ecosystems, as well as of the interactions between their inherent artificial and natural agents. Yet the assortment of behaviours and decisions in societies of urban agents needs to be integrated with more synthetic and manageable formal models of urban space and ecosystems understanding. To this aim the ECOURB research work will be largely devoted for the next future.

References

1. Lin, C.-J., Ho, T.C., Chu, H.-w., Yang, H., Mojica, M.J., Krishnarajanagar, N., Chiou, P., Hopper, J.R.: A Comparative Study of US EPA 1996 and 1999 Emission Inventories in the West Gulf of Mexico Coast Region, USA. Journal of Environmental Management 75, 303–313 (2005)
2. Reible, D.D.: Fundamentals of Environmental Engineering. Lewis-Springer, Boca Raton, FL, USA (1999)
3. Newman, P., Jennings, J.: Cities as Sustainable Ecosystems. Island Press, Melbourne (2008)
4. Ferber, J.: Multi-Agent Systems: An Introduction to Distributed Artificial Intelligence. Addison-Wesley, London (1999)
5. Lindgren, M., Bandhold, H.: Scenario Planning: The Link Between Future and Strategy. Palgrave Macmillan, London (2003)
6. Camarda, D.: Beyond citizen participation in planning: Multi-agent systems for complex decision making. In: Nunes Silva, C. (ed.) Handbook of Research on E-planning: ICTs for Urban Development and Monitoring, pp. 195–217. IGI Global, Hershey (2010)
7. Ben Youssef, A., Lahmandi-Ayed, R.: Eco-labelling, competition and environment: Endogenization of labelling criteria. Environmental and Resource Economics 41, 133–154 (2008)
8. Brenner, M., Nebel, B.: Continual Planning and Acting in Dynamic Multiagent Environments, vol. 19. Springer, US (2009)
9. Kalapanidas, E., Avouris, N.: Air quality management using a multi-agent system. Computer-Aided Civil and Infrastructure Engineering 17, 119–130 (2002)
10. Bruse, M.: Simulating human thermal comfort and resulting usage patterns of urban open spaces with a multi-agent system. In: 24th International Conference on Passive and Low Energy Architecture (PLEA), Singapore, pp. 699–706 (2007)
11. Tanimoto, J., Hagishima, A., Sagara, H.: A methodology for peak energy requirement considering actual variation of occupants' behavior schedules. Building and Environment 43, 610–619 (2008)
12. Dastani, M., van Riemsdijk, B., Hulstijn, J., Dignum, F., Meyer, J.-J.: Enacting and Deacting Roles in Agent Programming. In: Odell, J.J., Giorgini, P., Müller, J.P. (eds.) AOSE 2004. LNCS, vol. 3382, pp. 189–204. Springer, Heidelberg (2005)
13. Ciliberti, T., Terrico, D., Terrone, A.: Rilievo Satellitare delle Temperature nella Città di Bari. Academic training report, ECOURB - Politecnico di Bari (2011)
14. Anderson, L.W., Krathwohl, J. (eds.): A Taxonomy for Learning, Teaching, and Assessing: A Revision of Bloom's Taxonomy of Educational Objectives. Longman, New York (2001)

15. Brancolini, A., Buttazzo, G.: Optimal networks for mass transportation problems. ESAIM: Control, Optimisation and Calculus of Variations 11, 88–101 (2005)
16. Borri, D., Camarda, D.: Spatial ontologies in multi-agent environmental planning. In: Yearwood, J., Stranieri, A. (eds.) Technologies for Supporting Reasoning Communities and Collaborative Decision Making: Cooperative Approaches, pp. 272–295. IGI Global Information Science, Hershey (2011)
17. Simon, H.A.: Models of Bounded Rationality. The MIT Press, Cambridge (1982)
18. Borri, D., Concilio, G., Selicato, F., Torre, C.: Ethical and moral reasoning and dilemmas in evaluation processes: Perspectives for intelligent agents. In: Miller, D., Patassini, D. (eds.) Beyond Benefit-Cost Analysis: Accounting for Non-Market Values in Planning Evolution, pp. 249–277. Brookfield, Ashgate (2005)
19. Minsky, M.L.: The Emotion Machine: Commonsense Thinking, Artificial Intelligence, and the Future of the Human Mind. Simon and Schuster, New York (2006)

LabVIEW Based Cooperative Design for Control System Implementation

Witold Nocoń and Grzegorz Polaków

Silesian University of Technology,
ul. Akademicka 16,
44-100 Gliwice, Poland
{witold.nocon,grzegorz.polakow}@polsl.pl

Abstract. In this paper an object-oriented approach to the cooperative process of designing and implementing control systems is presented. Such approach promotes code reuse, code encapsulation and polymorphism, which, in relation to control systems, result in a better way of designing the system to be robust, easy to maintain and clear to analyze. Class hierarchy of system blocks and variables is presented using UML class diagram. Implementation in a graphical programming language LabVIEW is outlined.

Keywords: Object-oriented design, cooperative implementation of control systems, IEC 61131, IEC 61499.

1 Introduction

Implementation of modern control systems often requires a number of engineers to cooperate. To accommodate for those cooperation needs, a number of solutions have been proposed. Agent-based technology has received a lot of attention recently, especially in manufacturing processes [1], but also in control of continuous processes [2]. Agent-based approach is especially applicable in case of distributed control systems [3], and in other engineering applications [4]. Supervisory control and data acquisition systems (SCADA) also benefit greatly from agent approach [5]. Since in the modern control technology, distributed control systems (DCS) play a major role, the cooperative validation in DCS has been discussed [6]. Many advanced control algorithms are well suited to be implemented using those software technologies [7], [8].

2 Idea of Cooperative Control System Implementation

To facilitate cooperation between control engineers designing a distributed control system we propose utilization of an object-oriented structure of components used in the control system's synthesis. Such approach should be beneficial in the following aspects:

Y. Luo (Ed.): CDVE 2011, LNCS 6874, pp. 137–140, 2011.

- **Code reuse.** Realization of control loops for different parts of the process involves implementation of the same control algorithms. By using the object-oriented methodology, the code reuse is greatly facilitated, since it is straightforward to implement a class representing the cascade control loop with a flow control loop class as a member of this class.
- **Code encapsulation.** Because the object-oriented programming paradigm greatly supports the idea of code encapsulation, it promotes a strict specification of interfaces between sub processes, explicitly defining certain parts of code as private, thus preventing any other code from using the functionality to which access should not be allowed.
- **Polymorphism.** A safety critical control system should allow a fault tolerant operation in case of hardware or software faults. Implementing all parts of the control system in an object-oriented methodology, enables references to all parts of the process to be kept in a specified container. This enables easy implementation of "emergency stop" feature.

3 Class Definition

The development of control systems is subject to the IEC 61131 standard. The standard focuses on the technical issues of the development process. Another standard, i.e. IEC 61499, puts the emphasis on the general idea of a control system and its architecture. According to this idea, an automatic control system consists of individual components, executed in spatially distributed hardware devices.

It was decided to put some ideas of the latter standard into the practice in a revised form, so the notion of the distributed individual components served as a mechanism supporting the cooperative control system design and development. The core of the idea is the carefully designed class hierarchy, shown in the figure 1 in the form of an UML class diagram. The most significant notion is the separation of the control system modules instead of developing it as the whole. The same notion is, in some way, implemented in block diagrams widely used in the engineering domain (as in [9]). Introduction of the modularity notion allows to divide the work on the control system development among many engineers, who can thus work on the separated modules independently and simultaneously. It should be noted that the components may be of purely software nature (such as a control algorithm), or they may be realised physically in a hardware form (such as a controlled object itself).

Since the components separately developed by many engineers have to be connected into a consistent and working system, the crucial issue is the definition of the interfaces between the components. The interfaces should be unequivocal to eliminate incompatibilities caused by misunderstandings, and, at the same time, flexible enough to provide a sufficient degree of freedom for the individual collaborators. In case of the control systems the universal interface between the components has the form of variables. The IEC 61131 standard defines a wide range of data types, ordered into a hierarchical structure. A subset of the standard data types was chosen, to be included in the presented class hierarchy (Fig. 1). The proper degree of freedom for the collaborators is provided in two ways i.e. by the methods converting the data types and by the inheritance from the abstract any... classes.

For example, if the developer of a given component expects numerical data to be required by one of inputs, he may define the input to accept `any_magnitude` class. The software for the final system will compile correctly as long as any numerical variable is connected to the input. The exact data type conversion will be performed automatically by one of the overloaded `to...()` methods, defined in the abstract `any_variable` class.

Moreover, the same advantage applies not only during the system design and development, but also when the control system is running. Such flexibility is especially welcomed in the educational applications, where students have no time to agree exact interfaces, but are required to develop a control system and test it with various control algorithms. The presented approach allows students to divide the work and solve the task in a collaborative manner.

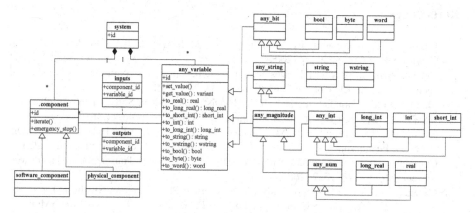

Fig. 1. UML class diagram of the proposed solution

4 LabVIEW Based Object-Oriented Design

Implementation of object-oriented methodology in LabVIEW is somewhat limited. Class data is always private, hence any call to the fields of a base class from a child class involves calling accessor methods (similar to the `get` and `set` methods in C#) of this base class. Similarly, interfaces are not currently supported in LabVIEW. Nevertheless, the presented application framework may easily be implemented using a well-known LabVIEW design pattern, known just as the **continuous loop** [10]. The structure of the algorithms stored in the collection of blocks may even be dynamically changed at run-time, if necessary. In such a case, the application may be realized using any variant of the **state machine design pattern** in LabVIEW. Therefore, the application may be well suited for the implementation of hybrid control systems that also accommodate cooperativeness of control system design and implementation [6].

5 Concluding Remarks

The system is run by iterative execution of distributed methods, which can result in certain side effects. Specifically, it is possible to construct systems of connected methods in which the results may depend on the order of blocks placed in the collection. Hence, the dependence is simply of a technical nature. This problem however is typical in distributed and parallel solutions, not just in the solution presented in this paper. For example it exhibits itself in systems built of blocks according to the IEC61499 standard. However, it is fair to assume, that in continuous control systems, the order in which blocks are connected is not critical as long as those connections make sense and sampling period in the system is sufficiently small. Nevertheless, future work should analyze this problem thoroughly.

Acknowledgments. This work was supported by the Polish Ministry of Science and Higher Education, grants no. N N514 471539 and BK-214/RAu-1/2011.

References

1. Bussmann, S., Jennings, N.R., Wooldridge, M.: Multiagent Systems for Manufacturing Control. Springer, Heidelberg (2004)
2. van Breemen, A., de Vries, T.: Design and implementation of a room thermostat using an agent-based approach. Control. Eng. Pract. 9, 233–248 (2001)
3. Maturana, F.P., Carnahan, D.L., Hall, K.H.: Distributed Agent Software for Automation. In: Nof (ed.) Springer Handbook of Automation. Springer, New York (2009)
4. McArthur, S.D.J., Davidson, E.M., Catterson, V.M., Dimeas, A.L., Hatziargyriou, N.D., Ponci, F., Funabashi, T.: Multi-agent systems for power engineering applications - Part I: Concepts, approaches, and technical challenges. IEEE Transactions on Power Systems 22(4), 1743–1752 (2007)
5. Metzger, M., Polakow, G.: A Study on Appropriate Plant Diagram Synthesis for User-Suited HMI in Operating Control. In: Forbrig, P., Paternò, F. (eds.) HCSE/TAMODIA 2008. LNCS, vol. 5247, pp. 246–254. Springer, Heidelberg (2008)
6. Choiński, D., Metzger, M., Nocoń, W., Polaków, G.: Cooperative Validation in Distributed Control Systems Design. In: Luo, Y. (ed.) CDVE 2007. LNCS, vol. 4674, pp. 280–289. Springer, Heidelberg (2007)
7. Metzger, M.: Fast-mode real-time simulator for the wastewater treatment process. Water Science and Technology 30, 191–197 (1994)
8. Nocoń, W., Metzger, M.: Predictive Control of Decantation in Batch Sedimentation Process. AICHE Journal 56, 3279–3283 (2010)
9. Polaków, G., Metzger, M.: Web-based visualization of student cooperation during distributed laboratory experimentation. In: Luo, Y. (ed.) CDVE 2009. LNCS, vol. 5738, pp. 317–324. Springer, Heidelberg (2009)
10. Blume, P.A.: LabVIEW Style Book. Prentice Hall, New Jersey (2007)

Improving Collaboration in the Construction Industry through Context-Aware Web Services

Jack C.P. Cheng and Moumita Das

Department of Civil and Environmental Engineering,
The Hong Kong University of Science and Technology
{cejcheng,mdas}@ust.hk

Abstract. Collaboration technologies have been increasingly used for supporting the requirements of a multi-disciplinary construction project team in recent years. In particular, web services technology has been leveraged in the construction industry for distributed communication and information management through message exchanges. However, the current standardized web services are unsuitable for typical construction information, which is large in magnitude and diverse in scope. This paper presents our proposed context aware web service framework that uses standardized ontologies to facilitate efficient and faster exchange of construction information in real time. This paper also presents an example scenario illustrating the collaborative environment facilitated with the proposed web service framework.

Keywords: Building information exchange, Construction Collaboration Technology, Context Awareness, Building Information Modeling (BIM), Web Services Technology.

1 Introduction

The construction industry is fragmented and information dependent in nature. Fragmentation hinders collaboration and therefore affects the productivity of the overall project. In addition, construction information is often diverse and the stakeholders involved in a construction project have different backgrounds in terms of expertise, education, computer knowledge, and working environment.

Web service frameworks have been leveraged in the construction industry for applications such as supply chain integration [1] and interoperability in electronic product catalogues [2]. SOAP (Simple Object Access Protocol) and WSDL (Web Service Description Language), developed by the World Wide Web Consortium (W3C), are the standards that facilitate communication between individual web service units through the exchange of XML messages. Although technologies like Message Transmission Optimization Mechanism (MTOM) supported by Microsoft WSE 3.0 (Web Services Enhancement) exist for sending large quantities of data (in multi-gigabytes), the structure of the current web services is simple and is not sufficient to manage the complex information stored in building models efficiently.

Y. Luo (Ed.): CDVE 2011, LNCS 6874, pp. 141–144, 2011.
© Springer-Verlag Berlin Heidelberg 2011

To overcome these shortcomings, in this paper we propose an ontology based context aware web service framework. Building information modeling (BIM) ontologies like Industrial Foundation Classes (IFC), CIMSteel Integration Standards (CIS/2), and Green Building XML (gbXML) are used in the framework to define the structure of building models which can be shared among different parties according to their access rights. In this way, all parties see only one "version of truth" and the parties can collaborate more efficiently, leading to saving in time, labor, and money.

2   Background

The application of context awareness is catching up in the construction industry in recent years [3]. Context from the perspective of the service client or service providers could be the client's location, hardware and software configuration, profile information, and connection preferences. Ontologies are used for structuring and specifying the context information being exchanged. BIM ontology like IFC defines the building objects, their properties, and the inter-relationship between them. The use of BIM ontology could make information standardized in format and therefore facilitate information exchange in an efficient, multi-directional manner. Due to this, exchange of the entire building model is not needed; instead, exchanging only a part of the model is sufficient to make additions and modifications to the building model. It makes the data exchange lighter and more secure.

3   Proposed Web Service Framework

As illustrated in Fig. 1, the proposed web service framework consists of a three-tier architecture. Each of these tiers is a group of web services with specific functionality. The individual web services are orchestrated using the BPEL standard (Business Process Execution Language).

The framework accepts three inputs for processing the requests – structured data, modification command, and context data. The structured data can be parts of a building model in standardized formats like IFC and CIS/2, or distinct values like the location coordinates and dimension. The modification command specifies the type of modification intended to be performed to a particular building object. The context information describes the end user characteristics such as location, role, and software environment. Once the first tier of the framework receives these inputs, the request is routed to the respective web service in the Data Mapping Tier according to the type of the structured data. This layer classifies the modification command into addition operation, deletion operation, or modification operation (e.g. changing location and/or dimensions), and routes the control to the respective web service unit in the Model Editing Tier. In this tier, through a complex series of operations, the updated building information model is outputted. Logging information of the modifications including the user, modification command, and the respective version of building model is stored in an update log table in a database.

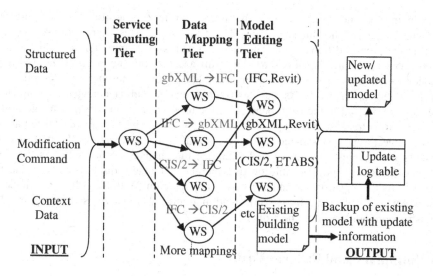

Fig. 1. Context aware web service framework

4 Example Scenario

This section presents an example scenario, as illustrated in Fig. 2, which demonstrates the use of the proposed framework to add walls in a building model. In this scenario, the designer, site engineer, contractor, and owner in a construction project could submit the wall addition command on the Internet using a web browser as the front end. The front end requires the users to login. Different people may have different access rights and therefore different available commands in the framework.

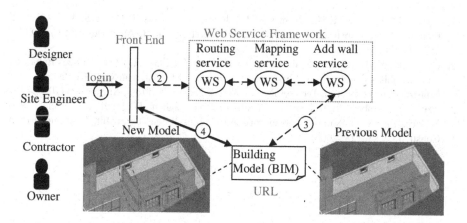

Fig. 2. Schematic diagram showing the collaboration between construction parties with the use of the proposed web service framework

Depending on the access rights, the users can make modifications or just get information out of the building model. The front end invokes the routing web service unit in the proposed framework. The mapping web service unit and the wall addition web service unit are then invoked. The wall addition unit connects to the building model which is located in the server and makes changes through API (application programming interfaces). As the central building model is changed, the updated version is reflected in the front page of all the users in real time. Every change in the model can be tracked in the update log table and all the users may be notified about the change through automated emailing system. Upon notification, the parties may discuss the changes if required and authorize the changes accordingly. As the web service framework is accessible on the Internet, with the required inputs, it can be invoked by the construction end users from any location. With the collaboration using the framework, rework due to information duplication which is common in the construction industry could be reduced.

5 Summary and Future Work

The proposed framework, which uses context awareness and web services technology, promotes collaboration by centralizing the data and therefore minimizing miscommunication among construction project teams. The scenario presents the wall addition using the proposed framework. Modification of other building objects like windows, doors, and floors can be performed similarly. However, since the representation of geometry and location varies for different building objects, further work is required in this area. Furthermore, in the future, the mapping between the building ontologies in the framework may be done by semantic approach rather than driven by manual rules.

References

1. Cheng, J.C.P., Law, K.H., Bjornsson, H., Jones, A., Sriram, R.D.: A Service Oriented Framework for Construction Supply Chain Integration. Int. J. Automation in Constr. 19, 245–260 (2009)
2. Kong, S.C.W., Li, H., Liang, Y., Hung, T., Anumba, C., Chen, Z.: Web Services Enhanced Interoperable Construction Products Catalogue. In: International Conference for Construction Information Technology, pp. 343–352. Elsevier Press, Amsterdam (2004)
3. Aziz, Z., Anumba, C.J., Ruikar, D., Carrillo, P., Bouchlaghem, D.: Intelligent Wireless Web Services for Construction–A Review of the Enabling Technologies. Int. J. Automation in Constr. 15, 113–123 (2006)

From Collaborative Business Practices to User's Adapted Visualization Services: Towards a Usage-Centered Method Dedicated to the AEC Sector

Gilles Halin[1], Sylvain Kubicki[2], Conrad Boton[1,2], and Daniel Zignale[1,2]

[1] FRE MAP-CRAI, Research Centre in Architecture and Engineering,
2 rue Bastien-Lepage B.P. 40435 - 54001 Nancy Cedex, Nancy, France
`Gilles.Halin@crai.archi.fr`
[2] Henri Tudor Public Research Centre,
29, avenue John F. Kennedy, Luxembourg-Kirchberg, Luxembourg
`{Sylvain.Kubicki,Conrad.Boton,Daniel.Zignale}@tudor.lu`

Abstract. Visualization of the cooperation context is an important issue, especially when applied to complex and unstable collective activities, as it is the case in the field of Architecture, Engineering and Construction (AEC). With the aim of assisting cooperative construction projects it is important to propose business services and user views adapted to user's business requirements. This paper presents the concept of "adapted visualization service" and a usage-centered method that enables to design visualization services adapted to actor's business needs.

Keywords: collaborative practice, visualization services, adapted visualization, usage-centered method, cooperative context, business requirement.

1 Introduction

Service-oriented groupware systems supporting the cooperative activities are emerging. They propose IT services that can be used by all the actors during projects of a significant size. Most of these 'large projects' use this type of platform to improve communication between stakeholders. The organization of the actors involved in these projects tends to make uniform the methods of work and the resources management. In most cases, "custom-made" software solutions are implemented and used efficiently in the framework of these contexts of durable cooperation between organizations. However such standardized methods are not common in Architecture, Engineering and Construction (AEC) industry [1].

Indeed, AEC projects involve temporarily teams of heterogeneous actors (architects, engineers, contractors, etc.) able to respond to the customer's requirements. Each of these heterogeneous firms has its own internal processes, methods and IT infrastructures. Then cooperative activities in the AEC sector are different from one project to another. Each project generates its own cooperative context, i.e. a set of specific stakeholders, particular processes or communication practices.

Y. Luo (Ed.): CDVE 2011, LNCS 6874, pp. 145–153, 2011.

Visualization of such cooperation context is an important issue, especially when applied to complex and unstable collective activities, as it is the case in the field of AEC. In order to consolidate the cooperation context, it is important to propose business services and user views adapted to user's business requirements. Therefore, the concept of "business visualization service" is developed in order to take into account such requirements in service systems developments. Our main hypothesis is that visualization in services systems user interfaces have to fit actors' usages. Indeed, actors have specific practices according to their roles in an activity.

This approach suggests a usage-centered method to design Adapted Visualization Services (AVS), describing collaborative practices, usages, and visualization services, and the relationships between their concepts. This method, inspired from UI design methods from software engineering [2] or HCI domains [3], integrates an innovative visualization service design process which guides the AVS configuration according to the identification of a set of collaborative practices needed in a collaborative project.

2   Towards a Method to Design Adapted Visualization Services

To design adapted visualization services for each actor business needs in a collaborative tool, a method based on a 4-steps process is proposed (Fig. 1). Each step of the method is supported by appropriate meta-models. Indeed, Model Driven Engineering approach recommends the use of meta-models to define domain languages, thus each model has to be conformed to its meta-model [4,5].

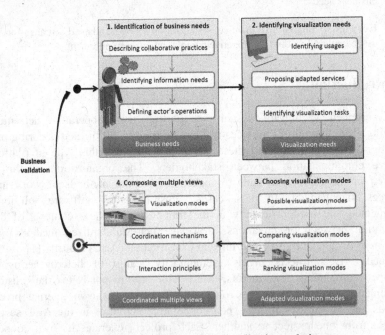

Fig. 1. Method to compose adapted visualization techniques

2.1   Identifying Actor's Business Needs (Step 1)

The first step identifies the business needs of actors. This consists in formalizing the collaborative practices and decomposing them in more role-specific practices. Knowing these practices helps to better define the business needs. Collaborative Practices (CPs) are defined as the behaviors of groups of actors (at least two) working together in various organizational situations according to business objectives [6]. These objectives are related to the AEC project requirements. Then, such CPs can be repeatable until the objectives achievement. CPs are decomposed focusing on each actor and defining their own practices: the Individual Practices (IPs). Each IP is defined by a business individual goal and composed of several Operations. Finally, usages - defined by an instrumental nature - confront actors to specific tools which support their operations. Each usage has its own context depending on the device used, its usual localization, or its frequency... (Fig 2).

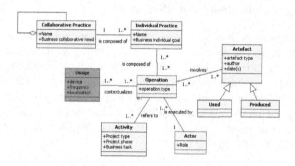

Fig. 2. Usage Meta-Model (UMM)

The Usage Meta-Model (UMM) characterizes this description. The concept of usage defines the context of execution of business operations (device used, localization, frequency...). The aim is the identification of standards operations performed in business activities, like "share", "consult", "create", "modify", "require"...One can see in the UMM which actors are responsible of each operation. The actors are defined by their business role in the project. The UMM also precises which artefacts are used or produced (i.e. documents like plans, meeting reports but also objects like materials or not formalized artefacts like reactions or validations). These artefacts can be characterized by their author(s) and some related dates (date of creation, modification, sharing...). Finally, operations are related to project types, phases and tasks. All these elements describe the business specificities that have to be considered.

The particularity of this approach is that the business-related concepts (actors, artifacts, activities) are already identified in a domain model, i.e. the Cooperative Context Meta-Model (CCMM) of a construction project [5]. There is no need to redefine them. A part of this CCMM illustrated in fig.3 represents how business-related concepts (here the concept of artefact) are described.

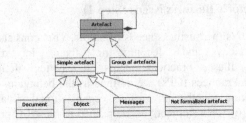

Fig. 3. The artifact concept characterized in the cooperative context meta-model

Based on the meta-models defined, each collaborative situation can be described accurately. The second step of the method consists of defining visualization tasks for each role-specific operations and corresponding usages identified in a CP.

2.2 Identifying Visualization Needs (Step 2)

When the collaborative practices are identified and decomposed into standard operations with their related usages, the corresponding visualization needs can be identified. Indeed, this is very important in order to adapt visualization services that will be provided to support actor's needs. In our specific context, visualization needs are the visualization tasks and interactions that a user will need to perform in front of a computer-supported tool. Visualization tasks are the "analytic and exploratory tasks that he might need or want to perform on the data" [6]. A visualization tasks meta-model is proposed (Fig 4), relying on [9].

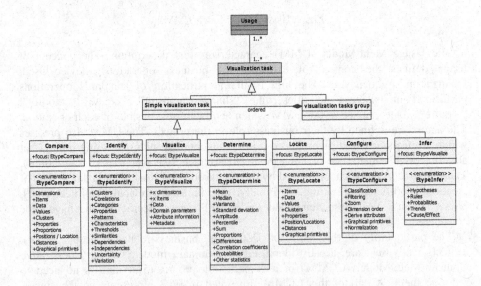

Fig. 4. User's visualization tasks meta-model

2.3 Choosing Adapted Visualization Modes (Step 3)

As one knows, many visualization techniques can exist to represent the same information. For example, both Gantt chart and PERT network can depict an activity planning. Whenever possible, we will appeal to business view. "Business views" are the visualization modes that practitioners use in their daily work. The purpose of this step is to choose the most adapted views for given usages. Firstly, it is useful to describe possible visualization modes in order to compare them. To this end, a business view meta-model is proposed (Fig. 5). That will help in describing possible business views according to the same formalism.

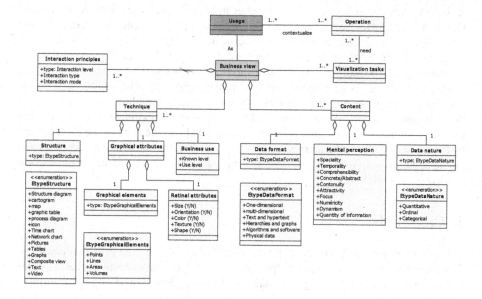

Fig. 5. Business view meta-model

But even if this description is necessary, it is not sufficient to choose the most adapted among the possible visualization modes. It is then useful to be able to rank them. A ranking system is proposed and enables to attribute a score for each business view.

This *adaptation score* (*As*) is calculated for each actor and each Usage with the formula below. The business view properties (fig.5) are used as criteria. The Meta-Model characterized these criteria and the matching between Business view and Usage through the *As*.

$$As = \frac{\sum_{i=1}^{n} Nc_i}{n} \quad \text{with} \quad Nc_i = \frac{\sum_{j=1}^{m} P_j}{m}$$

As is the average of the *Nci* and n is the number of criteria while m is the number of proprieties for a criterion *i*. The score (Nc_i) of a criterion i is then the average of its properties relevance (P_j) scores according to a visualization requirement. The visualization requirement is both an information need and a need for visualization tasks. The properties relevance scores (P_j) are -1, 0 or 1 depending on whether the property *j* is clearly unsuited, poorly adapted or well suited to the sub-practice. Each Nc_ivalue may vary between -1 and 1.

2.4 Composing Adapted Visualization Services (Step 4)

When the most adapted visualization modes are chosen for each business need of an actor, it is then possible to put them together in order to propose coordinated multiple views. An Adapted Visualization Service (AVS) is a set of adapted services proposed with appropriate coordinated multiple views to display information. So, for each business role, the appropriate coordination mechanisms and interaction principles will be determined. Exploration techniques and coordination control are two of the fundamental areas of coordinated and multiple views [8]. The utility of multiple coordinated views comes from users' ability to express multidimensional queries through simple forms of interaction [11]. To compose coordinated views, the 2x3 taxonomy of multiple window coordination from [11] and the state of the art proposed by [8] are some interesting starting points. So, relied on these literature references and our specific needs, work is ongoing in order to propose an adapted visualization service meta-model.

3 Case Study

Eleven Collaborative Practices [12] were distinguished during the principal phases of a construction project realization (preparation, design and execution phases). This distinction has emerged through an analysis of project descriptions and brainstorming with professionals. Depending on the context, each Collaborative Practice can be specified and divided in sub-practices. In this case study the CP related to the "execution preparation and management" is considered. This CP gathers site scheduling, material management, feedback formulation from contractors, etc. Attention will particularly be focused on the "site scheduling" collaborative sub-practice.

Table 1 considers both step 1 and 2 of our method. It represents the "site scheduling" collaborative sub-practice, decomposed in Individual Practices and Operations with their related Usages. Then, it defines corresponding visualization tasks.

When visualization tasks are known, possible visualization techniques comparison is needed in order to choose the most adapted one according to these needs. In instance, for the individual practice "Activities sequencing", actor need to visualize the dates, the activities durations and a building representation. The building representation could be a 2D plan or a 3D representation (Fig. 6).

Table 1. Site scheduling collaborative practice and related usages and visualization tasks

Collaborative practice	Individual practices	Operations	Usages	Visualization tasks
Collaborative site scheduling	Building elements listing	Consult elements pre-list	- Architect consults documents from his office	Visualize (focus: *data*)
		Look for appropriate elements	- Architect edits listings from his office	Locate (focus: *items*)
		Create elements listing	- Architect shares listings information from his office	Configure (focus: *classification*)
	Activities definition	Consult activities pre-list	- Supervisor consults documents and items from his office	Visualize (focus: *data*)
		Consult building elements	- Supervisor edits listings from his office	Locate (focus: *items*)
		Look for appropriate activities	- Supervisor shares listings information from his office	Identify (focus: *correlations*)
		Create activities listing		Configure (focus: *classification*)
	Activities duration estimation	Consult activities	- Sub-contractor consults items from his office	Visualize (focus: *data*)
		Understand activities consistency	- Sub-contractor draws conclusions from his office	Configure (focus: *filtering*) Determine (focus: *means*)
		Estimate activities duration	- Sub-contractor shares activities duration from his office	Infer (focus: *hypotheses*)
	Activities sequencing	Consult activities and durations	- Contractor consults documents from his office	Visualize (focus: *data*)
		Study relationships and dependencies among activities	- Contractor looks for information from his office	Identify (focus: *correlations*) Identify (focus: *dependencies*)
		Verify conflicts	- Contractor edits planning information from his office	Infer (focus: *trends*)
		Associate start/end dates	- Contractor shares conflicts and dates information from his office	Configure (focus: *classification*)
		Define site planning		Configure (focus: *normalization*)
	Schedule development	Consult activities listing	- Supervisor consults documents and items from his office	Visualize (focus: *data*)
		Consult actors listing	- Supervisor edits planning information from his office	Visualize (focus: *data*)
		Associate actors and activities	- Supervisor shares project plan information from his office	Identify (focus: *correlations*)
		Include planning		Infer (focus: *trends*)
		Realize project plan		Configure (focus: *classification*)

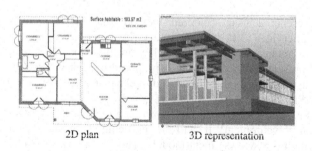

2D plan   3D representation

Fig. 6. Proposal for building representation modes

After describing them, their adaptation score (As) can be calculated following the step 3. Results for the present case study are represented in table 2. The score in this table are not validated yet and future works will focus on it and, more generally, on practitioner's evaluation of business views according to their experience. However, the example in table 2 can show that the 3D representation is more adapted than the 2D plan.

Table 2. Calculation of visualization modes adaptation score

Criteria	Proprieties	3D rep.	2D plan
Technique	Structure	0	-1
	Graphical elements	1	0
	Retinal attributes	1	0
	Business use	0	1
	Nc_1	0,5	0
Content	Data Format	1	1
	Mental perception	0	-1
	Data nature	0	-1
	Nc_2	0,33	-0,33
Interaction principles	Interaction level	1	-1
	Interaction type	0	-1
	Nc_3	0,5	-1
Visualization tasks	Visualisation tasks	1	0
	Nc_4	1	0
	As	0,58	- 0,33

Same work for each other usages will lead to know all the needed adapted visualization modes for each actor. In the last step, interactions and coordination mechanism will be associated in order to build adapted visualization services for all the actors.

4   Conclusion

The paper presents a usage-centered method that enables to design "Adapted Visualization Services". It considers actor's business Usages related to the "Collaborative Practices" (CP) in which they are involved. The models that support each step are presented and a formula is proposed to rank visualization modes. This method is illustrated through a case study related to the site scheduling business Collaborative Practice.

In the future, focus will be on the fourth step of the method which is still in an early stage of development. It will be particularly formalized by proposing a coordinated multiple views meta-model. The advantage of this model-driven approach is the possibility to support it by software tools. The design of such tools that will support the method will allow us to 1) extend it to other case studies and 2) confront it to professionals in order to validate both the method and the final propositions in terms of Visualization Modes. The possibility to represent graphically the CPs through diagrams is explored using the Eclipse environment and particularly the GMF framework (Graphical Modeling Framework).

Acknowledgment. This article is supported by the National Research Fund, Luxembourg.

References

[1] Nitithamyong, P.: Web-based construction project management systems: how to make them successful? Automation in Construction 13, 491–506 (2004)

[2] Constantine, L.L., Lockwood, L.D.: Usage-centered engineering for Web applications. IEEE Software 19, 42–50 (2002)

[3] Coutaz, J., Calvary, G.: HCI and Software Engineering: Designing for User Interface Plasticity. In: Sears, A., Jacko, J.A. (eds.) The Human Computer Interaction Handbook, pp. 1107–1125. Lawrence Erlbaum Associates, Mahwah (2008)

[4] Favre, J.M.: Towards a basic theory to model model driven engineering. In: 3rd Workshop in Software Model Engineering, WiSME, Citeseer (2004)

[5] Sottet, J.S., Calvary, G., Favre, J.M., Coutaz, J., Demeure, A.: Towards mapping and model transformation for consistency of Plastic User Interfaces. In: Computer Human Interaction, Workshop on The Many Faces of Consistency in Cross-platform Design, Citeseer, pp. 9–12 (2006)

[6] Schmidt, K.: Cooperative Work and Coordinative Practices. In: Computer Supported Cooperative Work, pp. 3–27. Springer, London (2011)

[7] Kubicki, S., Bignon, J.C., Halin, G., Humbert, P.: Assistance to building construction coordination – towards a multi-view cooperative platform. ITcon 11, 565–586 (2006)

[8] Valiati, E.R.A., Pimenta, M.S., Freitas, C.M.D.S.: A taxonomy of tasks for guiding the evaluation of multidimensional visualizations. In: BELIV 2006: Proceedings of the 2006 AVI Workshop on Beyond Time and Errors, pp. 1–6. ACM, New York (2006)

[9] Boton, C., Kubicki, S., Halin, G.: Method to design coordinated multiple views adapted to user's business requirements in 4D collaborative tools in AEC. In: Proceedings of 15th IEEE International Conference on Information Visualization, London, United Kingdom) (2011)

[10] Roberts, J.C.: State of the Art: Coordinated & Multiple Views in Exploratory Visualization. In: Fifth International Conference on Coordinated and Multiple Views in Exploratory Visualization (CMV 2007), pp. 61–71 (July 2007)

[11] Wang Baldonado, M.Q., Woodruff, A., Kuchinsky, A.: Guidelines for using multiple views in information visualization. In: AVI 2000: Proceedings of the Working Conference on Advanced Visual Interfaces, pp. 110–119. ACM, New York (2000)

[12] North, C., Shneiderman, B.: A Taxonomy of Multiple Window Coordinations, University of Maryland, College Park, Dept. of Computer Science (1997)

[13] Zignale, D., Kubicki, S., Ramel, S., Halin, G.: A model-based method for the design of services in collaborative business environments. In: Proceedings of IESS 1.1: Second International Conference on Exploring Services Sciences, Geneva, Switzerland, p. 15 (2011)

An Augmented Reality Application Framework for Complex Equipment Collaborative Maintenance

Wei Wang, Yue Qi, and QingXing Wang

State Key Laboratory of Virtual Reality Technology and Systems,
Beihang University, Beijing 100191, China
{wangwei09,qy,wangqx}@vrlab.buaa.edu.cn

Abstract. Complex equipment maintenance process usually involves massive amount of components. It requires collaborative manipulation by many technicians. Therefore, traditional maintenance is difficult to meet the needs of these processes. *Augmented reality* technology has been demonstrated as an useful solution. This paper introduces an augmented reality application framework applicable to various complex equipments. In the framework, the difference of different equipments maintenance processes is extracted as *task-driven work flow*, and the functional interfaces of augmented reality are the collective base. We can create a new application as long as we can place the work flow and associated virtual resources within the application. Context-aware tutorial information and hands-free voice commands are provided in the generated applications by the framework. By using the application, the multi-user cooperative operations are well supported. We demonstrate our framework by showing the applications for key aircraft components. We also present a distributed virtual learning tool based on the framework.

Keywords: Augmented Reality, Task-driven Work Flow, Collaborative Maintenance.

1 Introduction

Maintenance is essential for industry products maintaining performance and extending lifetime. However, the maintenance process of complex equipment usually involves massive amount of components, and requires many technicians adhering to stringent cumbersome guidelines. Therefore, inconspicuous operation errors and long maintenance terms are inevitable. Recent statistics [1] on aero accidents demonstrate that many accidents occur due to improper maintenance, and the proportion is up to 30 percent according to GE's experiential statistics on commercial aircraft engines.

Traditional maintenance is difficult to meet more and more complex industry products. And augmented reality(AR) is an useful technology to build advanced interfaces using interactive and wearable visualization systems to implement new methods to display tutorial information for maintenance technicians [4].

Y. Luo (Ed.): CDVE 2011, LNCS 6874, pp. 154–161, 2011.

Neumann [5] also figured out how AR techniques could benefit the tasks of maintenance by interacting with human. Nevertheless, developing a particular augmented reality application for each complex equipment will be exhausting.

Our main contribution is an augmented reality application framework for various complex equipments collaborative maintenance. In the framework, we extract the respective difference of all the maintenance processes as task-driven work flow, and the augmented reality functional interfaces are the collective base. A new AR application will be generated as long as we can place the work flow and associated virtual resources within the application. Rich context-aware multimedia and 3D virtual information are displayed in the generated applications according to users' voice commands, based on the task-driven work flows. What is more, the multi-user cooperative operations are well supported in the framework.

2 Related Work

In the industrial field, many AR applications have been developed for assisting maintenance since the idea of AR systems was presented in the early 1900's. Caudell and Mizell [2] constructed wire harness for airplanes such as Boeing 747s with an AR system instead of real boards, manuals and paper templates. Feiner et al. [3] at Columbia developed a laser printer maintenance application to introduce and demonstrate the idea of knowledge-based augmented reality for maintenance assistance. Regenbrecht [9] introduced an augmented reality system for automotive maintenance, while Crescenzio [10] applied AR technique in aircraft maintenance.

Conventional augmented reality applications usually focus on creating a tool or system for a certain type of products, while all the AR applications generally share the same functional foundation that is the AR functional interfaces, including interacting, rendering and tracking etc. According to previous work [5], all kinds of multimedia information and 3D virtual objects displaying can provide more intuitive understanding than conventional ways to users. Compared to [13], we adopt a relatively simple hand-free voice-command interactive approach in the framework. The typical tracking method is using special pattern images as optical markers [12]. Such methods are simple and efficient, but it's obvious that placing markers seems to hinder the effective implementation of AR systems. Crescenzio [10] described markerless camera pose estimation based on matching feature images, which cannot ensure accuracy and speed simultaneously. Wang et al. [7] used infrared projector to project infrared markers onto the surface of equipments for recognition, which was swift and stable, but it also had constraints: equipments have to stay still during the entire maintenance process, and the dimension of the workspace is limited by the amount of cameras they used. In this paper, a mixed tracking approach integrating infrared and optical methods is employed to accurately estimate the pose of concerned objects, including participants, equipments etc.

Complex equipment maintenance process usually requires multiple participants manipulating cooperatively, so multi-user paradigm should be taken into consideration while developing these AR applications. Ismail [8] presented the idea of collaborative AR which allowed for multi-user simultaneously sharing the real world surrounding them and a virtual world. Our framework also well-support multiple collaborative operators.

3   Our Framework

The architecture of our framework is shown as Fig. 1, which is mainly composed of three parts: the task-driven work flow, the augmented reality functional interfaces and the multi-user management server. The work flow represents the respective process of different AR applications as well as different maintenance processes, while the collective AR functional interfaces contain mixed tracking, rendering engine, interaction, network transmission and work flow analysis.

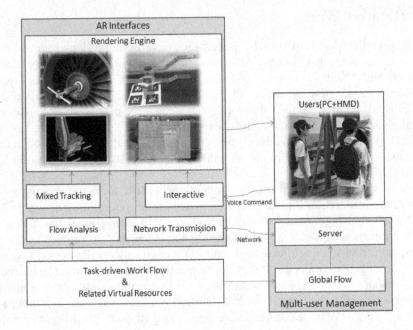

Fig. 1. Framework Architecture Diagram

A Head-Mounted Display(HMD) which is connected to a wearable PC, is requisite to users for watching the display, including the real scene and the virtual overplays. Participants interact with the applications through voice-commands that are pre-defined based on the maintenance events, such as turning on or off 3D animations, jumping to next or previous step, switching the tutorial information, and so on.

The framework employs distributed client/server structure to manage and synchronize the participants, and a communication protocol is defined based on the maintenance events.

3.1   Task-Driven Work Flow

As the types of complex equipment are greatly various, it is unreasonable that developing a particular augmented reality application for each type. We realize that the difference of different maintenance processes can be extracted as the task-driven work flows, and the same part can be interpreted as the common functional interfaces. So we can create new applications by replacing the task-driven work flows and related virtual resources.

Every maintenance process can be expressed as a sequence of tasks, and every task can be further divided into a sequence of steps, whose context relationship is serial, parallel or collaborative. The serial steps must be carried out in serial sequence while the parallel steps can be executed simultaneously. The collaborative steps are composed of several serial or parallel steps in some specific order, and require multiple participants manipulating cooperatively, while serial and parallel steps can also be completed by one person. The above "process-task-step" hierarchical depiction of maintenance processes is defined as the task-driven work flow. With maintenance experts' help, we perform the flow of the aviator seat maintenance process as Fig. 2. The task1 is composed of a sequence of serial steps, and in the task "Parts check" step1 and step2 are parallel while step7 is step6's cooperative subsequence.

When designing these work flows, we should integrate practical experiences. For instance, the potential error risks provided by maintenance experts will become useful warning information(Fig. 1), showed before every step in the maintenance process.

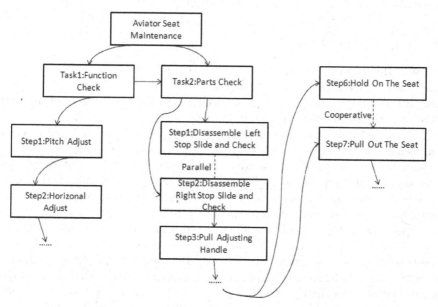

Fig. 2. The work flow of aviator seats maintenance

3.2   Multiple Operators Management

Towards the operators, the collective real scene is captured by their own camera. In the framework, we set a distributed server to control the process and synchronize all the members according to the global flow that is the subset of the task-driven(local) work flow. The global flow only contains the context sequence and relationship depiction of all the steps, while the local work flow also contains the detail information of every step, such as the path of related virtual resources, warning information, and so on. If the process only has one participant, we can also manage it by local without the server.

The server assigns the steps to participants over the network according to the global flow. Participants that received assignment are permitted and required to complete the step, meanwhile the others becoming aiders or observers synchronously, and give feedback to the server when they finish the step. When all participants are idle, the server assigns steps to participants. Otherwise, it will wait. Serial steps will be assigned to one, while parallel steps will be assigned to different ones simultaneously. Cooperative steps are organized with some specific order, and based on the above assignment rules the server assigns the subsequent steps after receiving the current steps' feedback.

In the maintenance processes, the crew members need keep synchronized. Besides all the clients having the same local work flows, the server notifies the current status when it executes assignment. When receiving the notice from the server, the client updates their status. What is more, when some clients are busy as well as the server being waiting, the busy clients will broadcast the transformation that need to share with the other clients. Therefore, we ensure the synchronization of the crew members throughout the whole process.

3.3   AR Functional Interfaces

Tacking Interface. The tracking quality directly affect the intuition of 3D augmented reality applications. We implement a mixed tracking interface with both optical and infrared methods to accurately estimate the 6 degree-of-freedom (DOF) pose of all the concerned objects.

The NaturalPoint OptiTrack infrared tracking tool [11] is employed as chief approach in the framework, while other accurate realtime tracking methods are the effective substitute. Retroreflective markers are attached to the target objects, allowing them to be tracked in full 6DOF by the infrared tool. However, to track the operator's view, a calibration step is required to pre-compute the transformation matrix between the attached retroreflective marker and the camera. Especially for binocular HMD, both the transformation matrices of the two cameras are needed. In the calibration step, we attach another retroreflective marker to a special pattern image, and gain the view matrix of the calibrated camera in the coordinate system of the special image, and directly measure the transformation from the new marker to the origin of the image. We can get the transformation matrix between the two retroreflective markers with OptiTrack. The product of above matrices is the target matrix.

For some special target objects, like "help browser", a 2D image/vedio player (Fig. 1) with fixed spatial position, optical tracking methods based on special image patterns are more convenient, such as ARToolkitPlus [12].

Rendering Engine. The rendering engine is employed to display the real environment captured by the cameras and all the virtual objects, including text, image, video, 3D model and 3D animation. Towards binocular HMD, we split two viewports for rendering the corresponding contents of the two cameras. The engine obtains virtual resources according to the result of the flow analysis, and accepts voice commands to adjust the rendering status based on the output of mixed tracking interface.

We display 2D information such image and video as texture images mapping to a virtual screen. 3D virtual objects including models and animations are overlayed on the correct position with DirectX3D or OpenGL. The virtual scene is organized with Scene Graph [14], and a resource manager is created to preload some resources to avert "loading data" delay and avoid resource objects generated repeatedly. To improve the speed of rendering, the framework supports Level Of Detail(LOD) and occlusion culling techniques [6].

Interactive Interface. The applications' behaviors are controlled by voice commands instead of keyboard-mouse actions, which free both hands of users to take the maintenance operations. Certain instructions from the pre-defined voice commands will be identified, and then activated according to the current maintenance context like which step in the task currently, status of virtual objects etc, and enqueued the instruction queue, and finally interpreted as transition in pre-defined state machine of the target object, leading to corresponding activities such as switching assistance information, reporting maintenance status, and so on.

4   Results and Discussion

4.1   AR Applications

We create the AR applications for jet engine and aviator seat quickly through designing the work flow and related resources. The jet engine application has been successfully applied in the jet engine course. Most students express it is impressive in improving learning outcomes, and ten students who are divided into five groups because of two persons' cooperative steps, are invited to measure the practical effect in the initial ten steps of the engine maintenance process after familiar with the application. Fig. 3(a) shows the average operation time reduced to 15mins from 21mins, and the average errors decreased to 0.4 from 3.2. The application for aviator seat has been tested by three technicians in a factory workshop, and Fig. 3(b) demonstrates that the average workload rate is low and the effect rate is high. The reason of different impact on maintenance speed in the two experiments is their different technical background. The students are novices, while the technicians are skilled. The above results demonstrate that our framework has great applicability and utility.

4.2 Expanded Application

Generally, a novice need spend a long term for learning until getting the certificates. With extending the network transmission interfaces, we can create an intuitive assembly/disassembly teaching tool, combining with a virtual assembly/disassembly software. Teachers use the virtual software to control the whole process, while students synchronously apply the AR application to observe and experience the procedures. Fig. 3(c) shows the virtual software interface and Fig. 3(d) is the case that two students are learning.

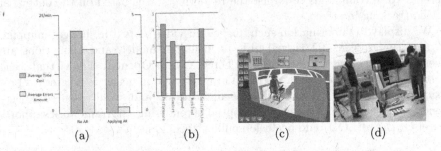

(a)   (b)   (c)   (d)

Fig. 3. (a)Jet Engine Application Measurement;(b)Aviator Seat Application Measurement;(c)Virtual Assembly/Disassembly Software;(d)Students Learning

5 Conclusions

We have explored an augmented reality framework for complex equipment collaborative maintenance. The framework expresses the maintenance processes with task-driven work flows integrating practical experiences, and rich context-aware multimedia and 3D virtual information are displayed according to voice commands. What is more, the multi-user synchronized cooperative operations are well supported. In our experiments, we demonstrate that the fast generated applications for key aircraft components really improved the maintenance efficiency. The framework also has great expanded applications. Combining with a virtual assembly/disassembly software, we create a distributed intuitive learning tool, which plays a significant role in training and teaching.

In this paper, we focus on applicability and utility, and ignore the rendering reality of virtual scene. It is known to all that the realistic rendering of virtual scene has large magnitude computation so that being far from realtime, because the complex materials and detailed natural illumination. As future work, we consider exploring fast realistic rendering methods to further improve the intuition of augmented reality.

Acknowledgments. This work was supported by the National Natural Science Foundation of China(Grant No.60773153), the National High Technology Research and Development Program of China(Grant No.2009AA012102), and the Beijing Natural Science Foundation(Grant No.4102037).

References

1. Statistical Summary of Commercial Jet Airplane Accidents: Worldwide Operations, 1959-2009, http://www.boeing.com/news/techissues
2. Caudell, T., Mizell, D.: Augmented reality: an application of heads-up display technology to manual manufacturing processes. 2, 659–669 (1992)
3. Feiner, S., Macintyre, B., Seligmann, D.: Knowledge-based augmentd reality. Commun. ACM 36(7), 53–62 (1993)
4. Haritos, T., Macchiarella, N.D.: A Mobile Application of Augmented Reality for Aerospace Maintenance. In: Proc. 24th Digital Avionics Systems Conf., DASC, vol. 1, pp. 5.B.3-1–5.B.3-9 (2005)
5. Neumann, U., Majoros, A.: Cognitive, performance, and systems issues for augmented reality applications in manufacturing and maintenance, pp. 4–11 (1998)
6. Grundlhofer, A., Brombach, B., Scheibe, R., Frohlich, B.: Level of detail based occlusion culling for dynamic scenes. In: GRAPHITE 2005, New York, USA, pp. 37–45 (2005)
7. Wang, T., Liu, Y., Wang, Y.: Infrared marker based augmented reality system for equipment maintenance. In: 2008 International Conference on Computer Science and Software Engineering, vol. 5, pp. 816–819 (December 2008)
8. Ismail, A.W., Sunar, M.S.: Collaborative Augmented Reality: Multi-user Interaction in Urban Simulation. In: 2009 Second International Conference on Machine Vision, ICMV, pp. 309–314 (2009)
9. Regenbrecht, H., Baratoff, G., Wilke, W.: Augmented Reality Projects in the Automotive and Aerospace Industry. IEEE Computer Graphics and Applications 25(6), 48–56 (2005)
10. Crescenzio, F.D., Fantini, M., Persiani, F., vStefano, L.D., Azzari, P., Salti, S.: Augmented Reality for Aircarft Maintenance Training and Operations Support. IEEE Computer Society, Los Alamitos (2011)
11. Optical Motion Capture Solutions, http://www.naturalpoint.com/optitrack/
12. http://studierstube.icg.tu-graz.ac.at/handheld_ar/artoolkitplus.php
13. Goose, S., Sudarsky, S., Zhang, X., Navab, N.: Speech-enabled augmented reality supporting mobile industrial maintenance. IEEE Pervasive Computing 2(1), 65–70 (2003)
14. http://www.sgtconker.com/2009/10/article-creating-a-scene-graph-in-xna/

Faculty-Wide Information System for Energy Saving

Yuya Ogawa, Seisaku Shinoda, and Younosuke Furui

Faculty of Information Science, Kyushu Sangyo University,
3-1 Matsukadai 2-chome, Higashi-ku, Fukuoka 813-8503, Japan
younosuke.furui@gmail.com

Abstract. It is difficult to persuade university students to voluntarily access data in which they are not currently interested, such as electricity consumption data. This paper describes the concept and design of a faculty-wide information system that aims to draw students' attention toward electricity consumption and to motivate them to save energy. It visualizes the data on a three-dimensional map, and displays it with other information such as announcements.

Keywords: Visualization, three-dimensional map, energy saving.

1 Introduction

Today, energy saving is one of the most important issues in the world. Many institutes and universities all over the world are making efforts to save energy by means of new digital equipments and information technologies. One of the major approaches is the visualization of electricity consumption [1-2]. The visualized data can motivate people (e.g., university students) to reduce the amount of electricity they consume.

Kyushu Sangyo University is also making efforts to save energy. When the Faculty of Information Science, to which the authors belong, was established in 2002, an electrical power measurement (EPM) system was installed in the faculty's building for the purpose of supporting energy saving. It collects the data on electricity consumption from all over the building. The EPM system, however, has been unsuccessful in drawing the students' attention. There are three problems: 1) Most of the students are not currently interested in energy saving. 2) A privacy and security issue prevents the system from being widely accessible. 3) The data management, analysis, and personalization functions of the system are poor.

This paper describes the concept and design of a faculty-wide information system that we have been developing since May 2010 in order to solve these problems. This system currently implements three functions: managing the electricity consumption database, visualizing the data on a three-dimensional (3D) map of the faculty's building, and integrating the visualized data with other information such as announcements. Our plan also includes user authentication, user authorization based on the permission list of each room's electric lock, collecting data on students' locations and activities for data analysis, and supporting awareness of other students not only to help a student find his/her friends but also to obtain noteworthy information cooperatively.

Y. Luo (Ed.): CDVE 2011, LNCS 6874, pp. 162–165, 2011.

2 Case Study on Kyushu Sangyo University

The central unit of the EPM system is EcoServer II, an energy efficiency data collection server developed by Mitsubishi Electric [3]. All the rooms in the faculty's building are equipped with one or more electric power meters. A teacher's private office, for example, has only one meter, while the largest classroom—capable of seating 240 people—has five meters: four for air conditioners and one for everything else, such as the lights, video projectors, and portable PCs. EcoServer II collects data from the meters and preserves them in its storage for up to 24 months. EcoViewer II, the software for EcoServer II, also works as a web server that provides data in the form of tables, graphs, and CSV files through the local area network.

During the five years from 2005 to 2009, eight students worked on the EPM system in their research to obtain fruitful results. Several methods for saving energy were proposed, but none have been yet put into practice. We notice that the reason for this unsuccessfulness is owing to the following problems:

1) Most of the university students are not interested in energy saving. When we conducted a questionnaire survey of sixteen students (the faculty has approximately 500 students in total), ten students answered "not interested," four answered "fair," and only two answered "interested." Thus, it is difficult to persuade the students to pay attention to energy saving. In addition, it is difficult to find students who could continue the research.

2) There is a privacy and security issue. For example, each teacher has his/her own laboratory and several rooms, and most of the teachers do not want to have their rooms' data accessible to outsiders. To resolve this issue, some kind of access control policy is needed. Currently, the access to the web server, EcoViewer II, is permitted solely to a limited number of laboratories (including the authors' laboratory), and only for research purposes. Thus, most of the students cannot access the collected data. In fact, some students are totally unaware that such a system exists.

3) The data management and analysis functions are poor. EcoViewer II provides data in the form of CSV files, tables, and graphs, but does not provide any explanation or implications. The collected data expire after the 24 month preservation period. In addition, there is no personalization function; whenever a student wants to view the data of a particular room on EcoViewer II, he/she has to begin at the search page by filling the room number in the web form, which he/she might not always remember.

3 Faculty-Wide Information System

We have been developing a faculty-wide information system in order to solve the above three problems. We think that the system should have all the following functions, although the current version of the system implements only A–D functions:

A) Visualize the electricity consumption data in the form of the building's map.
B) Display the map with other information, such as announcements, which would serve to draw the students' attention more than electricity consumption.

C) Reside on each student's PC and be activated by a simple operation. Functions A and C make the electricity consumption data more accessible to the students.
D) Periodically download the electricity consumption data from EcoViewer II and store them in a relational database.

The following functions are not yet implemented, but included in our plan:

E) Recognize who is using the system and provide him/her with the data collected from the places where he/she can enter, that is, where he/she can make efforts to save energy. This function would resolve the privacy and security issue. Since the faculty's building is equipped with an electric key system, this function is possible by using the permission list of each room's electric lock.
F) Collect data on students' locations and activities. This function would be helpful not only for analyzing the relationship of their activities and electricity consumption but also for providing the students with awareness of others.

This system is based on the client-server model shown in Fig. 1. The server consists of two parts: a web server application and a batch program. The batch program downloads not only the electricity consumption data in the form of CSV files from EcoViewer II but also the announcement data from the university's portal site, and stores both of them into a MySQL database.

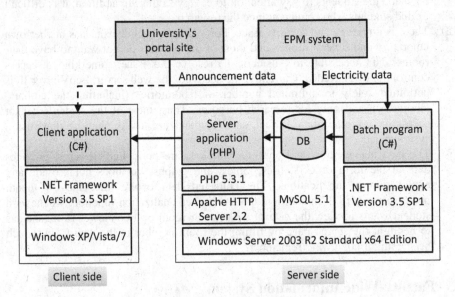

Fig. 1. Overview of system architecture

Every student in the faculty has their own portable PC; our goal includes installing the client application on every PC used in the faculty building. The client application runs as a system tray-resident program on the Windows OS, displays a scrolling ticker on the Windows desktop, and shows the titles of announcements one after another. When the student notices and double clicks one of the titles, the client window pops up as shown in Fig. 2. This window not only lists all the titles of announcements on the right pane but also shows a 3D map of the building on the left pane. Each place on the map is painted in blue, yellow or red; blue indicates that the amount of electricity consumed in the place in the recent one hour is less than 3 kWh; yellow indicates 3–5 kWh; red indicates more than 5 kWh. When the mouse pointer is moved onto the place, the amount is displayed on the upper area of the left pane.

We also conducted an experiment to evaluate the client application. Sixteen students participated in this experiment. The results indicate that nine students rated the usability of the 3D map as easy, while the rest rated it as fair.

Fig. 2. Snapshot of client application window

4   Conclusion and Future Work

We developed a system that visualizes electricity consumption data and integrates them with other useful information. The results of the experimental indicate that the system could be positively accepted by the students. Our future work includes the implementation of the rest of the functions and a long-term evaluation of the system.

References

1. Green University of Tokyo Project, http://www.gutp.jp/en/
2. Microsoft Collaborates with Osaka University on Green IT Project, http://blogs.msdn.com/b/see/archive/2011/01/14/microsoft-collaborates-with-osaka-university-on-green-it-project.aspx
3. Mitsubishi Electric – Global Environmental Portal – Fukuyama Works: Managing Specific Consumption, http://www.mitsubishielectric.com/eco/activities/production/activities/japan/fukuyama.html

Cooperative Visualization Based on Agent Voting

Dariusz Choinski, Mieczyslaw Metzger, and Witold Nocoń

Silesian University of Technology, ul. Akademicka 16, 44-100 Gliwice, Poland
{Dariusz.Choinski,Mieczysław.Metzger,Witold.Nocon}@polsl.pl

Abstract. In this paper a cooperative system for visualisation of a biotechnical system is presented. Some of the events associated with the state of metabolic reactions are indistinguishable, mainly due to lack of appropriate sensors and measurement capabilities. Therefore, a solution is needed to identify the state in which the reactor currently is, based on partial information and selected measurements available in real time. Those partial identification results are than used to provide a cumulative result by means of a voting mechanism between the cooperating agents.

Keywords: Voting, Multi-Agent Systems, Monitoring of Biotechnological Processes.

1 Introduction

In many industrial processes, especially in the field of biotechnology, classical control algorithms are not capable of providing a satisfactory maintenance of the process. This is because such processes are difficult to fully observe and monitor in real time. Some of the events associated with the state of metabolic reactions are indistinguishable, mainly due to lack of appropriate sensors and measurement capabilities.

Therefore, a solution is needed to identify the state in which the reactor currently is, based on the information and measurements available in real time. The solution presented in this paper is based on a multi agent system, in which particular agents identify the state of the process based on selected measurements. Those partial identification results are than used to provide a cumulative result by means of a voting mechanism between all the particular agents.

It is possible to distinguish basic goals of industrial controls systems. Those are:

- maintaining the industrial installation in a properly safe state,
- achieving the quality and efficiency goals,
- maximization of profit.

Therefore, control of industrial installation requires optimization on different layers of abstraction. Parameters responsible for those goals are concurrently observed (Fig. 1). Observation of parameters by many operators may be disturbed by the presence of Φ^{uo} events, that are not observable by the supervisory control and data acquisition system. Based on the measurements defining particular state variables Ω, autonomic applications of particular agents alone capable of generating events that may be

Y. Luo (Ed.): CDVE 2011, LNCS 6874, pp. 166–169, 2011.

divided into observable events Φ^o and non observable events Φ^{ou}. Such a division of events relates to pure physical situations, in which some of the events are not passed within the multi-agent system into the supervisory system due to constraints in measurements devices. Those events are eliminated based on conditions specifying the accepted confidence level.

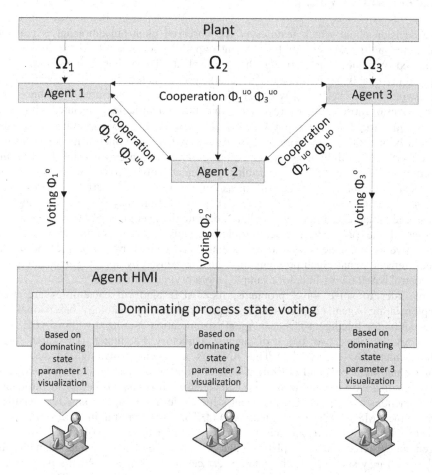

Fig. 1. The idea of cooperative voting mechanism in multi agent system

Parts of the observed measurements, that relate to non observable events caused by disturbances in measurements and control are verified based on cooperation with other agents. However, for such constructed agent no to cause the dependence of results on the history of agents cooperation and on the order in which information is passed between agents, the information is only read and the derived results are not passed. For each agent, the information gathered from other agents is used to find correlation between concurrent events present in different measurements. Agents are not informed about the results of this correlation finding, but each agent grades its own reasoning results based on previously specified grading. This grading together with a set of observable events relating to the current state of the plant is passed to the HMI agent. This agent is responsible for deciding, based on the majority voting of agent, which state of the plant is the most probable.

2 Cooperative Voting

The decision about which features of the observed plant are dominant is realized within the multi-agent system. Each Agent's application is responsible for observing a specified variable characterizing the pilot plant. Those applications implement algorithms enabling identification of characteristic states. States are specified by piecewise affine system PWA [1]. Dependencies of measured variables and derivatives of those variables, together with controlled variables associated with those measured variables, create polyhedrons Ω corresponding to particular states that should be identified and monitored by Agent applications. Such a model is further described in [2]. Monitoring of state changes is based on events, that describe the fulfillment of dependencies describing particular polyhedrons. However, due to physical constraints associated with measurement noise and disturbances, some state changes are not observable. Therefore, the application may identify a change in measured variable still not being able to generate the event described by crossing the border of the polyhedron. Such problem usually arises from the fact, that the derivative is computed with a substantial error caused by noise present in the measurement signal. Such problems may also be caused by applying manual control or control based on off-line, for example laboratory, measurements.

In order to solve those problems, the JADE platform capabilities are used, implementing Agent cooperation [3]. Agent cooperation ontology based on FIPA (Fundation for Intelligent Physical Agent) specification is utilized within JADE. This ontology specifies two types of agents: Directory Facilitator (DF) and Agent Management System (AMS). The AMS is an agent providing the service of controlling the access and utilization of agent platform. One and only one AS agent may run on a working platform and it is mandatory. It is responsible for identification and functions associated with the agent's life cycle. Every agent must register itself within the AMS in order to obtain an AID id. This id is stored in the AMS in order to create a catalog of all agents and in order to monitor those agents' states. Since the agent is registered within the platform and possesses a global and unique id, name and address, it may subscribe to the catalog services of other agents. What's important is that the environment enables access to the services at a specified time. This condition enables control and constraining of the granted resources.

The possibility of obtaining catalog information about other Agents, about states monitored by those agents and about their resources, enables cooperation. This cooperation is defined as exchange of information gathered by individual agents, about observations about detection of states that were reached without actually detecting observable states. The cooperation regards only the exchange of information describing the current states. If the current change occurred in a way, that the defined and observable events occurred before, other Agents are in possession of similar information regarding the current state. This enables to identify the actual state describing the system to be identified by means of cooperation.

With help from the HMI Agent and by means of the voting mechanism, the dominant state characterizing the object is determined. The information regarding particular parameters of the plant that is presented to the user is enhanced by specifying the feature of the plant, even if the particular parameter is not alone sufficient to determine this feature. The voting is based on a previously specified grading that is based on additional measurements, the purpose of which is to determine the uncertainty of determining the given states described by the polyhedrons Ω by the measurements available for particular agents. This grading, together with the set of observable events relating to the current state of the object is sent to the HMI Agent, whose responsibility is to select the most probable state of the object based on voting and previously specified weight factors. This state will then be considered as a basis for evaluating the object.

3 Concluding Remarks

The presented mechanism has been tested on a biotechnological pilot plant for the purpose of determining the current state of the metabolic flux. Therefore, each user, although not possessing the full picture of the object, may collectively make decisions based on the critical issues concerning the state of the object. This in turn enforces cooperation even for distant users. As mentioned previously, such a multi-agent system has been tested for supporting a biotechnological process maintenance in distant locations based on particular measurements, having different dynamical properties and sampling periods.

Acknowledgments. This work was supported by the Polish Ministry of Science and Higher Education, grants no. N N514 471539 and BK-214/Rau-1/2011.

References

1. De Schutter, B., Heemels, W.P.M.H.: Modeling and Control of Hybrid Systems. Lecture Notes of the DISC Course. Delft Center of Systems and Control, Delft University of Technology, Netherlands (2008)
2. Choinski, D., Metzger, M., Nocoń, W., Polaków, G.: Cooperative Validation in Distributed Control Systems Design. In: Luo, Y. (ed.) CDVE 2007. LNCS, vol. 4674, pp. 280–289. Springer, Heidelberg (2007)
3. Choinski, D., Senik, M.: Multi-Agent oriented integration in Distributed Control System. In: O'Shea, J., Nguyen, N.T., Crockett, K., Howlett, R.J., Jain, L.C. (eds.) KES-AMSTA 2011. LNCS, vol. 6682, pp. 231–240. Springer, Heidelberg (2011)

Comparing Static Load Balancing Algorithms in Grid

Sherihan Abu Elenin and Masato Kitakami

Graduate School of Advanced Integration Science, Chiba University,
1-33 Yayoi-cho, Inage-ku, Chiba, 263-8522 Japan
sherihan@graduate.chiba-u.jp,
kitakami@faculty.chiba-u.jp

Abstract. The ability to monitor and manage Grid computing components is critical for enabling high performance distributed computing. The Grid Monitoring Architecture (GMA) specification sets out the requirements and constraints of any implementation. There are many systems that implement GMA but all have some drawbacks such as, difficult to install, single point of failure, or loss of control message. So we design a simple model after we analyze the requirements of Grid monitoring. We propose grid monitoring system based on GMA. The proposed grid monitoring system consists of producers, registry, consumers, and failover registry. The goals of it are the management and failure recovery. Load balancing (LB) should be added to the system to overcome the message overloaded. Load balancing algorithms can be static or dynamic. This paper evaluates the four types of static load balancing algorithms. We evaluate the performance of the system by measuring the response time, and throughput. Central Manager algorithm introduces the smallest response time and the highest throughput. So it is the best static load balancing algorithm.

Keywords: Grid computing, Security; monitoring system, load balancing, response time, throughput.

1 Introduction

Grid computing focuses on large-scale resource sharing, innovative applications, and high-performance orientation [1]. In this environment, the security problem is a hot topic in Grid research due to the dynamics and uncertainty of Grid system. The Grid security issues can be categorized into three main categories: architecture related issues, infrastructure related issues, and management related issues [8].

This paper is focused on Grid management. The ability to monitor and manage distributed computing components is critical for enabling high performance distributed computing. Monitoring data is needed to determine the source of performance problems and to tune the system for better performance [9]. Monitoring is the act of collecting information concerning the characteristics and status of resources of interest. Monitoring is also crucial in a variety of cases such as scheduling, data replication, accounting, performance analysis and optimization of distributed systems or individual applications, self-tuning applications, and many more [8].

Y. Luo (Ed.): CDVE 2011, LNCS 6874, pp. 170–177, 2011.

Most existing monitoring systems work with network or cluster systems. There are several research systems implementing the Grid Monitoring Architecture (GMA) [6]: Autopilot, R-GMA, MDS, etc.   Autopilot [11] is a framework for enabling applications to dynamically adapt to changing environments. It aims to facilitate end-users in the development of application. R-GMA [12] combines grid monitoring and information services based on the relational model. Although the robustness of R-GMA, it has three drawbacks: flow of data, loss of control message, and single point of failure. The Monitoring and Discovery System (MDS) [3] of the Globus Toolkit (GT) is a suite of components for monitoring and discovering Grid resources and services. It has many problems such as it is too difficult to install.

In this paper, we focus on monitoring management in Grid system. The proposed Grid monitoring system is also based on the GMA [6]. GMA is the basis of most of monitoring system. The goal of GMA is to provide a minimal specification that will support required functionality and allow interoperability. We design a simple Grid monitoring system. The proposed system components are producers, registry, consumers, and failover registry. The goals of this system are to provide a way for consumers to obtain information about Grid resources as quickly as possible, and to recover any faults in the system.

In the proposed Grid monitoring system, we observe that there may be overloaded in Registry if the number of requests is large. So load balancing should be added to the proposed system in order to get better performance. Load balancing is a technique applied in parallel system that is used to reach optimal system condition, which is workloads are evenly distributed amongst computers, and as its implication will decrease programs execution time. Load balancing is dividing the amount of work that a computer has to do between two or more computers so that more work gets done in the same amount of time and, in general, all users get served faster. Load balancing can be implemented with hardware, software, or a combination of both [5].

Load balancing can be static or dynamic [10]. Static load balancing algorithms are Round Robin algorithm, Randomized algorithm, Central Manager algorithm, and Threshold algorithm. Dynamic load balancing algorithms are Central Queue algorithm, and Local Queue algorithm. In this paper, we apply the static load balancing algorithms in the proposed system to get better performance. In the end, we compare the four static load balancing algorithms to select the best one that can work well with the proposed system.

2 Static Load Balancing Algorithms

In static load balancing, the performance of the processors is determined at the beginning of execution. Then depending upon their performance the work load is distributed in the start by the master processor [4]. The slave processors calculate their allocated work and submit their result to the master. A task is always executed on the processor to which it is assigned that is static load balancing methods are non-preemptive. The goal of static load balancing method is to reduce the overall execution time of a concurrent program while minimizing the communication delays. There are four types of static load balancing: - Round Robin algorithm, Randomized algorithm, Central Manager algorithm, and Threshold algorithm.

Round Robin algorithm [13] distributes jobs evenly to all slave processors. All jobs are assigned to slave processors based on Round Robin order, meaning that processor choosing is performed in series and will be back to the first processor if the last processor has been reached. Processors choosing are performed locally on each processor, independent of allocations of other processors.

Randomized algorithm [13] uses random numbers to choose slave processors. The slave processors are chosen randomly following random numbers generated based on a statistic distribution. Randomized algorithm can attain the best performance among all load balancing algorithms for particular special purpose applications.

Central Manager algorithm [10], in each step, central processor will choose a slave processor to be assigned a job. The chosen slave processor is the processor having the least load. The central processor is able to gather all slave processors load information, thereof the choosing based on this algorithm are possible to be performed. The load manager makes load balancing decisions based on the system load information, allowing the best decision when of the process created. High degree of inter-process communication could make the bottleneck state.

In Threshold algorithm [10], the processes are assigned immediately upon creation to hosts. Hosts for new processes are selected locally without sending remote messages. Each processor keeps a private copy of the system's load. The load of a processor can characterize by one of the three levels: underloaded, medium and overloaded. Two threshold parameters t_under and t_upper can be used to describe these levels. Under loaded: load < t_under , Medium : t_under ≤ load ≤ t_upper , and Overloaded: load > t_upper.

3 Proposed Grid Monitoring System

3.1 Overview

We design a simpler model after we analyze the requirements of Grid monitoring, and implement it. The proposed Grid Monitoring System is based on the Grid Monitoring Architecture (GMA) [6] as shown in fig. 1.

In order to satisfy the requirement of Grid monitoring, Global Grid Forum (GGF) recommend Grid Monitoring Architecture (GMA) as Grid monitoring mechanism [6]. The GMA specification sets out the requirements and constraints of any implementation. In GMA, all of monitoring data are events which are based on timestamp for storing and transferring. The Grid Monitoring Architecture consists of three types of components: Directory Service (Registry), Producer and Consumer.

The architecture of proposed Grid monitoring system and the Communications between the Producer and the Consumer is shown in fig. 2. The proposed Grid monitoring system consists of producers (P), registry, consumers (C), and failover registry. The main aim of proposed system is to provide a way for consumers to obtain information about Grid resources as quickly as possible. It also provides fault tolerance system supported by failover registry. The structure of proposed Grid monitoring system depends on java Servlet and SQL query language.

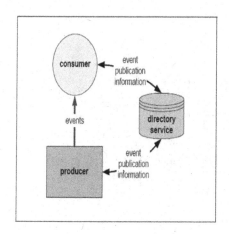

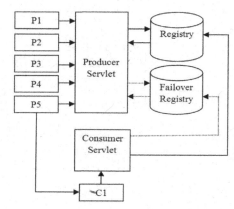

Fig. 1. GMA components   **Fig. 2.** Proposed Grid Monitoring System

3.2   Components of Proposed Grid Monitoring System

Producers are Grid services which register themselves in registry, describe the type and structure of information by SQL CREATE TABLE and SQL INSERT TABLE, and reply to the query of consumer as shown in fig. 3. So the producers in our Grid monitoring system are source of data. Each producer has interface and Servlet. Producer interface communicates with producer Servlet to build data base. The functions that are supported by the producer are creating tables, inserting data into tables, deleting data from tables, and updating data in tables.

Registry acts as a discovery Grid service to find relevant producers matching the query of a consumer. Registry schema consists of four layers: register layer, data layer, service layer, and republish layer. Register layer is responsible of registering all producers and consumers in the system. Data layer as shown in fig. 3 contains the description of data base exist in all producers. Service layer and republish layer take request and get reply, respectively. The functions that are supported by the registry are registering both producers and consumers, adding entry from producers, updating entries from producers, removing entries from producers, and searching about suitable producer for consumer. The overall purpose of the registry is to match the Consumer with one or more Producers. This is achieved by that Producers publish information about themselves and then Consumers search through the registry until they find the relevant match and then the two communicate directly with each other. The registry is not responsible for the storage of database, but only the index of it.

Failover registry is a backup version of all layers in registry. It acts like registry in the situation of failure of registry. It also has all the functions of registry. The proposed Grid monitoring is the only system that has Failover registry. Other Grid monitoring systems like R-GMA has drawback in single point of failure in directory server. However, Ganglia, MDS, or Hawkeye haven't any solution for failure.

Consumers can be software agents or users that query the Registry to find out what type of information is available and locate Producers that provide such information. The function of consumer is sending request to registry to find data by SQL SELECT statement in browser interface.

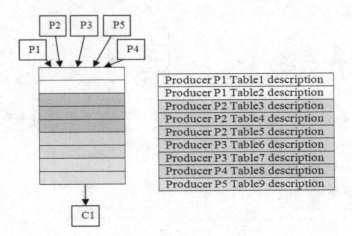

Fig. 3. Data layer in Registry Schema

3.3 The Overall System

Our Grid system is divided into Grid domains (GDs). GD consists of application domain (AD), resource domain (RD), client domain (CD), and Trust Manager (TM). TM's operations consist of Trust Locating, Trust Computing, and Trust Updating. This system was proposed and tested in [7]. We add another operation to TM. This operation is Registry to manage the relationship between producers and consumers.

After analyzing the architecture of proposed Grid monitoring system, we observe that there may be overloaded in Registry or Producers if the number of requests is large. So Load Balancing (LB) should be added to the proposed Grid monitoring system to get better performance. It is important in order to get optimal resource utilization, maximize throughput, minimize response time, and avoid overload.

4 Results

The performance of the Grid monitoring with Load balancing is evaluated by measuring response time, and throughput. We measure these two performance metrics twice. One depends on the message sizes in the system, and the other depends on the number of users.

4.1 Experimental Platform

Our Grid platform consists of: 1) Hardware Components: Nodes: 5 PCs (Intel Pentium4 2.2 GHz processor, Intel RAM 256 MB) and 10 PCs (Intel Atom 1.66 GHz processor, Intel RAM 2 GB), and Interconnection Network: Gigabit Ethernet 1000Mbps. 2) Grid Middleware: Globus Toolkit 4.2.1. 3) Software Components: Operating System: Linux Fedora 10, and Tools: Programs written in Java, Apache Ant for Java- based build tool, and Microsoft SQL server 2008.

4.2 Response Time (RT)

Response time is the average amount of time from the point a consumer sends out a request till the consumer gets the response. We measure response time twice; one as a function of message size as shown in fig. 4 and one as a function of number of users as shown in fig. 5.

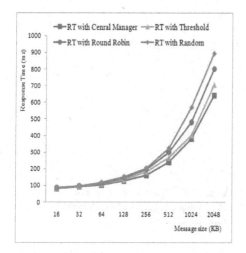
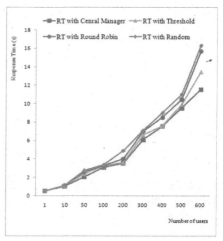

Fig. 4. Comparing Response Time for 4 static load balancing algorithms depending on the message size

Fig. 5. Comparing Response Time for 4 static load balancing algorithms depending on the number of users

We measure response time depending on message size with fixed number of requests; 15 requests. In fig. 4, Randomized algorithm gives the highest response time in all message sizes. This is because there is no steps or any calculations of loaded in the system. Central Manager algorithm is the best in all results because it introduces the smallest response time and it increases very simply; especially when message size is less than or equal 512KB.

In fig. 5, Central Manager algorithm gives the smallest RT. So it is also the best algorithm. Threshold and Round Robin algorithms give mediate results. We observe that RT in all four algorithms until 300 users is small. When number of users is more than 300, the response time in all algorithms are largely increased.

4.3 Throughput

Throughput is the amount of data transferred in one direction over a link divided by the time taken to transfer it, usually expressed in bits or bytes per second. The throughput is then calculated by dividing the file size by the time to get the throughput in megabits, kilobits, or bits per second. We measure the throughput as a function of data (message size) in Mega Bytes Per Second (MBPS) as shown in fig. 6 and as a function of number of users as shown in fig. 7.

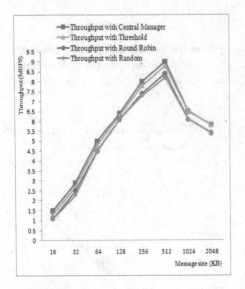
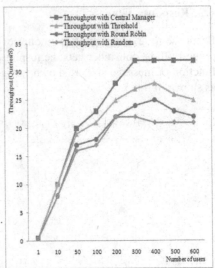

Fig. 6. Comparing Throughput for 4 static load balancing algorithms depending on the message size

Fig. 7. Comparing Throughput for 4 static load balancing algorithms depending on the number of users

In fig. 6, Round Robin and Randomized algorithms give the smallest throughput. Low throughput means low data flow. On the other hand, Central Manager algorithm introduces the highest throughput. We observe that the throughput is increased when message size is less than or equal 512KB in all algorithms. But it decreased when message size is more than 512KB in all algorithms.

In fig. 7, in Central Manager algorithm, throughput is increased with number of users until 300 users. It is constant after 300 users. In Round Robin algorithm, throughput is increased with number of users until 400 users. It is decreased after 400 users.

5 Conclusions

There are few researches on the monitoring system in Grid. Previous works over monitoring system is interested in cluster computing, network, or P2P systems. In the proposed Grid monitoring system, we focus on the system management by controlling the relationship between the producers, consumers, and registry, and its fault tolerance by adding failover registry in every domain. The overloaded is a big problem in the system, so load balancing should be added. The load balancing algorithms are two types: static or dynamic. The performance of four types of static load balancing is evaluated by measuring the response time, and throughput. Round Robin, Randomized, Central Manager, and Threshold algorithms are evaluated in the proposed Grid monitoring system twice from point of view of message sizes and number of users. Central Manager algorithm is the best and has introduced good performance. Randomized algorithm has introduced bad results.

Acknowledgment. The authors are grateful to Prof. Hideo Ito for his discussions and advices.

References

1. Foster, I., Kesselman, C., Tuecke, S.: The Anatomy of the Grid: Enabling Scalable Virtual Organizations. International Journal of High Performance Computing Applications 15(3), 200–222 (2001)
2. Yao, Y., Fang, B., Zhang, H., Wang, W.: PGMS: A P2P-Based Grid Monitoring System. In: Third International Conference of Grid and Cooperative Computing (GCC), China (2004)
3. Globus Toolkit, http://www.globus.org/
4. Eager, D.L., Lazowska, E.D., Zahorjan, J.: Adaptive load sharing in homogeneous distributed systems. IEEE Transactions on Software Engineering 12(5), 662–675 (1986)
5. http://www.cyquator.com/Html/load.html
6. Tierney, B., Aydt, R., Gunter, D., et al.: A Grid Monitoring Architecture (2004), http://www-didc.lbl.gov/GGF-PERF/GMAWG/papers/GWD-GP-16-2.pdf
7. Elenin, S.A., Kitakami, M.: Trust Management of Grid System Embedded with Resource Management System. IEICE Transaction Information System E94-D(1), 42–50 (2011)
8. Chakrabarti, A.: Grid Computing Security, 1st edn., pp. 33–45. Springer, Heidelberg (2007)
9. Tierney, B., Crowley, B., Gunter, D., Holding, M., Lee, J., Thompson, M.: A Monitoring Sensor Management System for Grid Environments. Cluster Computing 4(1), 19–28 (2001)
10. Sharma, S., Singh, S., Sharma, M.: Performance Analysis of Load Balancing Algorithms. Academy of Science, Engineering and Technology (38), 269–272 (2008)
11. Ribler, R.L., Vetter, J.S., Simitci, H., Reed, D.A.: Autopilot: adaptive control of distributed applications. In: Proceedings of the Seventh IEEE Symposium on High-Performance Distributed Computing, pp. 172–179 (1998)
12. Bhatti, P., Duncan, A., Fisher, S.M., Jiang, M., Kuseju, A.O., Paventhan, A., Wilson, A.J.: Building a robust distributed system: some lessons from R-GMA. In: International Conference on Computing in High Energy and Nuclear Physics (CHEP 2007), Victoria, Canada (September 2007)
13. Rahmawan, H., Satria, Y.: The Simulation of Static Load Balancing Algorithms. In: International Conference on Electrical Engineering and Informatics, Malaysia (2009)

A Model for Collaborative Scheduling Based on Competencies

Tomasz Kajdanowicz

Wroclaw University of Technology, Wroclaw, Poland,
Faculty of Computer Science and Management

Abstract. The paper presents a proposal for scheduling human resources among projects. In the situation when multiple number of projects needs to be planned in an organisation and only available human resources can be used for their completion, a group of managers needs to align scheduling and work collaboratively. The planning problem in such situations requires considering appropriate employee assignment to tasks, according to their specific skills and time constraints, which makes it very complicated. The paper describes a proposal of a model that provides the staffing solution optimisation for the given objective function,e.g. maximising the increase of competencies of the staff. Modelling is based on the quantitative description of tasks and employees.

Keywords: collaborative scheduling, staff scheduling, competence scheduling model.

1 Introduction

The resource-constrained staff scheduling in projects continues to be an active area of research. Recently this study gathered growing interest from researchers and practitioners trying to provide better models and solution methods[2,5]. The problem of planning a set of projects is in fact a collaborative scheduling problem as it requires interactions between managers to interchange information about constraints in projects and availability of resources[3]. In general such class of problems involves finding a feasible staff schedule by optimising objective functions that describes desired outcome[5].

The problem becomes more difficult when such scheduling is based on additional constraints such as the competencies required to fulfil the tasks. Staff scheduling in such a situation requires additional information about the competencies of employees [1,2].

Companies often are in a situation when they need to develop a set of projects at the same time. Obviously, the organisation has limited resources and needs to answer the question if, within available resources, it is able to accomplish whole set of those projects. Moreover projects necessitate exact competencies and the staff scheduling problem needs to address such requirements. Additionally, while preparing the staff schedule, it is usually desired to optimise some objective function, e.g. minimising the execution time, maximising the increase of competencies of the staff, maximising the economic outcome, etc.

Y. Luo (Ed.): CDVE 2011, LNCS 6874, pp. 178–181, 2011.

2 A Model for Collaborative Scheduling Based on Competencies

Based on the collaborative work of project managers resulting in time and competency constrains on projects, the model is able to provide the scheduling solution maximising the increase of competencies of the staff.

2.1 Problem Formulation

The staff assignment problem is considered given a fixed time interval composed of T periods indexed as $t = 1, \ldots, T$. Each of the projects $i = 1, \ldots, n$ being staffed are decomposed into a set of interdependent tasks $k = 1, \ldots, K$ and each project itself consist at least of one task (therefore $K \geq n$). Tasks are assigned to a particular project by $c_{ik} \in \{0, 1\}$ indicators, where 1 denotes that a project ith consist of kth task and 0 otherwise. Moreover a single task k may belong only to one project. According to ordering dependencies between tasks each kth task is characterised by the earliest possible starting time $\rho_k \in \{1, \ldots, T\}$ and the latest finish time $\delta_k \in \{1, \ldots, T\}$. It is assumed that ρ_k and δ_k are obtained from critical path analysis and therefore the duration of each kth task is known at time $t = 0$.

Assuming that during all periods $t \in [0, T]$ the set of employees remains fixed, they may be indexed by $j = 1, \ldots, m$. It means that during the whole time no changes in the staff are considered. Each employee is characterised by a set of competencies $r = 1, \ldots, R$ which describes different fields of expertise, knowledge or skills. Each rth competence possessed by jth employee at a given time period t is quantitatively indicated by a real number z_{jrt} called competency expertise. According to phenomena of knowledge depreciation, which states the nature of human beings, the value of z_{jrt} may change over time. By learning, the value of z_{jrt} grows and such process in enterprises is usually considered when an employee j works for a task requiring rth competence. In other words, when an employee j does not work in certain task requiring particular competency r, his competence expertise z_{jrt} decreases. Obviously the initial values of z_{jr1} are given. The competence expertise refers to an employee ability to solve a situational and targeted task alone. Moreover, it is emphasised that theoretical knowledge is not always necessary to solve a task and, what is more, practical experience and practical knowledge derived from it must always be there to address the task.

Each task requiring a given competence r may be done by an employee j with certain efficiency c_{jrt}. This is a relative indicator of the share of work done by jth employee on task requiring rth competence in one period, in comparison with an employee with the highest possible competency expertise at time t=0. For the convenience and the model clarity it is assumed that the level of competency expertise is directly correlated with efficiency. (Therefore it will be treated equivalently).

Each task k is characterised by work time performed with a given competency d_{kr} and denotes the time required by an employee to complete the task in a situation when the employee has the highest possible competency expertise. According to previously mentioned critical path analysis it is assumed that all work times for all tasks are known in advance. Therefore, all possible changes of a project, in response to unexpected events, compel to reapply the whole calculation process according to the model.

It is obvious that each employee has a limited work capacity. Therefore, the jth employee capacity in period t is indicated by $a_{jt} \in [0,1]$. Moreover due to technical and organisational constraints, effective work time in a task k and in a given competence r may be limited to b_{kr} value, known in advance.

In order to provide the solution for scheduling and proper staff assignment to a task requiring particular competences $x_{kjrt} \in [0,1]$, a decision variable is introduced and is interpreted as the time the employee j works in task k in competence r in period t. This constitutes the 4-dimensional matrix of working times.

Reflecting the process of competence expertise growth and decay it is assumed that if an employee j worked during x time in competence r his competence expertise grows by $\alpha_r \times x$ and α_r is a constant related to competence r. Knowledge depreciation in competence r is reflected by forgetting factor β_r. Under such assumptions the z_{jrt} might be obtained from Eq. 1.

$$z_{jrt} = z_{jr1} - \beta_r(t-1) + \alpha_r \sum_{k=1}^{K} \sum_{s=1}^{t-1} x_{kjrs} \tag{1}$$

where: z_{jr1} is the competence expertise at the beginning of planning horizon, $\beta_r(t-1)$ reflects knowledge depreciation, and $\alpha_r \sum_{k=1}^{K} \sum_{s=1}^{t-1} x_{kjrs}$ is the competence expertise grow.

2.2   Objective Function

The problem may be represented in terms of work time arrays $x = (x_{kjrt})$ by the objective function in Eq. 2.

$$g(x) = \sum_{r=1}^{R} \sum_{j=1}^{m} (z_{jr(T+1)} - z_{jr1}) \tag{2}$$

The function from Eq. 2 represents the benefits in competence expertise obtained by whole staff in the planning horizon T. The problem under consideration is now to find a solution $g(x)$ that is maximal.

Obviously, there exist some constraints in the problem. First of them is the fact that in one period t an employee j can not work above his capacity, according to Eq. 3.

$$\sum_{k=1}^{K} \sum_{r=1}^{R} x_{kjrt} \leq a_{jt} \tag{3}$$

Additionally, the required overall work time d_{kr} for each competence r in each task k must be allocated with proper amount of work time provided by employees, Eq. 4.

$$\sum_{\rho=1}^{\delta_k}\sum_{j=1}^{m} x_{kjrt} = d_{kr} \tag{4}$$

As there exist technical and organisational constraints, the effective work time in task k and in competence r must be limited to b_{kr}, see Eq. 5.

$$\sum_{j=1}^{m} x_{kjrt} \leq b_{kr} \tag{5}$$

Finally, it is required that all tasks are performed in planned time (between start and due time). It is fulfilled by constraint in Eq. 6.

$$(t - \rho_k)x_{kjrt} \geq 0 \text{ and } (\delta_k - t)x_{kjrt} \geq 0 \tag{6}$$

3 Conclusions

A model for competence-oriented staff scheduling problem was proposed. It allows staffing schedule to be designed and is obtained by optimisation of a given objective function, such as competence increase maximisation of the whole staff. The proposed solution for staff scheduling is static and the decision about whole schedule is taken at time t=0.

Further studies will be focused on experimentation concerning the real world staff scheduling problem across distinct projects.

Acknowledgement. The work was supported by Polish Ministry of Science and Higher Education, the research project, 2011-12 and Fellowship co-financed by The European Union.

References

1. Alba, E., Chicano, F.: Software project management with GAs. Information Sciences 177, 2380–2401 (2007)
2. Eiselt, H.A., Marianov, V.: Employee positioning and workload allocation. Computers and Operations Research 35, 513–524 (2008)
3. Greenstad, R., Smith, M.: Collaborative scheduling: Threats and promises. In: Workshop on Economics and Information Security, Cambridge, England (2006)
4. Gutjahr, W.J., Katzensteiner, S., Reiter, P., Stummer, C., Denk, M.: Competence-driven project portfolio selection, scheduling and staff assignment. Central European Journal of Operations Research 16, 281–306 (2008)
5. Kolisch, R., Hartmann, S.: Experimental investigation of heuristics for resource-constrained project scheduling: an update. European Journal of Operational Research 174, 23–37 (2006)

Towards a Functional Characterization of Collaborative Systems

Jaime Moreno-Llorena, Iván Claros,
Rafael Martín, Ruth Cobos, Juan de Lara, and Esther Guerra

Department of Computer Science, Universidad Autónoma de Madrid, Spain
{jaime.moreno,ivan.claros,ruth.cobos,
juan.delara,esther.guerra}@uam.es,
Rafael.Martinj@estudiante.uam.es

Abstract. In this paper we present major results of a detailed study about the functionalities that are present in different collaborative systems, realized as collaborative components. We have used this study to establish a methodology for the automatic generation of collaborative applications supporting group needs. The methodology is directed to any community of end users, who do not need to have any programming skills.

Keywords: CSCW, Collaborative Features, Collaborative Design, Web 2.0.

1 Introduction

Web tools such as Google sites, weblogs and wikis provide a usable interface to facilitate the configuration of a web application by an end user. Nowadays, these applications are mostly for individuals, but not for groups.

Collaborative systems (CS) design is a complex task [7], because the requirements from the end user community are critically required by the CS designers, and there is a growing number of new collaborative features (CF) available. Web end users are becoming increasingly involved and familiarized with the configuration of Web tools. Therefore, it would be desirable to have a collaborative tool to facilitate the creation of collaborative applications, which takes advantage of existing experience and facilitates end users' participation.

With the aim to automatically build collaborative applications, we have defined the concept of collaborative component (CC) as a software entity that gives functional support to individual or group actions inside a groupware environment to improve collaboration processes. A desirable characteristic of this kind of components is the independence of the environment and a wide flexibility in its configuration. The web 2.0 is a suitable environment to implement CCs and to collaboratively integrate CSs with them.

This article presents a study about the functionalities/features –that are managed by CCs– which are present in different CSs. The purpose of this study is to establish a methodology for proposing a Web 2.0 tool that provides to any community of end users the automatic generation of a collaborative application that supports its collaborative work, using a Web 2.0 CCs repository and a knowledge base of its application and use modes.

Y. Luo (Ed.): CDVE 2011, LNCS 6874, pp. 182–185, 2011.

2 Study of Collaborative Features Supported by Collaborative Systems

Several authors have presented their taxonomy of CSs. Noble [10] proposes general purpose communication tools, special purpose facilitators of group processes, shared work and group sense making tools, and process support tools. Datta [8] identifies four categories based on user-needs: communication, organization, writing/editing, and engaging/networking. In the line with our approach, some collaborative processes were proposed by Bolstad [4]: planning, scheduling, tracking information, brainstorming, document creation, data gathering, data distribution and shared situation awareness, where CS categories were called to our vision of CC.

Our proposal extends Bafoutsou's work [2] and introduces a new category: the online social network one, due to the special attention of academic and industry researchers in these spaces [1, 3]. Below, the proposed five categories of CS:

File and document group handing systems: they facilitate the management of files and documents in group. They usually incorporate features such as files/documents management and storing in a central database, shared-view, individual editing and synchronous work with files/documents, as well as collective authoring and revision of these resources [2, 4]. Sometimes they facilitate basic communication services such as notifications and e-mail in form of messaging.

Teleconferencing or computer conferencing systems: they support synchronous and asynchronous discussion, messaging and audio/video conferencing [2]. They usually allow sharing files/documents, where users can see and work on them simultaneously through shared screens or shared whiteboards [5].

Electronic meeting system: they combine computer communication and decision support technologies to facilitate the formulation and solution of problems by a group [4]. According to [2] they support synchronous and asynchronous meetings. They typically provide support for slide presentations, anonymous collaborative whiteboard, meeting agenda, surveys, file/document sharing, collaborative file/document editing, application sharing, automatic generation of meeting minutes, messaging and synchronous discussion.

Electronic/collaborative workspace: the main aim of these systems is to provide teams a common working space [2]. Usually this includes a file repository, discussion support, task management, address book, and access to project workspaces.

Online social networks systems (OSN): they facilitate the linking between users, sharing and finding content, and disseminating information. According to [4], OSNs are based on a network formed by nodes which represent individuals or other entities linked by some kind of relationship, such as friendship, kinship, taste, common interests, among others. OSNs enable users to have a public or semi-public user profile, to manage lists of linked users, and to view and traverse these lists inside the system [4]. Bulletin board and synchronous/asynchronous messaging are often provided as well.

Table 1 shows the probability to have a particular collaborative feature (CF) in a collaborative system category (CSC). We have called to this probability feature presence index (FPI). Its value is calculated as:

$$FPI\ (CF_i, CSC_j) = \#\ CS\ in\ CSC_j\ with\ CF_i\ /\ \#\ CS\ in\ CSC_j \qquad (1)$$

For instance, FPI (bulletin board, online social network) is 0,71, that is, the probability to have a bulletin board in a CS of category online social network is 0,71. In order to generate these values, we have started from the data included in the works of Bafoutsou [2] and Mayrhofer [9], and we have analyzed additional CSs.

Table 1. Functional characterization of collaborative system categories

Collaborative Systems Categories / Collaborative Features	Doc& File Group Handing	Computer Conferencing	Electronic Meeting Systems	Electronic Workspace	Online Social Network
i) Messaging/ Notification	1,00	0,30	0,65	0,71	0,94
ii) Bulletin Board	0,75	0,00	0,00	0,07	0,71
iii) Asynchronous Discussion	0,75	0,00	0,20	0,64	0,94
iv) Synchronous Discussion	0,25	1,00	0,75	0,43	0,59
v) Collaborative Whiteboard	0,00	1,00	0,75	0,29	0,00
vi) Screen/ Application Sharing	0,00	1,00	0,70	0,14	0,00
vii) Audio/Video Conferencing	0,13	1,00	0,75	0,29	0,06
viii) Surveys/ Polling	0,50	0,70	0,70	0,14	0,06
ix) Sched. Tools/ Task Manag.	0,38	0,80	0,85	0,64	0,41
x) Contact Manag./ Addr. Book	0,63	0,30	0,65	0,36	0,94
xi) Document Sharing	1,00	0,90	0,60	0,93	0,88
xii) Document Management	1,00	0,00	0,00	0,64	0,00
xiii) User ID/ Profile	1,00	0,90	1,00	1,00	1,00
xiv) Asynchronous Activity Ctrl.	0,75	0,00	0,75	0,43	0,00
xv) Synchronous Activity Ctrl.	0,50	1,00	0,90	0,57	0,42
xvi) Indexing Management	1,00	0,00	0,00	0,00	0,00
xvii) Rediffusion/ Syndication	0,88	0,00	0,00	0,00	0,94

We now provide a brief description of each CF: i) messaging communication services allow sending/receiving asynchronous messages from known senders; ii) bulletin board allows publication of messages on a public or semi-public board; iii) asynchronous discussion allows chronological organization of messages (e.g. forum); iv) synchronous discussion provides support to user discussion in real time (e.g. chat); v) collaborative whiteboard provides a shared workspace where several users can use text/graphic tools at the same time; vi) screen/application sharing provides a screen shared by several users that usually have some control; vii) audio/video conferencing, communication services with audio-video capabilities; viii) surveys/polling allows applying forms or elements for decision making (e.g. votes); ix) scheduling tools/task management allows managing tasks and organizing them over time; x) contact management/address book allows the organization of contacts with others users or organizations; xi) document sharing allows to manage personal or shared lists of files and documents, usually asynchronously; xii) document management extends the capabilities of document sharing with centralized organizational mechanism, versioning and change control; xiii) user id/profile allows managing a user identification and profile with information about preferences and interests; xiv) asynchronous activity control allows managing of historical information about user interaction with the system (e.g. awareness mechanisms like historical reports); xv) synchronous activity control allows managing of real time information about user interaction with the system (e.g. awareness mechanisms like radar view); xvi) indexing management facilitates the process of finding resources, and xvii) rediffusion/syndication offers summary information views that can be shared with other systems.

3 Conclusions and Future Work

In this article we have presented a study showing the likelihood of having a collaborative feature (CF) in a collaborative system category (CSC). These probabilities can give us evidence about how important is any CF in a CSC. The CFs of each CSC constitutes a CFCSC vector that describes the functional characteristics of the CSC.

We are working on using this study to establish a methodology and a Web 2.0 tool that provides to any community of end users, who don't need programming knowledge, the automatic generation of an application that supports its collaborative work, using for this purpose the above CFCSC vectors as a configuration guide. This Web 2.0 tool is called REUSES (Rapid End-User Synthesis of Collaborative Systems). REUSES uses mashup technology to integrate tailored collaborative systems with collaborative components using the Metadepth code generator [6].

Acknowledgments. This research was partly funded by the Spanish National Plan of R+D, project number TIN2008-02081/TIN and by the CAM (Autonomous Community of Madrid), project number S2009/TIC-1650.

References

1. Alexander, B.: Social networking in higher education. In: Katz, R. (ed.) The Tower and the Cloud, EduCause (2008),
   http://net.educause.edu/ir/library/pdf/PUB7202s.pdf
2. Bafoutsou, G., Mentzas, G.: Review and functional classification of collaborative systems. IJIM 22(4), 281–305 (2002)
3. Boyd, D., Ellison, N.: Social Network Sites: Definition, History, and Scholarship. JCMC 1(13), 210–230 (2008)
4. Bolstad, C.A., Endsley, M.R.: Tools for supporting team collaboration. In: 47th Annual Meeting Human Factors and Ergonomics, Denver, Colorado (2003)
5. Coleman, D., Ward, L.: Talking advantage of real-time collaboration tools. IT Professional 1, 25–30 (1999)
6. de Lara, J., Guerra, E.: Deep Meta-modelling with MetaDepth. In: Vitek, J. (ed.) TOOLS 2010. LNCS, vol. 6141, pp. 1–20. Springer, Heidelberg (2010)
7. Grudin, J.: CSCW: History and focus. IEEE Computer 27(5), 19–26 (1994)
8. Datta, L.: A Taxonomy of Collaboration Tools,
   http://allcollaboration.com/home/2010/4/19/
   a-taxonomy-of-collaboration-tools.html
9. Mayrhofer, D., Back, A.: Web-conferencing software tools: A comprehensive market survey. Arbeitsberichte des Learning Center der Universität St Gallen 128 (2004)
10. Noble, D.: Metrics for Evaluation of Cognitive-Based Collaboration Tools. In: Proceedings of 6th and Control Research and Technology Symposium, Annapalis, USA (2000)

Efficient System for Clustering of Dynamic Document Database

Pawel Foszner, Aleksandra Gruca, and Andrzej Polanski

Silesian University of Technology, Institute of Informatics,
Akademicka 16, 44-100 Gliwice, Poland
{pawel.foszner,aleksandra.gruca,andrzej.polanski}@polsl.pl
http://www.polsl.pl

Abstract. We describe in this paper, a system that groups, classifies and finds the latent semantic features in a database composed of a large number of documents. The database will be constantly growing as users who co-create it will be adding more and more new documents. Users require a system to provide them information, both about a specific document, and about the entire set of documents. This information includes statistical data about words in documents, information about aspects in which this words appears, classification, clustering, etc.

To meet these expectations we propose using methods for searching for hidden patterns in multivariable data. We apply machine learning algorithms for data analysis, useful in identifying local patterns in multivariate data. We consider two different algorithms described in the literature (1) Probabilistic Latent Semantic Analysis Method [2] and (2) Nonnegative Matrix Factorization algorithm described in [4] and used in the text analysis system [1].

Keywords: clustering, classification, NMF, semantic features, document database

1 Introduction

Unsupervised classification of documents is an area with large potential and numerous possible applications. However when designing text classification systems one encounters many problems. One of the most difficult problems is that the data are highly multidimensional. From the viewpoint of unsupervised classifier, which is taking as an input documents without any additional descriptions, each separate word will be a separate dimension. Even if we constrain the system to documents of a specific area (biological articles, reports in the company, etc.), number of words can reach tens of thousands. After an appropriate filtration of colloquialisms, words of similar meaning or words found in very large or very small number of documents the number of words could be reduced to a few thousand. Multidimensionality leads to problems in designing algorithms for grouping documents, both in the aspect of the algorithm efficiency and in the aspect of their execution times.

Y. Luo (Ed.): CDVE 2011, LNCS 6874, pp. 186–189, 2011.

In this paper we describe a system for efficient dynamical clustering of text documents. It is assumed that the system is exploited jointly by many users who can add new documents, extract and review existing ones. The functionality of the system is based on on-line grouping of incoming documents according to several aspects, detected in the past. Detection of the semantic aspects of the documents stored in the database is additionally supported by group of users with 'expert' status. The methodology of grouping documents and detecting/discovering their semantic aspects is based on using appropriate algorithms for searching for semantic features in the text documents. We implement these algorithms and we design their incremental versions applicable for on – line updating the semantic structure of the large text database.

In the following we present overview of the system construction and some elements of the algorithmic aspects of processing of the incoming data for the system.

2   System Overview

The system was intended as an intermediate layer between the documents database, and the user. There are two types of users: (1) a user with rights to add new documents to the database, and (2) an expert who analyzes added documents. Scheme of the system is shown in figure 1. The database will be a collection of text or PDF files containing documents. This set is subjected to pre-processing which is analyzed for the occurrence of words from the dictionary. The output of this treatment is a matrix D of occurrences in the which the value of occurrences a single word in single document is balanced by the number of documents in witch it is occurred.

$$D_{ij} = tf_{ij} * \log \frac{T}{t_j}$$

where tf_{ij} is a number of occurrences word j in document i, T is the total number of documents in database and t_j is number of documents that contains word j. The main element of the system will be part of the figure 1 described as a "processing engine". The main task of this part will be automatic detection of the

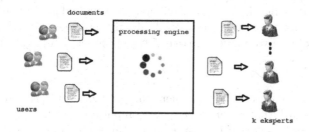

Fig. 1. System overview

semantic features of the submitted documents. Based on the detected semantic features the system can then display to users information related to documents that they add to the system, as well as direct the appropriate documents to the appropriate experts.

Due to the fact that when we have a large number of documents, the execution of both algorithms, PLSA and NMF is a costly in time. Calculation of matrices in the algorithms, e.g., W and H in NMF (see section 'Algorithms') should be designed in an incremental manner. The more documents in the database the less can be perform updates to the matrix W and H.

Values for documents added after the last update (class of document, aspects in the which words occurs) should be calculated based on the existing matrices W and H.

3   Algorithms

The first implemented algorithm for semantic feature detection is PLSA (Probabilistic Latent Semantic Analysis), described in the the articles [2] and [3]. The distribution of occurrences of words in documents is assumed to be modeled by a mixture of probability distributions corresponding to different semantic aspects encountered in the text documents. The word frequencies are assumed to follow from the random procedure of (i) selecting a document d_i with probability $P(d_i)$, (ii) selecting a latent class z_k with probability $P(z_k|d_i)$, and (iii) generating a word w_j with probability $P(w_j|z_k)$. This procedure leads to the following mixture distribution of the word frequencies

$$P(w_j|d_i) = \sum_{k=1}^{K} P(w_j|z_k)P(z_k|d_i). \tag{1}$$

The 'hidden' distributions $P(z_k|d_i)$ and $P(w_j|z_k)$ are estimated by the appropriately designed expectation - maximization (EM) procedure.

Another method to discover hidden patterns in the data is the NMF algorithm [5]. NMF method is based on the matrix decomposition. The task of finding the exact distribution of the factors is too costly in time. Thus arose the various methods used to find approximate factors based on quadratic programming. They differ in the way of obtaining the matrices W and H. This can be achieved either by maximizing the value of likelihood function and also by minimization of function of distance or divergence. NMF algorithm is based on the factorization of the matrix into two smaller matrices whose product should give initial matrix.

$$V \approx WH$$

Finding such a matrix W and H where the product corresponds exactly to the matrix V is a task that is very greedy for computational time. Existing methods focus on finding a solution by searching a local minimum of the function representing the difference between the original matrix and the product of matrices W and H.

In our case, the matrix V will contain information on occurrences each word in documents. Each column in this matrix will be a vector, whose components will represent the occurrences of words in a document which relates to this vector. Number of documents (denote it by n) will be therefore also the number of vectors. Each vector will have p components, where p will mean the total number of words in the dictionary. Dictionary in our case will be a collection of words that can occur in the documents, filtered with colloquialisms, words of similar meaning and words found in very large or very small number of documents.

From the system point of view, the most interesting are the matrices W and H, which respectively provide information about the words and documents. Lets assume that our system collects documents that can be classified into one of k areas, and we have k experts in these fields. Matrix H would contain then the information about how to classify a document into one of k areas. It could be useful to refer the document to the appropriate expert. Matrix W contains information about the words and aspects in which they occur and what aspects are present in the each k fields. It could therefore be helpful in finding documents.

4   Conclusions

The proposed algorithms are similar in terms of computational complexity and memory usage. We have been testing both these algorithms in terms of their computational complexity and performance. We have also applied these algorithms to the data sets from publicly available sources [1]. The obtained results and execution times were similar. Developing incremental versions of the algorithms highly increases their computational efficiencies.

Most important element of the design of the text clustering system is deciding on the (maximal) number of aspects allowed to be present in the analyzed text documents. In the present design we assume that the number of aspects is constant in time. In the future we plan to develop methodology to adapt the number of analyzed aspects to the structure of the incoming data.

Acknowledgments. This work was supported by the European Community from the European Social Fund.

References

1. Chagoyen, M., Carmona-Saez, P., Shatkay, H., Carazo, J., Pascual-Montano, A.: Discovering semantic features in the literature: a foundation for building functional associations. BMC Bioinformatics 7(1), 41 (2006)
2. Hofmann, T.: Probabilistic latent semantic analysis. In: Proc. of Uncertainty in Artificial Intelligence, pp. 289–296 (1999)
3. Hofmann, T.: Unsupervised learning by probabilistic latent semantic analysis. Machine Learning 401, 177–196 (2001)
4. Lee, D., Seung, H.: Algorithms for non-negative matrix factorization
5. Lee, D., Seung, H.: Learning the parts of objects by non-negative matrix factorization. Nature 401, 0028–0836 (1999)

Proposition of a Model Using Parametric Operations to Assist the Creation of Architectural Forms

Jean-Paul Wetzel

Architecture School of Strasbourg,
France
wetzel@strasbourg.archi.fr

Abstract. This article presents the use of form operators during the design phase. This case study of three projects of BAAM agency shows the relevance of their use of form operators. It also shows the variety of forms that can be obtained from the same idea. The aim our work is to apply operators on forms and geometries to vary randomly.

BAAM is an architectural firm that applies the work of our research laboratory.

Keywords. Decision tree, historical operations of forms, generative form.

1 Design Process

In the early stage of a project, the architect introduces and validates his assumptions by making many adjustments while designing. The use, during the sketching phase, of existing modelling tools is not compatible with the iterative nature of this process. As a result, the challenge lies in the definition of a model which will allow to take into account the whole creative process, with all its coming and going while it is being developed.

1.1 Design Process and Decision Trees

The process of a project is the result of a set of choices and actions. It would be possible to represent this evolution in a decision tree like the one described by Rowe [1].

This graph shows the evolution of the project from the initial stage to the final result, through a series of intermediate stages. Each node represents a stage of the project and each arc figures the act which transforms the current state into the next one. The design approach differs from other more classical approaches in that it needs to hold at the same time alternative solutions because all of them have their advantages and disadvantages, and it is often necessary to develop them in parallel before being able to finally pick one rather than the others. This requires maintaining simultaneously, in the decision tree, several potential paths which are variants of the project. We call this representation a design tree.

Y. Luo (Ed.): CDVE 2011, LNCS 6874, pp. 190–197, 2011.

1.2 Towards an Iterative Modelling Environment, the Design Tree

Based on previous observations, we propose here a data structure derived from the decision tree and historical modelling software. We will call this a design tree (fig. 1). The peculiarity of this tree lies in the simultaneous conservation of multiple design paths. These paths are as many variants in the making, which seems much more suited to a creation process.

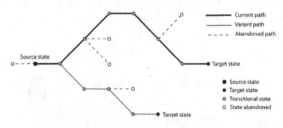

Fig. 1. The design tree

A node in the tree represents the state of the project at a certain time and arcs represent the transformation between two nodes. Only those deemed relevant statements are stored in the tree. Depending on the position of the node in the tree, we distinguish three states:

- Source state (root): stable condition, the earlier choices are no longer questioned,
- Transitional state (intermediate): relevant state could allow the development of multiple alternatives,
- State target (termination): final statement of an alternative design, which can exist in several, including one who is the current status of the project.

From the point of view of navigation in the tree, a hyperbolic representation [2] (fig. 2) depending on the context would allow to view the information on the current stage in comparison to the next and previous stages. Each node would have a sticker related changes made by the designer to be placed in direct relation with stages relatives. The designer could navigate these stickers according to revert to previous operations or to create a new branch.

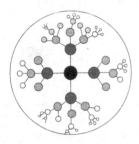

Fig. 2. Hyperbolic representation

2 Case Study

2.1 PER (Pôle d'excellence Rurale, Center of Rural Excellence) of Dolleren

BAAM agency is responsible for the design and construction of the Dolleren center of rural excellence by implementing an approach Low Consumption Building (LCB) approach type. This project involves the rehabilitation of a former holiday camp into a rural excellence center premises comprising training rooms, a business incubator and premises for a local television TV Doller (fig. 3).

Fig. 3. Initial building

The architects of this operation have decided to completely cover the existing building with insulation on the outer skin to meet the thermal performance of a LCB building. To reach this goal with the formal principle adopted for the roof that was of a pleated form, with an other major constraint that was to hold the television studio on the ground floor which should include a ceiling height of 4.50 meters (volume in red on the figure below).

Fig. 4. Example of three variants

To obtain this form with all of these objectives, the architects have used the operator "pleating"[3, 4]. Using this operator has enabled architects to obtain variants that

Fig. 5. Final design process state

have been evaluated according to aesthetic criteria and feasibility (fig. 4). After choosing the shape, the architects have clad the rest of the building with wood siding (fig. 5).

Using this "pleating" operator was very useful during the design of the building, and allowed the architects to get a multitude of variations in half a day's work. Today this project has been built, you can see the realization in Figure 5.

2.2   Designing a Museum about the Second World War in Bastogne (Belgium) by Using the Morphological Operator "Pleating" (BAAM Architecture)

BAAM agency has participated in a competition for the extension of the museum on world war II Bastogne (Belgium). The program included a 1,000m² extension to the star-shaped existing building which it surface area is about 1,100m² (fig. 6).

Fig. 6. Existing Museum.

The party chosen by the architects was to create a corridor corresponding to the surface of the programme and then change its shape with the operator "pleating". The purpose of this exercise was to get a loop that linked the extension to two branches of the existing building and thereby evoked the hardness of fighting during the Battle of the Bulge.

Fig. 7. Example of three variants

The application of the operator "pleating" has enabled the architect to obtain a variety of solutions (fig. 7,8). We can see that adjustments are necessary so that each end of the corridor should connect properly to the existing building. The creation of a new operator by introducing constraints at the ends of a geometry could be considered and then obtain solutions directly exploitable.

Fig. 8. Final design process state

The use of morphological operators "pleating" has enabled the architect to obtain variants of a project. The project, moreover, has been noted for its architectural merits by the jury of the competition.

2.3 Architectural Competition for the Construction of Louvain-la-Neuve Museum

The Baam architecture firm has participated at the end of 2007 in an architectural competition for the realization of a new museum in Louvain-la-Neuve in Belgium. In view of the programme and the available space on the ground, the architects decided to make a compact structure present on all of the buildable area of the plot of the competition. This principle has led to a formalization of the first project in the form of an extruded surface (fig. 9) that may contain the entire program.

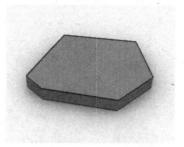

Fig. 9. Original form representing the maximum volume that can be occupied by the project

The architects were then focused on the roof. Their desire was to make available the 5th facade and revegetate it. On a conceptual level they wanted to give it a mountain form. The architects started devised it by using the generative system operator "pleating" with various alternatives obtained for this morphological Project. They then applied the operator on the upper surface of the geometry by declaring the following variables:

- Number of plies 3
- Amplitude 2m
- Harmony 50%.

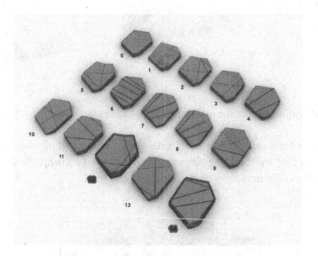

Fig. 10. Variations of roof shape by "pleating" operator

The generative system had created a multitude of forms more or less feasible. The designers then decided to hold the fourteen illustrated answers shown below. For further research work on the form, the architects have continued their study on two forms which seemed the most appropriate: the number twelve and fourteen. The criteria chosen by the architects are aesthetic and functional.

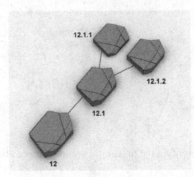

Fig. 11. Adjustment of the result of folds 12 located by the operator "pleating"

At this level, the architects adjusted forms twelve and fourteen by moving and shaping the folds that constituted the operation of "pleating" of the roof surface (fig. 11,12,13).

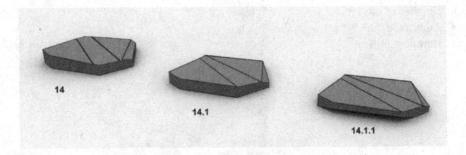

Fig. 12. Adjustment of the result of folds 14 located by the operator "pleating"

The form fourteen was chosen by the designers because it allowed better Visitors stroll on the roof of the building than number twelve. To complete this formalizing project work, the architects then worked in front and plan.

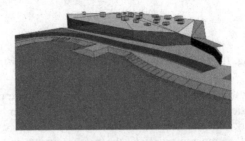

Fig. 13. Final design process state

By taking some parameters reflecting the idea of the project, it is possible to obtain a considerable number of alternatives. Indeed, the use by the architects of the operator "pleating" associated with a generative system that enabled a visualization and evaluation of a wide range of formal solutions.

3 Conclusion

The implementation in an architectural project of morphological operators implemented in 3D Studio Max is conclusive. The designer has a tool with which he can refine the shape of the project throughout the process of morphogenesis. It is possible to generate a variety of solutions, either randomly or in a controlled manner, which means that this tool is by no means a design system fully automatic. The choice of the final form of the project is done and the designer is guided not only by aesthetic criteria, but also and especially by the response forms obtained due to the constraints of the project.

However, this tool can also be used for a specific type of architecture where the designer wants to include in draft stage derived of operators implemented. Indeed, the limitations of this tool lie in the number of operators implemented.

A second limitation of our tool is because we have not yet specified exactly how the designer will navigate throughout the multitude of solutions given to him. Currently, we model projects with a number of adjustments and solutions. But whether a generative system is established or if the project becomes more complex, the problem will be to displaying all solutions with an intuitive and understandable representation to all variations of the project.

References

1. Rowe, P.G.: Design Thinking. The MIT Press, Cambridge (1987)
2. Spence, R.: Information Visualisation, Design for Interaction. ACM Press, London (2001)
3. Wetzel, J.-P., Belblidia, S., Bignon, J.-C.: Specification of an operator for the design of architectural forms: "Pleating". In: eCAADe, Frankfurt (2007)
4. Wetzel, J.-P., Belblidia, S., Bignon, J.-C.: Specification and implementation of a parametric operator: Folding. In: 9th International Conference on Design & Decision Support Systems in Architecture and Urban Planning, The Netherlands (2008)

The Digital Design Build Studio

Gernot Riether

Georgia Institute of Technology
gernot.riether@coa.gatech.edu

Abstract. The paper will discuss the "Digital Design Build Studio" as a potential model of interdisciplinary research and show how digital design and fabrication methods that become more affordable and available might open up new possibilities to connect academia with practice. The paper will use the AIA pavilion, a Digital Design Build Studio that were taught during the Fall semester of 2010 as case study.

Keywords: Education, Digital Fabrication, Scripting, Design / Build.

1 Introduction

Architecture schools have over the past 20 years been the primer incubators in the speculation of architecture that is informed by digital design and fabrication tools. Architecture schools changed their curriculum to become "Digital Laboratories." [1] In the Paperless Studios at Columbia University or the DRL, Digital Research Laboratory at the AA new design and fabrication tools have been tested at the University before they informed practice. Especially offices such as RUR, the office of Jesse Reiser and Nanako Umemoto or Asymptote, the practice of Hani Rashid and Lise Anne Couture, in New York or Zaha Hadid in London are offices that managed to take a digital design research from academia to practice.

Still the reality is that most architecture graduates don't find a job in offices that speculate with new design tools on a similar level then they might have experienced at the studio in school. Clients that can afford the luxury of cutting edge architecture are rare in an economic crises and the market for signature buildings seems to be saturated. As technology developed faster gaps between practice and the discipline became very large. This divide between the discipline and practice informed over the past years odd discussions weather we should train students for the practice or setting them up to become visionaries of the discipline of architecture.

Practice on the other hand seems to address different issues much quicker then academia. LEED certificates are requirements but there are no requirements for students in architecture schools to meet any particular standards in relation to environmental design and sustainability beyond "awareness" of these issues and a demonstration of "knowledge and understanding" within an integrated portfolio of work. [2] Projects designed in the studios of architecture schools show a distinct lack of evidence-based and integrated assessment of building performance factors such as energy efficiency, carbon dioxide emissions or resource use.

Y. Luo (Ed.): CDVE 2011, LNCS 6874, pp. 198–206, 2011.

New models to link the research that takes place at architecture schools with the practice of the discipline and the building industry need to be developed. After the excitement of digital modeling tools and scripting that allow the management of complex geometry the current challenge is to address pressing environmental issues through these tools and overcome pure formal experiments. We are researching the advantage of complex geometry to address environmental issues. Addressing environmental issues through complexity requires the support of experts including computer scientists and engineers. At an Institute of Technology we have the resources to formulate multidisciplinary teams around architectural problems.

Digital design and fabrication tools are also much cheaper then they were 10 years ago. Tools that cost $20,000 in the year 2002 when we first equipped our digital fabrication lab are now available for $2,000. With digital architecture becoming more affordable we have new opportunities.

Instead of making up projects and clients to create a make believe environment for students, a model that is very common in teaching architecture, it is suggested here to define and work on real projects. Rethinking building components for instance would allows the school to take on real issues on a small scale. The results from these new architecture labs might move the speculation about the future of architecture to a different level and bridge to the building industry or architecture offices that don't have access to resources one might have at an Institute of Technology.

Graduating students who can connect design ideas with material resources, efficient fabrication and production processes in an environmentally sensitive manner will not depend on the few architecture offices that are specialized in the realization of expensive digital experiments but can make his research available for every architecture office and clients. But what should be the skill set of these graduates?

Responding to environmental issues with complexity requires highly sophisticated tools and it is often the problem to get lost in specific tools. The architect, according to Vitruvius should be equipped with knowledge of many branches of study and varied kinds of learning. [3] Architecture education failed this promise already of denying its collapse into specialties and separated architectural design from landscape design, urban planning, interior design and structural engineering. The current development of digital tools might define and reflect in new specialties within the discipline of architecture. Technology always played a significant role in the process of the appearing of particular domains in disciplines, which explains the branching in medicine for instance in the years 1800-1814, when medicine was broken down into categories, specialties and subspecialists that generally limit their practice to problems of one organ system or to one particular area of medical knowledge. The increasing complexity of digital tools might require new experts: New courses, new faculty hires, new research laboratories and departments are needed. "Since only experts can deal with the problem", Laurie Anderson. [4] Architecture education is currently in this process of developing a new set of specialties, a process in which digital technology plays a significant role and it will be critical how architectural problems are defined and how frameworks of experts are organized around them.

The way we will break down architectural research in specialties will define the role of the architect in the future. Architecture graduates will have the choice of becoming Experts or Vitruvian Architects. The model of the Digital Design Build Studio will show a studio framework that allows the student to slip in both roles, the Vitruvian Architect and Expert.

2 The Digital Design Build Studio

Steve Badane's Jersey Devil design/build firm was launched in 1972, comprised of skilled craftsmen, architects and inventors. The idea of design/build has especially in architecture schools in the US influenced educational programs such as the Yestermorrow design/build school, founded 1980 by John Connell or the Rural Studio at the University of Alabama, founded 1993 by Dennis K. Ruth and Samuel Mockbee.

The main objective of these programs is to imparting practical experience to architecture students and to demystify the building processes. Using a hands-on experience students are taught not just design but also the skill of craftsmanship. design/build programs in some cases also serve helping a larger community to improve their living conditions with design and construction of small homes to larger community projects.

Other programs are challenging architecture schools to compete in design/build competitions. The Solar Decathlon founded 2002 by the U.S. Department of Energy is a competition to design and build solar-powered houses on the Mall in Washington that are cost-effective and energy-efficient. These projects have proven a large impact not just in the education of students but also in practice and a larger community. The Solar Decathlon webpage reports more then 300,000 house visits, more then 500 participants at workshops for professionals and millions of readers and viewers through various media worldwide during a 10 days event. [6]

The increasing availability of digital fabrication tools at architecture schools allows for a digital design build studios with a focus on the challenges and opportunities of automated production processes. A design build studio that is driven by these issues might not just teach architecture students about workflow from design to material, fabrication, assembly and construction that is driven by digital tools but can also become an important research for the discipline of architecture and the construction industry.

One approach for a studio framework that is integrating different research agendas is to fill the design studio with lectures and seminars in areas of climate, energy, construction, building assembly, material science and bombarding the students at the same time with workshops in digital tools. Another approach is to ask experts from other disciplines for consultation. A different approach is presented here: The Digital Design Build Studio:

In the first part of the studio the students work individually, defining and developing projects. In a second part projects will be discussed, compared, dropped or merged into larger projects. For the final part one project will be selected and developed further. Students will identify themselves as experts based on their interest and expertise. The Design Build Studio promotes a project based learning environment. Building on the experience of the Solar Decathlon Project the studio's goal is to test ideas on a 1/1 scale. The difference is that projects are smaller in scale and scope and focus on one building component rather then entire buildings. This allows the studio to fit in the existing curriculum but also allows for an investigation and research that goes beyond the regular design studio setting. Instead of leaving students thinking that they have a "good understanding" of a process to build high performance buildings, students in the Design Build Studio will develop a specific expertise within the context of a real project. Each student of the Design Build Studio takes on a specific part and responsibility in the project, which will stimulate a self-regulating learning process, a model that is described in detail by Boyer and Mitgang [9]. Growing into the role of an expert for a specific part in the project each student develops an individual research agenda which encourages students to "think for themselves" which is, as we know from Brewer, the aim of all higher education [10] The studio instructor's role is the guide that facilitates the dialogue between students from different disciplines. Students also learn to develop communication strategies. Valuing feedback and advice in a non – hierarchical environment can promote equal group discussions with a cross fertilization of ideas. The studio will develop into an environment in which students have to build trust in each other and learn how to effectively condense and connect ideas. The Research Studio also collaborates with experts form companies of the related building industry. In that way the entire studio not only shares the characteristic with a professional world it is also integrated in it.

3   AIA Pavilion, a Case Study for a Digital Design Build Studio

The project started with defining and developing different ideas for a pavilion for events hosted by the AIA in New Orleans. The pavilion had to be flexible enough to adapt to different site conditions that were not known at the beginning of the studio. Eight students developed different approaches to the problem that were presented in form of sketches, diagrams and small study models. After the first presentation different ideas were synthesized in more complex project that were developed further by teams of two to three students. These projects were presented as large models, renderings and scale 1/1 prototypes of building components. The projects were discussed as a group and with experts and external reviewers. Based on the comments one project was selected and developed in a group effort.

In the second design phase of the project students started to take responsibility for different tasks including developing the geometry, researching different materials and fabrication methods. Entering the fabrication phase students had developed an expertise in different areas including CNC or thermoforming. One student for instance was responsible to develop a script for numbering all the edges of the 320 different cells.

After the production of all components the studio relocated from Atlanta to New Orleans for the construction of the pavilion. With eight students the 320 different panels were assembled in less then two days. After the opening the studio met again to discuss the presentation of the project. Each student was given the format of a 22"/22" panel to present their individual part within the lager project. These diagrams and drawings together with the presentation of the final project and photographs informed a booklet and the final presentation of the Design Build Studio.

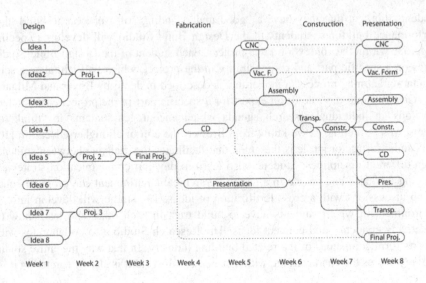

Fig. 1. The diagram shows the different responsibilities of students

4 Project Description

The AIA pavilion is developed from 320 variations of a single cell. Each cell is generated from different sets of attributes and their information that are derived from the modules unique position within the overall form, different architectural and structural requirements and unique site conditions. The geometry of the cells was transformed for instance into seating, foundation, light fixtures, plant holders and rainwater collectors. Informing each proto-cell with different, sometimes contradicting sets of information increased the unpredictability in of its final form. The final overall form and spatial qualities of the pavilion emerged from the cells variations. Using scripting allowed for the design but also for a rapid fabrication and assembly -- engraving instructions that helped to connect the different cells, numbering the edges and adding connection details that changed with each cell.

A cell geometry was developed that allowed combining structure and envelope in a single material system. The edges of each cell were folded differently based on each cells location within the overall structure. This provided stiffness within the cell. When connected the edges of all cells form a complex geodesic system. To minimize the amount of material used for the envelope and to create a lightweight structure, the envelope generates wormholes that act brace- and column-like and increase the surface tension. The formation of wormholes within the surface allowed for the lightweight structure of 123 kg.

Glycol-modified polyethylene terephthalate (PETG) was used as a single material. This material can either be produced from recycled plastic or sugar cane: The chemical industry is currently changing it's production of plastic from fossil-fuel plastic to bio-plastic. The pavilion is part of larger series of investigations in providing techniques and methods to build light weight structures with plastics and a

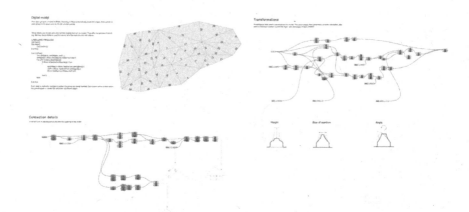

Fig. 2. The form of the pavilion was tessellated into 320 different triangles. More then 1,000 connection-details were located along the cell's edges. Based on information from program and environment each triangle was transformed differently.

Fig. 3. The triangular cells were assembled into lager groups

Fig. 4. The interior of the final pavilion

to provide new spatial and aesthetic qualities to change our perception of plastic from an environmentally problematic to an environmentally friendly material. The highly malleable nature of plastic made it suitable to the digitally derived form of the pavilion and its complex geometry and cell variations. The material is light, impact resistant and easy to fabricate.

The various triangular outlines of the individual modules were routed from PETG sheets. Each of the triangles was then thermoformed into a three dimensional shape. To save material a single flexible mold was developed that could be modified easily to produce different shapes from different triangles. Thermoforming, a technique used mostly in the packaging industry, was used to generate the final geometries of the cells. This technique involved fewer parts and tooling than other molding techniques, which allowed for cost and time effective production. It was also very precise, resulting in very small assembly tolerances.

Using a minimum amount of material to produce the pavilion the flexible mold was constructed from a digitally fabricated kit of parts. Its main components were a flexible frame and stamp. The frame held the material in place during the forming process. The stamp transformed each cell into different shapes. The mold combined three different thermoforming techniques: drape forming, vacuum forming and draping. Rearranging the few elements the mold was used to produce the 320 different building cells of the pavilion but could be further used to produce an infinite number of other variations. All cells were prefabricated and assembled into 6 larger components designed to stack and fit compactly into a small truck for transport.

5 Conclusion

Architecture schools have defined themselves as incubators for testing digital tools. The current challenge is the integration of the research in digital design and fabrication with environmental issues. The decreasing cost for digital design and fabrication – the total cost of the AIA pavilion was $2,500 -- is seen as new opportunity to inform praxis with digital design and fabrication methods and strategies. The Digital Design Build Studio is introduced to promote a research environment that is characterized by students that learn how to operate as architects and experts. I think that this model will allow to elevate the research in studios regarding digital tools to the next level, will empower the students and will help to define new ties between experts of different disciplines and departments at the school and the university level but also between academia and practice.

Acknowledgment. Studio Instructor: Gernot Riether

Project Team: Gernot Riether, Valerie Bolen, Rachel Dickey, Emily Finau, Tasnouva Habib, Knox Jolly, Pei-Lin Liao, Keith Smith, April Tann

Fabricated at: DFL, Digital Fabrication Laboratory at Georgia Institute of Technology
Special Thanks to: Russell Gentry and Andres Cavieres

References

1. Hollein, M.: Greg Lynn and Hani Rashid Architectural Laboratories, p. 7. NAi Publishers, Rotterdam (2002)
2. Stevenson, F.: Integrated sustainability through imaginative studio assessment. In: The Oxford Conference, A Re-Evaluation of Education in Architecture, p. 116. WIT Press, Southhampton (2008)
3. Vitruvius The Education of the Architect, Ten Books on Architecture, 1st chapter
4. Anderson, L.: Big Science, Audio CD (July 2007)
5. Design Develop Build, webpage, http://gbl.arch.rwth-aachen.de/ddb/ (January 09, 2010)
6. Solar Decathlon, webpage, http://www.solardecathlon.gov/ (January 09, 2010)
7. Pottmann, H., Asperl, A., Hofer, M., Kilian, A.: Architectural Geometry, p. 1. Bentley Institute Press, Exton (2007)

8. http://www.grasshopper3d.com/ (January 09, 2010)
9. Boyer, Mitgang: Building Community: A New Future For Architectural Education and Practice, Carnegie Foundation for the Advancement of Teaching. Princeton, NJ (1996)
10. Brewer, I.M.: Learning more and teaching less – A decade of innovation in self-instruction and small group teaching, p. 1 (1985)
11. Comese, architecture gallery, webpage, http://www.comese.me.it/eventi.html (January 09, 2010)

Author Index